Scientists, the Arms Race and Disarmament

Scientists, the Arms Race and Disarmament

A Unesco/Pugwash Symposium

General Editor
Joseph Rotblat

Taylor & Francis Ltd
London
1982

Unesco
Paris

LIBRARY
COLBY-SAWYER COLLEGE
NEW LONDON, NH 03257

JX
1974.7
,S34
1982

11/86

The ideas and opinions expressed in this book are those of the authors and
do not necessarily represent the views of Unesco.
The designations employed and the presentation of material
throughout this publication do not imply the expression of any opinion
whatsoever on the part of Unesco concerning the legal status of any
country, territory, city or area or of its authorities, or concerning the
delimitation of its frontiers and boundaries.

First published 1982
by the United Nations Educational,
Scientific and Cultural Organization,
7 Place de Fontenoy, 75700 Paris
and Taylor & Francis Ltd,
4 John Street, London WC1N 2ET.

© Unesco 1982

All rights reserved. No part of this publication may be
reproduced, stored in a retrieval system or transmitted, in
any form or by any means, electronic, mechnical,
photocopying, recording or otherwise, without the prior
permission of the copyright owner.

ISBN 92-3-102021-8 (Unesco)
ISBN 0-85066-234-6 (Taylor & Francis Ltd)

Typeset by C.P. Services Limited
Printed and bound in the United Kingdom by
Taylor & Francis (Printers) Ltd,
Rankine Road, Basingstoke, Hampshire RG24 0PR

08931

Preface

Arms for Peace? Arms or Peace?

Peace – a lasting peace based on justice and fellowship – is recognized ever more widely as an aspiration common to peoples throughout the world.

Sixty million killed and tens of millions disabled, orphaned and widowed during the Second World War; 130 armed conflicts throughout the world since 1945, leaving some 25 million dead, mostly in the Third World; human misery; land and property laid waste; the fruits of the imagination and the labours of several generations destroyed; economic losses and an incalculable squandering of resources – such is the dismal inventory of the last few decades.

Yet the dangers facing mankind today are even greater than those which have gone before. The destructive power of modern nuclear weapons and of chemical and biological weapons is such that a third world war could wipe out the entire human race.

Thirty-seven years after the explosion of the first atomic bomb at Hiroshima, five countries officially possess nuclear weapons, but others seem to be on the point of acquiring them or have the capacity to do so. The world is thus living in a kind of "balance of terror" that is becoming increasingly precarious as arms become ever more sophisticated, varied and numerous.

The arms race has a built-in tendency to accelerate. The average figure for annual military expenditure has almost doubled in a few years, rising from 370,000 million dollars in the 1960s to just over 500,000 million dollars in 1980. A million dollars are spent every minute on arms, and 500,000 scientists and engineers are engaged on military research throughout the world.

This is not only an appalling misuse of human and material resources, but is, in itself, a factor of tension, since the quest for supremacy in the field of armaments goes hand in hand with efforts to extend respective zones of influence, which have already led strategists to include outer space in their calculations. Furthermore, the development of instruments of destruction and death, by adding yet another dimension to problems of inequalities, misunderstandings and fears of our age, tends to foster intransigence and, when differences arise between nations, to encourage attempts to solve them by force rather than by negotiation.

It is moreover true that the arms race makes huge profits for certain exporting countries, allows them through mass production to acquire arms at minimum cost, and gives them an opportunity continually to perfect their techniques through the real-life laboratory of battlefields.

Nor can we overlook the actions of certain pressure groups, in particular military and industrial ones which aim to secure economic, political and social advantages for themselves in the various purchasing countries.

The effects of the arms race are, indeed, all too evident: growing instability among the poor nations, and their deflection from the path of progress; the danger of worsening conflicts between countries – and hence a world confrontation between the great powers – and the danger of a nuclear war that could lead to the annihilation of our planet.

Public opinion needs to be better informed of the burden and the risks implicit in the present situation, of the constraints it imposes on the economies of countries, and of the wastage of resources to which it leads. To arm impoverishes mankind and yet does not ensure its security.

As part of the efforts of the United Nations family to promote greater understanding both of the implications of war and of the promise of peace, Unesco has carried out a threefold programme of a normative, educational and informative nature. The aim is essentially, in the words of Unesco's Constitution, to establish peace "upon the intellectual and moral solidarity of mankind".

The General Conference at its eighteenth session (Resolution 11.1) pointed out that peace "cannot consist solely in the absence of armed conflict but implies principally a process of progress, justice and mutual respect among the peoples designed to secure the building of an international society in which everyone can find his true place and enjoy his share of the world's intellectual and material resources..."

At the close of the twentieth century, a lasting peace can only be established on a foundation of understanding and mutual respect, of honest co-operation between peoples, and hence of a continuing dialogue that sets the collective aspirations of mankind above the selfish ambitions of the few.

Amadou-Mahtar M'Bow
Director-General of Unesco

Contents

Introduction

Seldom has the search for disarmament seemed more difficult than it does at present, and the dismal record of accomplishment after the excellent Final Document of the first United Nations Special Session on Disarmament (UNSSOD I), held in 1978, gives us little reason for optimism concerning the results to be expected from the second session of UNSSOD (1982). However, the increased general awareness of the perils of the continuing arms race, and the growing tide of public insistence for its halt and reversal, provide us now with grounds for hope for the 1982 session which were lacking in 1978.

Efforts to rouse awareness have taken many forms. The United Nations and other organizations have repeatedly stressed the colossal wastage of human and material resources resulting from the arms race – about one million dollars per minute, and between 25-40 percent of all scientists estimated to be occupied on military problems. If we add to these facts others, that many of the weapons produced and stockpiled – atom bombs and chemical nerve gases – would, if used, produce effects on human minds and bodies too horrible to contemplate, and that a nuclear war would lead to the end of civilization as we know it, no sane person can avoid the conclusion that the present arms race must be halted and reversed, and the enormous expenditure on arms used to meet human needs.

Yet past experience shows that these tasks present immense problems, and dramatic progress cannot be expected in the presence of existing social, economic and political tensions which affect nearly all parts of the world. If we hope ever to achieve significant disarmament we must try to understand better than we do now the complex web of factors contributing to the arms race. Only then can we begin an effective counter-attack on the powerful forces – military, industrial, political and even academic – which are benefiting from the unparalleled growth in arms we are witnessing today.

Valid analyses of the problems concerned are difficult enough; finding the right answers and a correct strategy for counter-attack is even more difficult. This book, "Scientists, the Arms Race and Disarmament", sets out to map one central dimension of the problem, the role of the scientist, particularly with reference to nuclear weapons.

Political decisions are made by governments, and responsibility for the arms race rests squarely on their shoulders. However, scientists and their engineer colleagues have been depicted as arch villains, fuelling the arms race by putting their knowledge at the disposal of military prowess, with little or no thought as to anti-social consequences. This over-simplification is false, but to what extent? Scientists as a group are among the most highly educated in the population; many have thought profoundly and have written about different aspects of their involvement in military undertakings, especially after the advent of nuclear weapons in the Second World War. Albert Einstein is one of the clearest examples. He continually fought for peace, starting with his early opposition to militarism at the beginning of the First World War. Yet he advocated, at the beginning of the Second World War, the study of the military use of nuclear energy, which led to the production of the atom bomb. The rest of his life, spent urging world peace, led many scientists to follow him to work for disarmament, but all too many are left still unaffected by his vision.

The dynamics of the arms race is often viewed primarily from the stand-point of East–West relations and interests, without taking sufficiently into account the peoples of the Third World who comprise most of the globe. The central confrontation of the superpowers and their allies, and their combined potential for destroying most of the world if a full-scale nuclear war erupts, is of course a principal concern. What must be kept in mind, however, is that many in the Third World have quite a different perspective of the situation, and rightly so. Their countries have been the battlegrounds of numerous wars since the Second World War; and their political stability, economies and resources have been sacrificed in the struggle by industrial nations for power and influence in those countries. Thus, the central confrontation referred to above is being dangerously extended to peripheral regions which are already torn by wars and tensions.

This is the background against which the present book, prepared jointly by Unesco and Pugwash, is written. Its authors are a group of scientists and scholars, many of whom have been associated for years with one or both organizations in their efforts for disarmament. More importantly, all are concerned with the preparations for the success of the next United Nations Special Session on Disarmament.

Professor Joseph Rotblat, the editor, is eminently qualified for the difficult task he has undertaken. Rotblat worked as a physicist on the atom bomb at Los Alamos, and left his job as soon as it became clear that the Nazis were not making the bomb. He returned to the United Kingdom and soon thereafter began a long and distinguished career in radiation physics at St. Bartholomew's Hospital Medical College in London, from where he retired a few years ago as Professor Emeritus. He was the first Secretary-General of Pugwash (founded in response to the Russell–Einstein Manifesto) and served in this capacity for the first seventeen years of the existence of Pugwash, now in its twenty-fifth year. Rotblat has been a ceaseless fighter for arms control and disarmament, a position he shares with many of the authors of the various chapters of this book.

The authors of the different chapters themselves come from many countries, East and West, North and South, and have widely different experiences. There are several who, like Rotblat, worked on the development of the atom bomb before they were used at Hiroshima: Professors Bernard Feld (United States) and Mark Oliphant (Australia) from the West, and Professor Vasily Emelyanov (USSR) from the East. They have spent the rest of their lives working to prevent the bomb from ever being used again against human beings. There are some who have lived, at least for short periods, in both East and West. Professor Francesco Calogero (Italy) spent several years working at Dubna in the Soviet Union; Dr. Sergei Kapitza (USSR) grew up as a child in Cambridge before his parents returned home.

It must be admitted that in the individual contributions to this book there is a certain element of repetition – almost everyone feels compelled to state the whole problem at least in brief, not only his allotted portion of it. But these statements are written from such varied experiences and viewpoints that they add force to the whole in the common conclusion they reach.

The book begins with accounts of the dimensions of the problem, the enormous growth of nuclear and conventional armaments, both of which depend on many ingenious ideas and critical experiments by scientists not necessarily themselves involved in war research, since each new discovery can, through military pressure, be turned to destructive ends by others. Professor Francesco Calogero analyses the problems arising from the nuclear arms race, while Professor Karlheinz Lohs deals with the technology of other types of weapons, in particular with chemical warfare. The general role of military R&D and the armaments momentum is discussed by Dr. Marek Thee, and the aspects of particular interest to the Third World are taken up by Professor Essam Galal.

The different parts played by individual scientists both within and against war research are discussed in Part II. Professor Engelbert Broda, from his own life's experience, discusses the fundamental dilemma of scientists caught up in the major conflicts of our time. Dr. Herbert York and Allen Greb, through participation in the actual negotiations for arms control, give an account of the involvement of scientists, from both East and West, as government advisors from the Second World War to the present day. They show how many who began as advisors to assist the war effort turned later into strong critics of government actions. This theme is taken up by Professor Vasily Emelyanov who gives details of the many protests made by individuals and by groups of scientists against further development of nuclear weapons.

The history of scientific protest and the growth of movements of scientists, both national and international, to work for peace and disarmament are described in detail by Professor Rotblat in Part III, in a contribution which is central to the purposes of the book. It illustrates the extent of the involvement of many of the best brains of our time in organizations such as the World Federation of Scientific Workers and the Pugwash Movement. It shows that their efforts have had some success, though very far from the success they had hoped for. Meetings of scientists, however, which occur at intervals, necessarily leave many questions unanswered about methods to bring about disarmament. So Rotblat also deals with the growth of peace research institutes and particularly of SIPRI, which is closely linked with the Pugwash Movement.

Part IV returns to basic principles, as it raises the general problem of the social responsibility of scientists. Professor John Ziman has written and thought a great deal on the subject. Many of the points he raises in his outline are illustrated by the contributions of Professors Ivan Supek and Ignacy Malecki, and commented upon by Professor Mark Oliphant.

How to reverse the arms race through the active involvement of scientists is the subject of Part V. Professor Bernard Feld discusses the very practical part scientific research can play in the processes of verifications essential for successful arms control. Swadesh Rana and Sergei Kapitza, from their different points of view, write of the importance of education for disarmament at all levels, school, university and through the media, particularly television, for the whole population – in all of which scientists can certainly play a major part. Professor Röling's contribution is, however, sobering. So many difficult and fundamental questions are raised by peace research to which solutions must be found if nations are ever to obey international laws.

So we come to the final Part VI, to the United Nations, the organization on which our hopes for the future rest. The numerous contributions made by Unesco are described by Stephen Marks, who has been deeply involved in many of these contributions. This is followed by the role of the United Nations itself with two expert contributions on the immediate past, the Disarmament Decade, by Ambassador Olu Adeniji, and the preparations for the future, the next Special Session on Disarmament, by Ambassador Alfonso Garcia-Robles.

The conclusions from the book and the recommendations for future action were discussed by a group of 33 scientists from 25 countries at a symposium held in Ajaccio on 19–23 February 1982. These conclusions and recommendations have been transmitted to the Second United Nations Special Session on Disarmament. They are reproduced at the beginning of the book, immediately following this Introduction, to focus the attention of the reader on the tasks lying ahead. We hope that the book, as a whole, with its very varied attitudes and information about the past and present, will provoke many others to think seriously about the future and to help to bring about disarmament.

Dorothy Hodgkin, President
Martin Kaplan, Director-
General
Pugwash Conferences on Science
and World Affairs

Conclusions and Recommendations of the Unesco/Pugwash Symposium on "Scientists, the arms race and disarmament" Ajaccio, France, 19th-23rd February, 1982

1.   The nuclear arms race, which has resulted in the creation of an unprecedented and awesome potential for destruction, is one of the outcomes of the remarkable advances in science and technology during the past few decades. The achievements of science have momentous implications in all aspects of life of the world community, including a radical change of traditional concepts of security and national power. Yet, the call in the Russell-Einstein Manifesto that a new way of thinking is essential if mankind is to survive in the new situation that has arisen from the progress of science has largely gone unheeded. National security is still measured by the strength of military arsenals, and super power is equated with the capacity to inflict unimaginable damage on an adversary. As a consequence, the nuclear arms race accelerates its pace and engulfs an increasing number of nations, although everybody knows that it may lead to the annihilation of civilization.

2.   The arms race is primarily the product of political forces. But scientists themselves contribute to this disastrous trend in world affairs. About half a million scientists and technologists – a high proportion of the total scientific manpower – are directly employed on military research and development. They are continually devising new means of destruction, making the existence of the human species on this planet ever more precarious. In particular, the nuclear arms race feeds on the continuous input of scientific innovation, and there is a growing belief that the momentum of this arms race is determined by the actions of scientists. This belief is exaggerated; a multitude of factors, interacting with each other, is involved, commonly expressed as the military-industrial complex. But the introduction of any new weapon is an irreversible step, and in this sense the role of the scientists in the arms race is of crucial importance.

3.   This role of scientists is contrary to their traditional calling. The objectives of scientific endeavour should be a service to mankind, helping to better the fate of man and raise material and cultural standards. The basic unmet needs of a majority of the people in the world present a

challenge great enough to warrant a huge and sustained effort by scientists. For an enormous effort of scientists to be instead directed towards wholesale destruction, to a return to a state of primitive savagery among the survivors of a nuclear war, is an unforgivable perversion of science.

4.   This world would be a much safer place if scientists in all countries would simply refuse to engage in military research. While realizing that, as a professional group, the scientists alone cannot easily act in complete isolation from their political and economic context, we implore those who are employed in the military R & D establishments to ponder on the social implications of their work and then leave it to their conscience to dictate their further conduct.

5.   In any case, there is an urgent task for all scientists to help in stopping and reversing the arms race, and to work for genuine disarmament measures, ultimately leading to general and complete disarmament. Scientists have already demonstrated that their efforts in these directions can be fruitful and effective. Movements of scientists – such as the Pugwash Conferences on Science and World Affairs, which provide a forum for objective and informative debate between scientists from East and West, North and South – have made valuable contributions to the international negotiations on arms control. These negotiations have led to few agreements, but without them the arms race might have acquired even more catastrophic dimensions. The work of institutes of peace research, provides factual information of great value to those concerned with the implementation of disarmament measures.

6.   This urgent task can no longer be left to the small number of scientists actively involved in the effort to stem the arms race. It should be the duty of *all* scientists to acquaint themselves with these issues. There is a tremendous scope for scientists to counteract the arms race and seek means to reduce the threat of a nuclear war. If the drive towards avoidance of war is to make headway, it must involve a much larger number of scientists; an increase by at least an order of magnitude is necessary to make the number comparable with that of the scientists involved in military R & D.

7.   We call on the scientific community to give their time and thought towards these objectives. A determined effort is needed to promote collaboration for peaceful purposes in fields of research where there is now competition for destructive purposes; to elaborate specific steps of arms reduction; to give early warning on the dangers of new developments; to collaborate with current medical campaigns in informing the public of the likely consequences of a nuclear war; to take part in disarmament education.

8.   Specifically, we recommend the following tasks for scientists:
- maintain contact between scientists from different social and economic systems, drawing on the common interests and values of the international scientific community, and explore through such contacts all possibilities of resolving conflicts and fostering progress towards disarmament;
- study the technological aspects of the arms race so as to be able to offer expert advice on these matters to decision makers and the general public;
- support efforts to limit and eventually stop the nuclear arms race, in particular, to conclude without delay a Comprehensive Test-Ban Treaty;
- monitor destabilizing developments in the arms race and warn the public about them;
- contribute to the ongoing research on the economic consequences of disarmament so as to be able to allay fears about unemployment and to find alternative opportunities for the utilization of resources and manpower at present employed on military projects;
- participate in national and international meetings of scientists to debate and seek means of disseminating the findings of the studies mentioned above;
- encourage the setting up of an international committee of scientists to analyse the consequences of the nuclear arms race and report their conclusions;
- address lay audiences and mass media and provide them with factual information about the dangers and likely outcome of a nuclear war;
- use their influence in scientific academies and institutions to induce them to devote some of their activities and budgets to the above issues;
- urge editors of scientific journals to provide space for discussions on those issues;
- promote disarmament education and, in particular, the inclusion of disarmament-related issues in the curricula of schools and universities;
- seek the effective implementation of the Unesco recommendation on the status of scientific researchers.

9.   We further recommend that Unesco:
- intensify efforts to promote goals and means of disarmament education, in the most effective manner;
- mobilize the world scientific community to make its contribution to the scholarly study of the problems of the arms race and of disarmament in both developed and developing states, and to ensure the wide distribution of the results of such study.

10.   Finally, we recommend that the Second Special Session of the General Assembly devoted to disarmament:

    – assure that studies of armaments and disarmament are more closely linked with arms control and disarmament negotiations;

    – increase the usefulness of disarmament studies of the United Nations to ongoing or planned negotiations, and avoid duplication by reinforcing the role of the Centre for Disarmament as co-ordinator of these activities;

    – launch the World Disarmament Campaign under the responsibility of the Secretary-General, with special responsibilities for Unesco, in its field of competence, and involve, in the Campaign, the scientific community as well as appropriate non-governmental organizations such as Pugwash.

11.   The continuing arms race with no prospect for its reversal in sight, and the ensuing threat of a nuclear holocaust, produce fear, frustration and a feeling of helplessness and hopelessness among people, particularly in the young generation. They also lead to apathy and pessimism in the ranks of the scientific community. But a formulation of specific tasks may hearten and activate scientists to do something worthwhile and enable them to return science back to its true calling. We believe that the above recommendations, including those addressed to the United Nations and Unesco, if implemented, would provide the much needed optimism that it is still possible to prevent catastrophe; and the hope – indeed the conviction – that scientists have an important role to play in the creation of conditions for a secure and peaceful world.

PART I
Role of science and technology in the arms race

Chapter 1. Dynamics of the nuclear arms race

Francesco Calogero

Introduction

The dynamics of the arms race has been the subject of much debate. Is technological progress the driving force, or are the military applications of science and technology motivated by political conflicts? Is the arms race a primary source of conflict, or is it a consequence of a strategic confrontation rooted in political and ideological differences? Indeed, is there an arms race, or is this a figure of speech devoid of any real foundation?

The last of these questions cannot be taken seriously except as an indication of the degree of sophistry displayed by professional advocates of the allocation of more resources to military purposes. The first two questions, on the other hand, belong to the "chicken or egg" type of problem, a category that is hardly useful to address in general terms, but which nevertheless underlines a fundamental problem (like morphogenesis), requiring a lot of research before it can be properly formulated, let alone solved.

In this chapter such ontological and gnoseological questions will be bypassed; instead the focus will be on a few elementary facts and considerations, whose relevance cannot be belittled by emphasizing their triviality.

The arms race

World military expenditures, at constant prices, have doubled over the last 20 years (see figure 1). Over the last 10 years some 5000 thousand million US dollars (5×10^{12}) at 1980 prices, have been spent for military

13

"Scientists, the arms race and disarmament"

US $ thousand million, in constant (1978) prices and exchange-rates

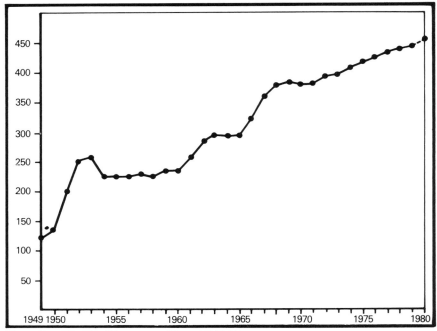

Figure 1.   World military expenditure, 1949–80
Source: World Armaments and Disarmaments, SIPRI Yearbook 1981, p.3.

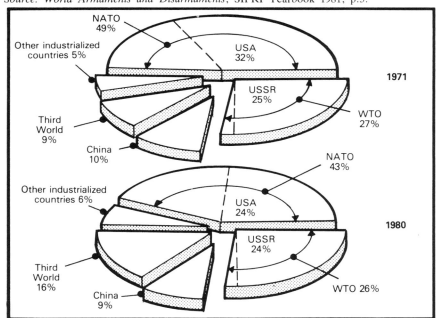

Figure 2. Distribution of world military expenditure, 1971 and 1980
Source: World Armaments and Disarmaments, SIPRI Yearbook 1981, p.XIX.

purposes; about $1000 per inhabitant of this planet. Of these expenses, nearly three quarters are attributable to the two main military blocs, the North Atlantic Treaty Organization (NATO) and the Warsaw Treaty Organization (WTO) (see figure 2).

As for data pertaining specifically to the *nuclear* arms race, the numbers of *strategic* nuclear warheads are probably the most significant indicator, although they represent only a fraction – about one third – of the total number of available nuclear warheads. According to official American estimates[1] these numbers have grown over the last 10 years by a factor of two for the United States (from 4600 in 1971 to 9200 in 1980), and by more than a factor of three for the Soviet Union (from 2100 in 1971 to 7000 in 1981). *Each* strategic warhead can destroy a city.

Nuclear proliferation

The number of nuclear-weapon States has by definition been frozen, at five, by the Non-Proliferation Treaty (NPT): United States, USSR, United Kingdom, France, China. But India, not a party to the NPT, exploded a "peaceful nuclear device" in 1974, and there are at least two other countries, Israel and South Africa, neither of them party to the NPT, that are widely credited as having some nuclear weapon capability. Several other countries, e.g., Pakistan, Brazil, Argentina, Iraq, Republic of South Korea, Taiwan, have nuclear energy programmes that are believed to be in part motivated by military considerations. The Libyan Arab Jamahiriya is often mentioned as seeking to buy a nuclear weapon option at any price (presumably in petrodollars), were such a bargain possible.

The NPT, to which 112 non-nuclear-weapon states, as well as three nuclear-weapon states are party (the other two, France and China, have stated their intention to abide by its provisions), still provides an international framework which makes it possible for the great majority of nations to resist the temptation to acquire an autonomous nuclear-weapon capability; and one hopes to see such a framework strengthened by nuclear-weapon-free zones. But the world-wide spread of nuclear know-how and materials, associated with the diffusion of nuclear energy, inevitably undermines the technological barriers to nuclear weapon proliferation; and, most importantly, the failure of the nuclear-weapon states, especially the two superpowers, to stop and reverse the nuclear arms race ("vertical proliferation"), to make good their commitment under Article VI of the NPT, is likely to lead to the crumbling of the NPT regime.

Moreover, the world-wide abundance of nuclear weapons and of nuclear materials generates a risk of non-governmental proliferation (or, less euphemistically, nuclear terrorism); this peril is hard to assess quantitatively, but it would be foolish to neglect it.

Prospects

If vertical nuclear proliferation continues at the current rate, and horizontal nuclear proliferation proceeds, it is likely that the actual use of nuclear weapons "in anger" will occur. It is not possible to give a clear-cut answer to the natural questions: when? and how? Nevertheless, it is important to consider these questions.

"When?" Clearly the relevant time-scale is measured in decades, rather than in centuries. The prospects refer to our own life-time, or at least that of our children or grandchildren.

This statement may be disputed, but should not be ignored. Let us restate it: a sober evaluation of the current trends suggests that, if they continue, nuclear weapons will be exploded to kill, probably within our lifetime, surely before the death of all the individuals alive now.

Another element to be kept in mind when assessing "prospects", is the occurrence of irreversible thresholds. It is generally agreed that the numbers of operationally available strategic nuclear delivery vehicles are verifiable; such verification constitutes a necessary condition for strategic arms limitations. But the advent of the long-range cruise missile – an ubiquitous weapon system that can be launched from the air, sea, or ground; can have strategic and tactical roles; can be nuclear or convention-ally armed; can achieve high accuracy by means of terminal guidance; and is fairly small (about 6m long and 0.5m in diameter) – is going to undermine drastically the verifiability of any strategic weapon limitation. As one of the advocates of this technological development admitted, strategic arms control, as we now understand it, will be made practically inapplicable. This sounds as ominous as a doctor telling a patient that medicine, as we know it now, can do nothing more for him.

"How?". From this point of view horizontal proliferation constitutes more of a danger than vertical proliferation. The overkill already available to the superpowers is so excessive that any addition to it makes little difference, although restraint in vertical proliferation is a necessary precondition to control horizontal proliferation. In the vertical prolifera-tion context, the actual use of nuclear weapons is more likely to begin at the so-called tactical level, than as a strategic first strike.

Another observation is relevant when discussing "prospects": over the last few years, there has been a deterioration of world security, by whatever parameter this is measured. This refers in particular to the two superpowers, in spite, or rather as a consequence, of their huge and escalating military investment and the quantitative and qualitative increase in their weaponry. It is a *leitmotiv* of the "hawks" as well as of the "doves", both suggesting different remedies, but generally agreeing on the seriousness of the predicament. And it constitutes the essence of several recent statements by highly respected elder statesmen[2]. The American Secretary of State, Alexander Haig has summed it up neatly: "The world is a less secure place than it was 10 years ago"[3].

How did it come about that a course of events which is against everybody's best interest has prevailed? This question brings us back to the central theme of this section, the dynamics of the nuclear arms race. But before going into this matter, one final point will be mentioned.

The picture we have outlined is of a world bent on a suicidal course. It is a reality few dare to face with intellectual honesty; hence this sort of argument is not welcome to "the experts", who simply ignore it with the polite hint that these are emotional considerations characterizing the "non-expert", or shrug it off with standard jokes: "in the long run we shall all be dead". Another aspect of the situation, implicit in the figures quoted earlier, is the contrast between the squandering of material and human resources on weaponry and means of destruction, and the misery and suffering of large sectors of the human population who are deprived of adequate food and shelter, basic medical care, elementary training, educational opportunities. And current trends point to an aggravation of these problems. But these prospects are also relevant to *the immediate present*; because they influence the ethos and spirit of many individuals, especially young people. This occurs mostly at the subconscious level, and is difficult to pinpoint with any accuracy; yet it lies at the root of the deep crisis of values which has many facets, from addiction to drugs and alcohol to terrorism, and which may eventually be the main motivation for mankind following the path of the lemmings.

Deterrence

As the analysis outlined above suggests, pure reason is probably not the main determinant of policy. Nevertheless it is important to understand the conceptual framework which provides the basic language for the arguments used within decision-making systems and in public to justify the decisions that determine the evolution of the nuclear arms race.

The core of the nuclear arms race, on which we shall now focus, is the confrontation between the two superpowers, in particular the central strategic systems by which these two countries threaten each other directly. At present these systems comprise: ground-launched fixed intercontinental ballistic missiles (ICBMs); submarine-launched ballistic missiles (SLBMs); and long-range bombers; see Table 1, which contains official data from the Memorandum of Understanding between the USA and the USSR attached to the SALT II Treaty. These data refer to the situation as of June 18, 1979, when SALT II was signed by Presidents Carter and Brezhnev.

Table 1.   Strategic systems of the superpowers

	USA	USSR
Fixed launchers of ICBMs	1054	1398
Launchers of ICBMs equipped with MIRVs	550	608
Launchers of SLBMs	656	950
Launchers of SLBMs equipped with MIRVs	496	144
Heavy bombers	573	156

The destructive potential of nuclear weapons is so huge that it defies the imagination: a single thermonuclear bomb can unleash in a fraction of a second more energy than the sum total of all the explosions that have occurred "in anger" throughout the entire history of mankind, since gunpowder was invented, including two World Wars, Hiroshima and Nagasaki, and the blanket bombings of Vietnam. As a consequence, there can never be any realistic prospect of *defence* against the threat from the fantastic number of existing nuclear weapons; about 16 thousands *strategic* nuclear warheads and about twice this number of "nukes", which are termed "tactical" in spite of the fact that a sizable fraction of them has a higher yield than the Hiroshima and Nagasaki bombs. Indeed, under these circumstances, any defence would have to be foolproof to an unattainable degree, if it were to prevent, in the face of a massive attack, the explosion of at least a few nuclear weapons near cities.

The scale of the cataclysm following a nuclear attack lies well beyond the capability of any society to cope with, indeed beyond our power to imagine, let alone plan for. This is recognized by those who have looked into the matter with professional seriousness; particularly the medical profession[4].

Since there is no possibility to *defend* from a nuclear attack, the primary goal must be to *exclude* the use of nuclear weapons. The surest way to achieve this would be to ensure that no nuclear weapons are available; hence the high priority which a policy of non-proliferation should command. But in the context of the confrontation between the superpowers, this option was forsaken long ago.

In the face of the perceived threat implied by the nuclear arsenal of the other side, an other alternative is to deter the "enemy" from using his nuclear weapons, by the assured prospect of a nuclear retaliation causing unacceptable damage. This requires the availability of a nuclear arsenal sufficiently extensive and secure, so that even after absorbing a "first strike" by the nuclear forces of the adversary, a retaliatory "second strike" capability, sufficient to cause unacceptable damage, would still remain operational.

Whenever the conditions outlined above apply to two contenders, there is a mutual inhibition against the use of nuclear weapons. This is the so-called "balance of terror", and is the situation that presently characterizes the confrontation between the two superpowers. This state of affairs has prevailed for at least twenty years, and presumably it has played a part in preventing the superpowers from engaging in a direct military clash.

It is impossible that such a situation continues *ad aeternum*. As long as nuclear weapons exist there is a non-negligible probability that eventually they will be used to kill. Moreover, the balance of terror is a policy based on the threat, backed by hardware, software, operational plans, to exterminate millions of individuals. The fact that the survival of human civilization is predicated on such a policy may, in the long run, result in the disintegration of the ethical basis of civilized society. On the other hand, there does not appear, in the near future, any realistic prospect of doing away with nuclear weapons completely. Therefore, the restraint against the use of nuclear weapons, resulting from the deterrence strategy based on the threat of mutual assured destruction, is, for the immediate future, the obvious policy. And it is in this conceptual framework that the dynamics of the arms race must be understood and, if possible, controlled.

While for the reasons outlined above the concept of deterrence by the retaliatory threat of assured destruction does not provide a satisfactory long-range secondary arrangement, it is important to realize that, in the near-term, this conceptual framework does provide a sound basis to restrain the nuclear arms race, because the strategic nuclear forces deployed by the superpowers are much in excess of what might be justified by the requirements of deterrence. We shall return to this important point below.

The drastic conceptual change in strategy caused by the advent of nuclear weapons has many implications; some of these appear paradoxical in the face of deeply ingrained ideas that have suddenly become obsolete after evolving through centuries and millennia of human history. Indeed, the most important cause of the overall decrease in security that characterizes the last few decades orginates from the inability of human society to adjust to such a major change of the strategic environment[5]. It is therefore appropriate to review some of these points.

Nuclear wars cannot be won; nor, for that matter, can they be fought. This runs counter to the martial rhetoric and ethos, which have played such an important role in history, and which still provide the back-bone of most military establishments. This fact is hard to accept and rational acceptance is often illusory, giving easy way to the prevalence of gut feelings, which often disguise themselves under the sophisticated jargon of strategic analysis[5].

Nuclear weapons are eminently useless, except for the specific, and untestable, single purpose, *deterrence*. Again, this runs counter to well-established conventional wisdom, since nuclear weapons appear as the ultimate instrument of power; and power, in international relations, is supposed to provide influence and the capability to promote one's interests. Indeed, such ideas provide one of the strongest incentives towards nuclear proliferation. Yet, there are glaring confirmations of the irrelevance of nuclear weapons (except for deterrence): for example, the defeat of the USA in Vietnam; and, did it make any difference to the predicaments of the United Kingdom, Italy, France, the Federal Republic of Germany and Japan, vis-a-vis the oil crisis, that two of these countries had an independent nuclear force, while the other three did not?

Stability

Although any novel weapon system should be viewed with distaste, as it adds to an already overloaded situation, it is important to distinguish weapon developments which are more destabilizing from those which are less destabilizing. There are, however, two aspects of stability, that are better discussed separately, although they are of course related.

Crisis instability

This refers to a situation that puts a premium on attacking first. Typically, this would be the case if one, or both, of the two opponents were vulnerable to a *disarming* first strike. The enormous retaliatory overkill available to each super-power (note for instance the largely invulnerable sea-based component of the strategic triad, comprising thousands of strategic warheads) excludes that any such eventuality would materialize, even if major reductions of nuclear forces were undertaken. Indeed, the idea that a nuclear war could be initiated by one side on the expectation that it would cause the death of "only" a few tens of millions of one's own people but many tens of millions of the enemy's – hence, victory! – cannot be taken seriously. Even if some paper strategists contemplate such fantasies, or rather nightmares, it is quite certain that no decision-maker takes any serious notice of such nonsense. It is appropriate to quote here McGeorge Bundy[6]:

"There is an enormous gulf between what political leaders really think about nuclear weapons and what is assumed in complex calculations of relative "advantage" in simulated strategic warfare. Think-tank analysts can set levels of "acceptable" damage well up in the tens of millions of lives. They can assume that the loss of dozens of great cities is somehow a real choice for sane men. They are in an unreal world. In the real world of real political leaders – whether here or in the Soviet Union – a decision that would bring even one hydrogen bomb on one city of one's own country would be recognized in advance as a catastrophic blunder; ten bombs on ten cities would be a disaster beyond history; and a hundred bombs on a hundred cities are unthinkable."

It is, however, undoubtedly true that certain types of weapons are more troublesome than others, since at a time of acute confrontation they constitute a potential source of anxiety due to the incentive to use them quickly, before they are destroyed. The more worrisome development in this connection is the possible adoption of a *launch on warning* doctrine, with the attendant risk that the catastrophic end of our civilization might be caused by a false alarm or a computer malfunction. (The possibility of such an event is denied by some technical experts, with the same assurance that other, no less reliable, experts used to exclude the possibility of an extended electric power blackout, before one did occur in New York and adjoining areas).

This negative quality of *vulnerable* strategic weapons refers not only to one's own weapons, but also to the weapons of the adversary. Thus, everybody's security is best served by phasing out such weapons, provided this can be done without upsetting the equilibrium based on deterrence, which, as already noted, is extremely stable, due to the enormous overkill capacity. Moreover, it is contrary to one's own security to deploy weapons that threaten the strategic weapons of the opponent, who might respond by adopting a launch on warning doctrine. In connection with this analysis, it is appropriate to mention the remarkable discussion that has recently raged in the United States, about the vulnerability of their land-based (1000 Minutemen and 52 Titans), caused by the increased number and accuracy of Soviet ICBM warheads. Incidentally, both these developments – especially the first – are associated with the introduction of Multiple Independently-targetable Re-entry Vehicles (MIRVs), a technological "advance" that might have been prevented by an arms control agreement (see p.25). This debate is based on scenarios of ICBM duels, ignoring – or paying only lip service to – the other elements of the strategic triad, as well as the enormous collateral damage that a nuclear attack, even if only aimed at ICBMs, would cause. Indeed, a Soviet attack against the American ICBMs would certainly cause terrible damage and millions of casualties, and would leave a retaliatory capability (for instance, at sea) sufficient to destroy completely the Soviet Union. Thus, this threat is predicated on the imputation to Soviet decision-makers of a lunatic behaviour, no more credible than, say, the idea that Mr. Gromyko might carry a nuclear weapon in his suitcase, when he attends the UN General Assembly in New York City. Yet, it is essentially on the strength of such arguments that the construction of the MX system (a major leap forward in the nuclear arms race) was advocated.

Arms race instability

Since the arms race is actually going on, while the scenarios of nuclear exchange are highly conjectural, and often quite unreasonable, this kind of instability is actually more significant. The issue is the impact novel weapon systems, or technological developments in weaponry, have on the nuclear arms race itself. Those developments which are likely to enhance the arms race should be seen as most undesirable. In the framework of the relationship based on deterrence, it is clear how to provide such an assessment. For instance, counterforce weapons are generally worse than countervalue systems; defensive systems, such as area anti-ballistic missile systems (ABMs), or even widespread civil defence, are bad; any development that might be perceived as a move towards the acquisition of a first strike capability (such as an increase in the accuracy or the number of nuclear warheads) is bad. On the other hand, technological developments that make more secure the second-strike retaliatory capability, such as advances in the invulnerability and reliability of nuclear submarines, are useful.

In this context, a development is rated on the basis of the reaction to be expected from the other side, possibly resulting in an additional escalation of strategic arsenals.

The examples mentioned above should be sufficiently self-explanatory to require no further elaboration. But let us mention that the agreement to ban ABMs, reached in the framework of SALT I, and widely recognized as the major achievement of strategic arms control to date, is congruent to this logic; and conversely, the recent advocacy of anti-ballistic missiles, with the implicit threat to terminate the ABM Treaty, constitutes an ominous development.

The paradoxical aspect of these considerations should be squarely faced: in the strategic nuclear field, attempts at defence are not only useless (no effective defence is possible), they constitute the worst possible policy, because they provide a potent stimulant for the nuclear arms race. By theatening to jeopardize the retaliatory second-strike capability of assured destruction possessed by the other side, they provoke a reaction to shore up that capability, i.e. to increase offensive capabilities. In fact, the long lead-times required for the development and deployment of operational strategic weapon systems, and the "prudent" practice ("worst-case analysis") to overestimate the capabilities of the adversary and to underestimate one's own – all this produces overreactions, as reflected by the present grossly excessive nuclear arsenals.

This paradoxical aspect is largely exploited by the professional advocates of "more" in nuclear weaponry, who often pose as proponents of a more defensive stance. It is from such circles that the pure deterrence theory, which, as stated above, does provide a sound logical basis to stop the nuclear arms race and to make major progress in reducing nuclear weapons, has been dubbed with the disparaging acronym MAD (Mutual Assured Destruction); the opposition to the ABM Treaty came from the same quarters. While one cannot exclude the good faith of some of the advocates of this line, scepticism is justified, at least in relation to those who also advocated going ahead with the MIRV programme. Indeed, the defensive employment of nuclear weapons has always been given as an excuse for developing and deploying more nuclear weapons than would be justified for deterrence. Since McNamara's time, the so-called "damage limitation" role of nuclear weapons has been used to provide some logical justification for the excessive quantities of nuclear weapons and for the drive to increase the accuracy of nuclear warheads as far as technology permitted. This role implied, of course, a counter-force targetting, which the other side, or at least the hawks on the other side, may interpret as an attempt to acquire a first-strike capability, responding with the call to develop more weapons of their own. And so on and on.

MIRVing has obviously been a most destabilizing technological development. Having on each missile many warheads, each of which might be targeted against a launcher of the other side, goes against the very grain of balanced deterrence. When coupled with the increased accuracy, brought about by technological advances such as terminal guidance, it appears to usher in the possibility to acquire a first-strike capability, thereby eliminating the likelihood of a strategic equilibrium based on deterrence. In fact, this threat might be relevant if only fixed ICBMs were in existence. In reality, the availability of the sea-based deterrent implies that this predicament is largely imaginary. The soundest way out would be simply the phasing out of ICBMs, perhaps associated with tacit or formal agreements, such as limitations on strategic anti-submarine warfare (ASW) and/or the creation of sanctuaries for strategic submarines, to reinforce the invulnerability of the sea-based deterrent against hypothetical future breakthroughs in ASW.

The introduction of MIRVs has caused a major advance in the nuclear arms race, to everybody's disadvantage; another ominous development is the introduction of the strategic cruise missile. These two are evident examples of a new technology operating as principal engine of the nuclear arms race. Unless some way is found to control this drive, the situation will continue to go from bad to worse, with decision-makers – and mankind – appearing simply unable to cope. "Unless military science is brought back under political control there is an increasing risk of a nuclear world war which, in the words of a recent UN report, would be the 'ultimate human madness'."[7].

Arms control

Although one could envisage an even worse situation than that existing today, for example, if neither the ABM nor the NPT Treaties had been concluded, it has also been argued that arms control negotiations have actually provided more of a stimulus than a restraint on the nuclear arms race[8]. We shall now review the relevance of arms control to the dynamics of the nuclear arms race.

Bargaining chips

Many rungs in the escalation of the development and deployment of nuclear weaponry have been justified on the grounds that they were essential in order to acquire a strong negotiating position (even the cruise missile was ushered in with such an excuse). It is not important whether this kind of argument is used in good or bad faith; what is important is that it carries an enormous political weight. Time and again, such arguments have provided the clincher to render untenable any advocacy of restraint in weapon developments and deployment, however justifiable such restraint appeared on the basis of sound strategic considerations.

It is difficult to overestimate the importance of this phenomenon.

Doves versus hawks

The classification of those who influence the decisions on weaponry in two groups, the "doves" and the "hawks", is obviously an oversimplification. Yet to understand such decisions it is essential to analyse the debate within the respective decision-making systems; these are easily observable in the United States and Western Europe, less so in the Communist world, although they presumably run along analogous lines. A schematization of these debates as a controversy between doves and hawks has some justification. In particular it is enlightening to realize that in terms of acquiring political influence, and therefore being eventually able to carry the argument, the hawks are generally in a more favourable position.

One mechanism by which this happens has been described above: indeed, the "bargaining chips" argument, in its more vicious usage, taints the doves with the accusation that they undercut the negotiating position of their own side. It is a subtle variant of the standard hawkish technique to smear the doves, explicitly or by innuendo, with the implication that they are sympathetic to the "enemy", or at least gullible to his arguments. This is most effective when the international situation is in a tense phase; or whenever patriotic sentiments are aroused, even if the causes of such militancy are largely unrelated to the confrontation between the two superpowers.

To elucidate this issue more specifically, let us look at two examples.

The first is, again, the introduction of MIRVs. This development originated in the United States mainly as a self-motivated technological advance[9]. But it was immediately evident that – unless the United States were prepared to exercise restraint and to negotiate a ban, that might have been verifiable by forbidding flight-testing – the Soviet Union would eventually also "MIRV" her missiles. The predictable result was a vast increase in the number of nuclear warheads, both American and Soviet, with all its unpalatable aspects, including the perceived vulnerability of American land-based ICBMs. It is important to note that not only did the American and Soviet hawks have it their way, i.e. they prevented the American and Soviet doves from forsaking MIRVs by mutual restraint, but having created a more dangerous situation, those very hawks acquired more political muscle by advertising the threat posed by the MIRVs of the enemy.

The second example illustrates even more clearly the perverse nature of the situation, which always puts the hawks in a favourable position.

The perspective deployment, agreed by NATO in December 1979, of 108 Pershing II and 464 Ground-Launched Cruise Missiles (GLCMs) in Western Europe, within range of Moscow and Leningrad, constitutes an unpleasant additional threat to the Soviet Union. However, had the Soviet Union been prepared, in 1978 or early 1979, to offer a bargain involving a substantial restriction on her nuclear missiles targeted on Western Europe, in particular on the SS20s, it is likely that the NATO decision could have been pre-empted (of course, against the wish of American and West-European hawks). Such an offer was no doubt debated in the Soviet Union; indeed, in October 1979 President Brezhnev mentioned such a possibility, but by that time it was too late. Thus, the Soviet hawks, who did not want any restriction on the ongoing deployments of the SS20s, had it their way. Is it likely they are now held accountable for the missed opportunity to prevent the NATO decision? Have they thereby lost their political leverage? No. Indeed, their advocacy of the pursuance of an extended SS20 programme is now reinforced by the perceived threat of the perspective NATO deployments. Moreover, now that Soviet-American negotiations have begun, they can claim credit for the "strong negotiating position" the USSR enjoys, with so many SS20s already deployed. Should an agreement result from these negotiations, they may argue that the continued deployment of SS20s was instrumental in getting a better deal. Of course, now the most probable outcome is that there will be no agreement. Past experience demonstrates the difficulty to reverse a decision to produce and deploy weapons; it is even more difficult to agree to eliminate missiles soon after they have been deployed. Thus, in the end, the chances for the Soviet Union and Western Europe, as well as the

United States, to be blown up, will have been increased. Everybody will probably agree with this assessment, but the hawks who had blocked the attempt to prevent these developments will have their influence increased in the more tense and less secure situation. So it goes on.

Unilateral initiatives

The analysis outlined above suggests that instead of arms control negotiations, the hope to restrain the arms race should be pinned on unilateral initiatives. Indeed, the robustness of strategic deterrence, implied by the enormous second-strike overkill available to both sides, allows ample scope for unilateral restraints and reductions. For instance, George Kennan suggested a 50% cut without incurring any real risk[10]. The hope, of course, is that such an approach, if undertaken by one side, would be reciprocated by the other side. Without such reciprocation, the unilateral restraint would soon become politically untenable; in any case, real disarmament cannot be achieved by one side only.

But, under the present circumstances, the political viability of unilateral initiatives is debatable; indeed, in an atmosphere such as prevalent today, there is a risk that unilateral actions may be undertaken merely as a propaganda gesture, to whip up a more belligerent stand by denouncing the lack of reciprocation.

One hopes that an approach based on unilateral restraints rather than on bilateral or multilateral agreements will eventually be motivated by the recognition that this is the best way to pursue one's own security; thus, the main emphasis should be on the uselessness of "more than enough" rather than on the quest for reciprocation. Indeed, the prevalence of this attitude is essential for progress towards disarmament, whichever approach is followed; as a matter of fact, one should not take a drastic view of the alternative between negotiations and unilateral initiatives, since these approaches may well complement each other, especially if one is aware of the possible shortcomings, and advantages, of each.

Format of arms control negotiations

Arms control negotiations have not succeeded in restraining the nuclear arms race; they may even have stimulated it. This is partly due to their format: they take a long time, and aim at setting numerical limits on weapon systems, on the basis of some notion of parity. It is precisely when the negotiations face the difficult problem of quantifying the agreements, that the hawks on each side, often masquerading as arms controllers, have the opportunity to sabotage any accord, or to permit only agreements that increase the level of armaments rather than reduce it.

Different approaches to arms control negotiations can be envisaged which might ease these difficulties[11]; the possibility of thereby achieving greater success in curbing the arms race should be explored.

Controlling technology

As some of the examples discussed illustrate, technological developments are the breeding ground on which the nuclear arms race flourishes; their pace appears to overtake the attempts to control armaments. It would be useful if the progress of science and technology could be guided so that, instead of fuelling the arms race, it contributed to controlling it. Indeed, technology can contribute in that direction as well, for instance, the advances in verification by national means, brought about by satellites, have made arms control more feasible (see p.208).

This problem, however, does not have a simple solution; once again it goes back to the contrast between doves and hawks within decision-making systems, because the direction of technological development depends largely on the influence of the provider of funds. The idea that scientists and technologists as a group should refuse to collaborate with weapon-oriented research is mere wishful thinking; moreover, it ignores the asymmetries that exist between different societal structures. This option is of course open to individual scientists but it amounts to a personal stand, unlikely to have much influence. On the other hand, much useful work can be done by scientists and technologists who muster a high level of competence on weapon developments, and who use such knowledge to monitor destabilizing developments and to provide sound technical advice to the doves.

Parity versus sufficiency

The concept of strategic deterrence based on the retaliatory second-strike threat of assured destruction provides a sound conceptual basis for restraining the arms race, and for disarming all the way down to a minimum deterrent posture requiring only a very small fraction of the present nuclear arsenals. Indeed, a logical corollary to the theory of deterrence is the concept of *sufficiency*: no more nuclear weapons are required than those sufficient to guarantee unequivocally the capability to inflict unacceptable damage in a retaliatory second strike, even after absorbing an all-out nuclear attack. Nuclear weapons in excess of these are redundant; they are not only useless, they constitute a liability, because any nuclear weapon implies some risk of accidental or unauthorized use. Moreover, strategic nuclear warheads that are clearly in excess of the requirements of the second-strike retaliatory mission are bound to be interpreted by the other side as first-strike weapons; they provide therefore the best arguments for the hawks on the other side to oppose any restraint and to advocate additional investments to upgrade qualitatively and quantitatively nuclear arsenals.

It is of course debatable what unacceptable damage means. In fact, no decision-maker would rate the destruction of even a single city as acceptable damage[6]. Yet, at the present level of armaments, there is really no need to debate this point, since either of the two superpowers could unilaterally eliminate more than one half of its strategic arsenal and still be left with the capability, after absorbing a hypothetical all-out nuclear attack, to respond with a retaliatory blow that would kill promptly tens of millions of people and wipe out the attacking country as a viable society[12].

Although many more strategic weapons are around than any sound reasoning justifies, there are professional strategists who make their living by concocting justifications ("damage limitation", "extended deterrence", "escalation dominance") for the existing arsenals, or even for the need to expand them even more. Space does not permit to go into these "theories" in any detail, indeed, it is doubtful whether this would be a useful exercise, since all these arguments, based on unreal scenarios, are merely *a posteriori* justifications for the available arsenals, but have no major influence on the decisions to develop and deploy weapons.

What does have a determining influence, are two kinds of considerations that are deeply rooted in conventional wisdom, and that linger on even though they have been rendered obsolete by the advent of nuclear weapons.

The first of these concepts has already been mentioned: the drive to be stronger, and to be able, if need be, to go to war and win. There has been recently a resurgence of the idea that nuclear weapons are actually usable for *war fighting*, rather than merely for *deterrence*. This is envisaged in the hypothetical context of a nuclear war being kept controlled and limited; something nobody seriously thinks is actually feasible [13]. Nevertheless, it provides a theoretical framework to justify upgrading the nuclear arsenals qualitatively and quantitatively, both in their strategic and tactical components. One must hope that these ideas are never really accepted by the decision-makers; otherwise, the end is nigh.

The second idea, which does have a determining influence on the nuclear arms race, in spite of its obsolescence, is that of *parity*. This concept has an enormous political appeal; or rather, the contention that "the other side is ahead", is a charge no decision-maker can afford to ignore. It constitutes some progress compared with the notion that one's own side, being good, must be *superior* in order to guarantee peace. But, in spite of the lip service paid to the idea that parity is an overall concept and does not require a precise matching of capabilities, category by category, in actual fact, once the need for parity is emphasized, the way is open for the hawks on each side to focus only on those strategic indicators which show their side at a disadvantage. Moreover, the format of arms control agreements, except those of a qualitative nature, like the ABM Treaty, focusses the limelight on the game of numbers, thus providing the best opportunity for the hawks to denounce any arms control agreement as a sell-out by concentrating attention only on those quantitative comparisons that show their side at a disadvantage. For example, the fact that SALT I allowed the United States a smaller number of ICBMs than the Soviet Union, justified as it was by other imbalances, has provided devastating ammunition for the American hawks to discredit the SALT process and arms control generally. This is another point of which the importance cannot be overestimated.

The military – industrial – bureaucratic complex

The military-industrial-bureaucratic complex designates a network whose interests are largely vested in the continuation of the arms race. Although this multifarious lobby is more visible in American politics, there is no doubt that an analogous influence exists in Soviet policy, in spite of the differences between the American and Soviet societies.

The political impact of the military-industrial-bureaucratic complex is pervasive; not only does it influence decisions, it affects the conceptual and ethical framework of society to a significant degree. The ideas of the people who make a living by developing, producing or managing weapons, are obviously biased in favour of an enhanced role of such activities, and this often colours their general outlook. Moreover, the internal dynamics of the military-industrial-bureaucratic complex, for instance, inter-service rivalries, may provide an additional stimulus to the arms race and/or an additional impediment to arms limitation. These are inevitable phenomena, but it is important to ensure that decision-makers and public opinion are subject to advice and pressure which differ from those coming from the military-industrial-bureaucratic complex.

It is also useful to explore and advertise the alternative opportunities to employ the human and material resources now wasted in the arms race (conversion); to pinpoint the missed benefits to society at large, and to allay the worries of those who fear that their economic security and social influence would be threatened by an eventual ending of the arms race.

A fact likely to play an increasingly important role over the next years is the pressure, both in the United States and the Soviet Union, of the overall socio-economic burden of the arms race, and the damage resulting from the diversion of such a large share of resources, and especially advanced research away from socially useful goals. One must hope that this will initiate within society, and perhaps even within the military-industrial-bureaucratic complex itself, the recognition of a need to change, which might reinforce synergistically the basic motivation to stop the arms race: the avoidance of a nuclear catastrophe.

What can be done

This chapter would be incomplete without an attempt to outline ways and means to stop and reverse the nuclear arms race.

Détente

A return to the international atmosphere of détente is essential. It is not a precondition for stopping the nuclear arms race, since these two goals are so closely related that success can only be achieved synergistically.

An essential component of détente should be the discussion at summit level of the substantive issues which create apprehensions and fuel the arms race. Moreover, such discussions should lead to the recognition of, and joint action on, common goals for humankind, such as global management of resources and major scientific and technological projects.

One positive aspect of the world today, which should not be belittled, is that the official rhetoric of both camps, as well as the feeling of most individuals, favour peace and even nuclear disarmament. This may be considered pure propaganda, or at best wishful thinking; nevertheless, it makes a great difference from the situation before the Second World War with Hitler in power in Nazi Germany. Peaceful coexistence is still the official policy of both superpowers.

The linkage of progress towards disarmament with "good behaviour" in all other conflicts is not a wise policy. The Nobel Peace Prize Laureate Andrei Sakharov is right in stating that nuclear arms control and disarmament must have priority, and no other consideration can justify forsaking any chance of progress in that direction. Yet the linkage is a fact of life; if belligerent confrontation rather than prudent restraint prevails in the world-wide behaviour of the superpowers, détente evaporates and so does, realistically, any chance of success in curbing the nuclear arms race.

Approaches to nuclear arms control and disarmament

It is hard to envisage a way out of the present predicament, without direct negotiations between the two superpowers. Some kind of resumption of the SALT process is probably expedient, although a different format might help to overcome some of the difficulties that have been discussed above. As for the transition from SALT to START, if this signifies a serious intention to consider Reductions rather than only Limitations, then it is of course welcome.

Proposals to precede any formal negotiation by a generalized freeze appear eminently sound. Also commendable, and certainly worthy of widespread international support, is the so-called "strategy of suffocation" of the nuclear arms race proposed by Canada, key elements of which are a comprehensive test ban, a cut-off of the production of fissile materials for weapon purposes and the banning of novel strategic weapon-systems.

Finally, it is high time the two superpowers recognized the priority of an effective non-proliferation policy, to avoid a nuclear catastrophe. Hence the need to curb vertical nuclear proliferation, as a precondition to tackle horizontal proliferation and to develop a common approach to this problem.

General and complete disarmament

General and complete disarmament must remain a fundamental goal of mankind; even though at present it appears as distant as the establishment of a World Government. Indeed, both these goals must be recognized as necessary for the survival of mankind. Difficult as they are to realize, they serve the important purpose of providing an alternative to despair, fear and demoralization, especially for the younger generation.

References

1. *World Armaments and Disarmament. SIPRI Yearbook* 1980, p.XLIII, and 1981, p.275.

2. Solly Zuckerman: *Science Advisers, Scientific Advisers and Nuclear Weapons*, the Menard Press, London, 1980. Lord Mountbatten: speech in Strasbourg on the occasion of the award of the Prize of the Louise Weiss Foundation to SIPRI, 11 May 1979. *Bulletin of the Atomic Scientists, October 1979, p.1.* G. Kennan: *A modest proposal. The New York Review of Books* (July 16, 1981).

3. Address before the Foreign Policy Association, New York, July 14, 1981.

4. See, for instance, the *Proceedings of the First Congress of*

International Physicians for the Prevention of Nuclear War, Airlie, Virginia, March 1981.

5. See, for instance, the lucid analysis by H.J. Morgenthau: The fallacy of thinking conventionally about nuclear weapons, in *Arms Control and Technological Innovation* (D. Carlton and C. Schaerf, editors). Croom Helm, London, 1977, pp. 255-264.

6. McGeorge Bundy, "To cap the volcano". *Foreign Affairs* vol.48 (1), pp.1-20, October 1969.

7. F. Barnaby, *SIPRI Yearbook* 1981, p.XV.

8. See, for instance, G.W. Rathjens, A. Chayes and J.P. Ruina: *Nuclear Arms Control Agreements: Process and Impact*. Carnegie Endowment for International Peace. Washington, D.C. 1974.

9. H. York: The origins of MIRV. In: *The Dynamics of the Arms Race* (D. Carlton and C. Schaerf, eds.). Croom Helm, London, 1975, pp.23-35. See also York's paper in the November 1973 issue of the *Scientific American, and the SIPRI Research Report No. 9, August 1973, ("The origins of MIRV")*.

10. G. Kennan *ibid*. (item 2).

11. See, for instance, F. Calogero: "A Scenario for Effective SALT Negotiations", *Bulletin of the Atomic Scientists* vol. 39, pp.16-22 (1973); "A novel approach to arms control negotiations?" in *Proceedings of the 27th Pugwash Conference on Science and World Affairs*, Munich, August 1977, pp.170-176.

12. See, for instance, the UN General Assembly document A/35/392, *Comprehensive study on nuclear weapons* (Report of the Secretary-General), September 1980.

13. See, for instance, the recent paper by Desmond Ball: Can Nuclear War be Controlled? *Adelphi Paper No 169*, International Institute for Strategic Studies, London, Autumn 1981.

Chapter 2. Other weapons and new technologies

Karlheinz Lohs

Introduction

Armament spending for 1981 is estimated by the United Nations Organization to amount to over US $500 billion, as compared with $400 billion ten years ago (at constant prices). One reason for this inexcusable increase in military expenditure is that about ten new kinds of systems of weapons are being developed every year.

According to estimates[1] some 500 000 scientists and engineers are at present engaged in the field of armament engineering, weapons development and military research. It is from their activities that new weapons are developed at such a rate and introduced into armed security. These developments range from new kinds of conventional weapon and redesigned incendiaries, to nuclear weapons of an ever-increasing destructive force or specialization, as is the case, for example, with the 'enhanced radiation weapon' (neutron bomb).

Chemical weapons, too, have undergone a particularly dangerous development in the past few years. They complement the background of the spectacular production of nuclear weapons and their stationing on land, on water and in the air, and of other exotic developments, such as the anti-satellite systems and particle beam weapons.

New weapons technology (NWT)

The situation with regard to chemical weapons can be seen as a microcosm of the whole, but before enlarging upon it in greater detail some comments need to be made about the problem of the new weapons technology. NWT will have fundamental effects on the full range of modern warfare, from conventional war to satellite and nuclear-missile

LIBRARY
COLBY-SAWYER COLLEGE
NEW LONDON, NH 03257

98931

war. NWT is largely a reflection or implementation of micro-electronics in military science. The factual situation as described by Richard Burt[2] in 1976 is still impressive today.

The substantially increased targeting accuracy achieved by new guidance techniques is a particularly striking development of NWT. A growing number of bombs, missiles and artillery shells, known generally as "precision-guided munitions" (PGM), is becoming available that have a single-shot-destruction probability which is 10 to 100 times greater than that of unguided munitions[3].

These techniques of guidance are being used or developed for weapons systems that include portable combat field weapons. Three groups can be distinguished: seeker guidance, precision positioning, and correlation guidance.

Seeker guidance, having been used so far primarily for missiles, is now also being applied to artillery and mortar shells with a final phase guidance such that impact accuracies of 0.3 to 0.9 metres were reached, with the help of laser target illumination, during test trials.

Precision positioning makes use of the signals emitted by synchronized transmitters or beacons in order to correct the accumulating errors of inertial navigation systems on board of means of deployment. More recent positioning systems, such as distance measuring equipment (DME), seem likely on their own to achieve the accuracy required for final phase guidance. An important line of development is the use of satellites to deliver data for course correction. The American Global Positioning System (GPS) with 24 in geostationary orbit satellites has made it possible for the deployment systems to determine their positioning with a deviation of less than 10 metres over intercontinental distances.

The systems of correlation guidance are based on a kind of comparison of maps with optical, radar, infra-red or microwave sensors, whereby course corrections are derived from the correlation of the image of the target area with stored reference images.

The long-distance cruise missiles developed by the United States are supposed to be targeted with the help of terrain contour matching (TERCOM), using radar altimetry for the cruising phase and a microwave radiometer for the final-phase guidance. This combination is thought to permit deviations of less than 30 metres over intercontinental distances.

For several years, development of remotely piloted vehicles (RPV) has paralleled that of PGMs. But only recently has progress in electronic data-transfer made it possible to give RPVs complex commands. The major fields of application of RVPs is reconnaissance of targets, allocation of targets, air raids and electronic warfare.

Directly related are improved ammunition technologies, including adaptation of conventional ammunition to the new method of identifying and striking targets, as well as a wide variety of strike means, such as chemical agents and incendiaries. Above all, conventional explosives have been continuously improved so as to enhance destructive effects but to reduce unwanted side-effects.

The increased reliability is considered to be an especially important development, obtained by minimum-maintenance warheads, missile fuels and fuse systems. Also to be observed is a trend away from general-purpose ammunition, exemplified by high kinetic-energy projectiles and improved hollow-charge projectiles for the attack of point targets. Shells with an accelerated final velocity serve, for instance, to penetrate concrete. "Earth penetrators" can reach deep into hard-core areas before detonating to produce a large crater. Today, conventional high-explosive ammunition is designed in such a way as to maximize the effects either of pressure or of fragments, or both, for concerted efforts on particular targets.

To achieve greater target-area coverage, clusters of munitions are used and dropped in greater quantities. In the wake of the new binary munition technology, diverse possibilities have also been opened up for the use of highly toxic chemical-warfare agents in this manner. Progress in cluster technology also includes the laying of mines to be dropped in containers holding up to 80 minelets from aircraft, or in artillery shells. Latest developments in mine technology allow activation and de-activation of mines from remote distances. Barrier weapons, such as mines, can also be filled with chemical warfare agents to create barriers which are difficult to surmount and thus considerably reduce the mobility of troops on the battlefield.

A brief reference should also be made to a new type of weapon that has become known since the Vietnam War, fuel – air explosives (FAE). These are dropped in canisters which rupture a few moments before impact. The liquid fuel from the canisters is distributed in fine droplets over a wide area and its resultant mixture with the surrounding air is then detonated to create an intense pressure wave. The military attraction of FAEs is that the energy released by pressure in the target area is more evenly distributed over the target than is the case with the explosion of a conventional composition, such as TNT. One kilogramme of ethylene oxide, a typical FAE fuel, produces the same pressure wave as 5 kilogrammes of TNT. Efforts are under way to increase this efficiency still further. The motion put forward by Mexico, Sweden and Switzerland, at the United Nations Conference on Specific Conventional Weaponry in 1979-80, to ban this weapon, was justified by the fact that the death rate with FAE is extremely high. The pressure wave ruptures the lungs, causes emboli in the brain and the heart, and those afflicted suffer a protracted and very painful death.

As becomes manifest, this is a specially macabre chapter of the military and technical perversion and the misuse of research work of science!

Finally, a few words on so-called electronic warfare. In the past ten years the following three major fields of electronic warfare have gained great importance: electronic reconnaissance, electronic counter-measures, and electronic protective measures.

It is obvious that these three related fields of armament technology have long been under active development because, given the present and still increasing use of electronics in weapons systems, even a small lead in the use, or interference with that use, or countermeasures against this interference, may result in decisive combat advantages.

In tactical operations, progress achieved in the miniaturization of electronic systems will permit even the smallest combat units to receive or transmit important information. The objective here is remote decision-making based on real-time information, and it appears that this will soon become feasible by the rapid development of computer technology.

The spectrum of the new command-and-control technologies covers the data transfer to individual weapons systems as well as that to world-wide systems, such as the American system WWMCCS (World-wide Military Command and Control System).

As scientists we must keep in mind that these new developments in the field of command, control, communication and intelligence will have a profound effect on the pace of future war and on the character of the future battlefield. It may have even a greater effect than that of new weapons, from strategic to the tactical level, and for conventional as well as nuclear wars. Should tactical guidance of ballistic missiles become possible – which is likely to occur in the mid-1980s – both sides would be under greater pressure to destroy each other's satellite systems during the first minutes of the war in order not to lose their major assets, like aircraft carriers and submarines. The same urgency would prevail on the tactical level with sensor/computer-based fire-control because counter-artillery radars would be able to locate the original shells and make it possible to interfere before they reached their target. Such automatization would speed up the pace of the battle to an unforeseen degree.

Chemical weapons

Since the mid-1950s, military chemical research has been conducted intensively in the United States on the development of a new warfare agents technology within the framework of so-called binary weapons programme[4].

As a result of the emergence of these new chemical warfare agents, a further escalation has been reached in rearmament with chemical mass destruction weapons, making the existing acute danger to peace even more threatening[5].

By 'binary' chemical agents is meant those substances that can be separately stored, transported and filled into shells as two relatively low-toxic chemical compounds; only after the firing of the shell or missile do the two components mix to undergo a chemical reaction producing a highly toxic warfare agent. This process happens within a few seconds.

The idea of "defusing" a warfare agent which otherwise could be managed only with great risk, by allowing it to be handled as two comparatively harmless precursors up to the moment of discharge, is not entirely new. In 1909 this idea was put forward in the first of chemical explosives in the form of a binary principle for the stockpiling and use of nitroglycerine. Similar concepts were advanced during the Second World War for the use of high explosives materials and for special arsenic warfare agents (magnesium arsenide and sulphuric acid). Several field tests with binary substances were carried out during the Second World War, but, because of technical defects, these binary weapons did not become operational. At present there is no reliable information available about a binary weapon programme in the USSR.

In the United States, the beginning of the present development of binary chemical weapons can be traced back to 1954. The development was initially focussed on massive aircraft bombs for generating VX-type agents, and later on smaller munitions for sarin, both these agents being neurotoxic components based on organic phosphorus compounds. 'Big eye' is the latest embodiment of the binary VX bomb.

At the beginning of the 1970s the United States still had substantial stockpiles of sarin and VX chemical warfare agents which would remain utilizable up to the middle of the 1980s at least, so that at that time the United States was not so much pressed to adopt the binary weapons technology. It would appear that in the 1970s the binary weapons remained in a stage of a stalled technical development, i.e. a stage which would make it possible to start production immediately in the event of a "favourable" political situation.

On 27 June 1980, the American House of Representatives, without debate and without a formal request by the President, voted approval of a factory for binary weapons production at Pine Bluff Arsenal. Since then the new Administration has endorsed the programme and stepped it up by the allocation of additional funds.

Is there any real military justification for new chemical weapons? An attempt is made below to provide an answer to this question, but it should be remembered that this attempt is made from the point of view of a civilian toxicologist.

1. Unlike other kinds of weapon, chemical weapons have become cheaper because of the use for civilian purposes of chemicals utilizable in the new binary weapons technology. Moreover, with that technology, cost-intensive storage problems no longer exist for the supply and

the regular renewal of stockpiles of chemical ammunition.

2. Binary technology makes it theoretically possible to reach a new qualitative development by enhancing the effects and the specific action of chemical warfare agents.

3. The possibilities of using those poisons that so far have been considered useless for military purposes have now become real because of binary technology. At the same time the boundaries between an agreement on chemical weapons and the already existing agreement on biological weapons are no longer clearly distinctive. The juridical definition of chemical weapons as conventional, or as mass destruction weapons, has also become rather elusive. The problem of precursors may make the definition and control more complex and therefore more difficult.

4. In general, there is an ever-increasing range of possibilities for the misuse of highly toxic products of the civilian industry also for military purposes (e.g., pesticides and some other agents noxious to the environment). The spectrum of civilian products used in the military chemical field is much wider today than 20 or 30 years ago.

5. The scientific insights into molecular biology suggest that it is possible to develop completely new kinds and systems of chemical and biological weapons of mass destruction (such as ethnic weapons or new psychotoxic warfare agents).

6. The military opportunities for covert warfare and for the use of sabotage agents have continuously increased and thus have become more threatening (e.g. the purposive destruction of domestic animals in industrialized agriculture, cattle breeding, damage to harvest crops, to drinking water and so on).

7. The medical protection of the civilian population from the effects of an attack with chemical weapons has continuously become more complicated and expensive. Only a very limited number of persons can effectively be protected against chemical weapons. This is tantamount to a temptation that should not be underrated.

In view of these military attractions of chemical warfare agents, the scientifically substantiated counter-arguments should be taken seriously. Historical experience has shown that an appeal to higher moral principles rarely has a salutary effect on people with aggressive minds. Whoever has been in the possession of a new weapon has believed that he is superior to those who lack the weapon.

The binary weapons technology, however, does not lack disadvantages. Although several binary components are available in countries with a developed chemical industry, or can be used there as civilian products, the total expenditure involved in converting chemical warfare ammunition to binary technology would be large. For example costs of conversion in the United States may well exceed some $8 billion.

In addition, there are costs required to adapt the structure of the civilian chemical industry to the requirements of this military binary programme. But there are still other disadvantages affecting the military value of binary weapons. Here are some examples, arbitrarily selected. A binary shell or bomb is bound to carry with it a higher potential incidence of faults and defects than do non-binary systems; there is more to go wrong. Moreover, consideration has to be given to the invariably long reaction periods for the binary components; with the current types of warfare agents they account for 10 to 20 seconds. As a result, an immediate attack against nearby targets would be difficult, even rendered impossible. The effective "payload" of a binary chemical weapon is smaller than that of a non-binary one because the binary components are at most utilized only to 70 to 80% during the process of chemical conversion. This would mean that the area that would be attacked or poisoned would diminish. Another negative aspect is the intensity of odour of several binary components which facilitates chemical reconnaissance by those to be attacked with these weapons.

Most of these shortcomings can be offset by appropriate military planning, but problems of transport and logistics would remain. An army equipped with binary weapons has to ensure that both components are available at the same time at the theatre of operation in the quantities necessary. Under the conditions of a military conflict this may be difficult to organize. Therefore, the probability of technical losses and organizational disturbances will increase considerably.

Despite these difficulties, and despite the costs of conversion of the existing chemical weapons, the American leadership has unequivocally endorsed binary weapons technology. There is cause for apprehension that other countries might follow this example. The United Kingdom has already shown signs of moving in this direction.

In this context a remark on principles appears to be appropriate. The modern weapons of our time, whether they be nuclear or chemical, are different in principle from the weapons of past centuries. The difference lies in the self-infliction of danger by the possessor of weapons. Normally rifles and guns fire only in the direction of the enemy. Although the production and possession of rifles and guns is an economic burden, there is at least no immediate danger of self-destruction. This is quite different with nuclear weapons and chemical warfare agents, a fact known by everybody even if the advocates of these modern systems of weapons are anxious to deny it, or to play it down.

In the case of nuclear weapons it is recognized that even the handling of the weapons may turn out to be dangerous to their possessors. But with regard to chemical weapons, the corresponding dangers are not yet sufficiently recognized by the public, nor even by the military. Binary weapons technology has been instrumental in bringing about the erroneous belief that this type of chemical weapon can be safely handled in public and by the military. However, the actual improvement of technical safety of binary warfare agents during production, stockpiling and use does not at all run parallel to the improvement of security in health standards for those who are continuously concerned with the components of binary warfare agents.

It is in the nature of almost all toxic compounds that they produce acute effects. However, delayed lesions, in more or less pronounced forms, can also result from ostensibly harmless concentrations. The greater the transition to the acceptance of increasingly complicated biochemical principles of operation that may characterize the likely development of new chemical warfare agents (and this transition has to be achieved by an aggressor intent on eliminating the enemy's defences and the medical protection available), the greater will be the risk of delayed side-effects and of long-term damage to man[6] and his environment[7].

Therefore, much more has to be done to make the public aware of the extent of the danger involved in chemical warfare agents. It is really paradoxical that, on the one hand, there is world-wide alarm about the threat which certain civil chemical agents that are increasingly necessary for human society pose to the environment; on the other hand, in many countries highly toxic substances are produced and stockpiled for use as chemical warfare agents. The politicians and the military of these countries are well advised not to reveal their potential danger.

Whenever there is news about the scope of the danger arising from military toxins to man or to the environment – as with the dioxin-caused injuries, or the lesions among the Vietnam war veterans, or the ecological devastations in Vietnam – the press has tended to bypass such controversial stories, suppressing them and covering them with a cloak of secrecy, passing instead to the reporting of political trivialities.

When describing and assessing the scope of danger to man and to environment in a chemical war, it is necessary also to take into account another factor which is not immediately related to the military use of poisons. This lies in the dangers threatening a densely populated and highly industrialized country in the event of the destruction of civil chemical plants by shells, bombs, or missiles. The quantities of highly toxic industrial chemicals released into the open air could well create a catastrophic situation comparable to the use of warfare agents. The term "secondary environmental weapons" has been suggested to describe the effects of civil chemical compounds. Since superiority in chemical warfare agents for military uses can only be achieved and maintained on the basis of a continuous transition to permanently higher toxic compounds – and here the existing security systems appear to be inappropriate – even at the highest stage of technical development the infliction of danger upon oneself continues to exist, thus making chemical weapons an unsafe warfare agent even in this military respect. Of course, the military staffs for chemical planning will not accept this view. But it is probably safe to assume that the military leaders are also aware of it. Notwithstanding this fact, the chemical strategy of deterrence is maintained.

Convention to ban chemical weapons

We turn now to the effects produced by the introduction of binary weapons technology on the current chemical weapons disarmament negotiations. Many resolutions have now been adopted by the United Nations, endorsing these negotiations. In addition, state-parties to the 1972 Biological Weapons Convention are now committed under international law to conduct such negotiations. This commitment is derived from Article IX of the Convention, which reads as follows:

> "Each State Party to this Convention affirms the recognized objective of effective prohibition of chemical weapons and to this end, undertakes to continue negotiations in faith with a view to reaching early agreement on effective measures for the prohibition of their development, production and stockpiling and for their destruction..."

This formulation does not expressly prohibit the new development of chemical weapons and their introduction, but it can be interpreted to indicate that the further development of chemical weapons is inconsistent with the continuation of negotiations in "good spirit". From this standpoint the introduction of binary weapons technology must be seen as tantamount to disregarding the obligations of international law. The effects of such a step would accordingly be a strain on all on-going disarmament talks.

Apart from this general and fundamental strain there are several peculiarities affecting the disarmament talks on the banning of chemical weapons in a substantive manner as well. Some of them must be referred to here.

The problem of defining chemical weapons and the scope of a Chemical Weapons (C-weapons) Convention is immediately affected. This is not the place to go into detail about the very complex problems of definition; they are discussed in the literature. The Geneva Protocol of 1925 does not provide a detailed definition of chemical weapons, but instead prohibits the use of poisonous, asphyxiating or similar materials without any reference to concrete data on the toxicity of these substances. The prohibition thus rests on a general purpose criterion that refers to virtually all substances deployable as chemical warfare agents. However, during the current disarmament negotiations in Geneva, Western and American representatives have suggested supplementing the general purpose criterion in the projected C-weapons Convention by an effects criterion based on toxicity. Substances above a certain limit of toxicity are to be considered warfare agents, whereas less toxic substances are not to be so classified. The socialist states, as well as a number of neutral and non-aligned states have consistently advocated a comprehensive ban on preparations for chemical war, but have nevertheless taken account of the position of the United States to a certain extent. Thus, in the joint statement of the Soviet Union and the United States of July 1980 concerning the bilateral negotiations on a joint initiative for a C-weapons Convention, there may be found, in addition to the general purpose criterion, supplementary toxicity criteria.

One problem with binary chemical ammunition, among others, is that the lethal nerve gas is present in the shell only in the target vicinity; before that it exists only in a potential form, as low-toxicity precursors. For this reason it has to be ensured that any toxicity values that may be specified in a CW Convention for lethally acting warfare agents will also take account of the binary technology and will include binary precursors.

Another very complex disarmament problem refers to the control of the C-weapons Convention: the question of verification. This matter has long been in the focus of discussion by experts. As to the problem of verification, a fundamentally new situation has arisen in conjunction with the development of binary weapons and the move towards their production. To understand the factual situation reference must be made here to the most essential control mechanisms of a future Convention.

A number of countries, notably the United States, demand on-site control and inspection undertaken by international inspection groups, i.e. a detailed inspection of the production centres and stockpiling installations. This would appear to be virtually impracticable in this form. It has been suggested that the United States relates such an inspection exclusively to its national sector and excludes private chemical enterprises from the control mechanism.[8] But since in the Soviet Union, as well as in some other countries, the entire chemical industry is state-owned, such rigorous international control measures with on-site inspection would open the gates for all-out industrial espionage. Binary technology would aggravate this situation, because some components of binaries are used as starting materials and intermediate products in the civilian industry.

It appears to be indispensable to combine national and international control mechanisms in a purposive manner. On-site inspections will have to be limited to a few exactly defined instances (e.g. to stockpile-destruction activities, or to really dubious cases), with full acceptance of reciprocity and equality of commitments. Supplementary control mechanisms will also have to be considered with a view to guaranteeing a sufficiently secure verification process. A number of suggestions have been put forward to this end and discussed within the Geneva Disarmament Committee.

In this context, the statistical analysis of economic data and near-site inspections, as well as the analysis and investigation of industrial safety measures, have assumed special importance.

However, all these mechanisms would be affected to a large degree by the introduction of the binary technology, since this would entail a substantial expansion of the range of substances to be verified by economic monitoring, by telemetering methods, or by near-site inspections. The limitations to national and international control methods that are presently feasible are acknowledged. However, these methods will have to be considered effective, since, on the one hand, they allow for the legitimate economic interests of states and preclude industrial espionage and, on the other hand, allow for a sufficient amount of safe indications of the existence or non-existence of production facilities for modern chemical warfare agents.

In summary, the introduction of binary weapons will have an incriminating and confidence-diminishing effect on the controllability of a future Convention on chemical weapons. It is therefore essential for the United States and the Soviet Union to consider this question and resolve it in principle in their bilateral negotiations. Even then, additional protracted negotiations will still be required.

Finally, there is the matter of the proliferation of chemical warfare agents. Under international law the proliferation of chemical weapons and initiation of production in those countries not now possessing such weapons have so far not been banned. It has to be assumed that several states in the developing world have an interest in acquiring these weapons.

It is a matter of fact that chemical weapons have gained special importance in exactly these regions of the Third World. While the well-equipped and trained armies in Europe are prepared for chemical attack, with the availability also of limited civil defence measures, chemical warfare waged under the conditions of the Third World would have devastating effects. Let us recall the use of chemical warfare agents in the Vietnam war. This chemical war was waged "exclusively" with the use of herbicides, but one can well imagine the effects produced in a chemical war in similarly unprotected countries, if chemical warfare agents of the type of sarin or VX were used.

Barriers that existed hitherto in the technical difficulties of manufacturing chemical weapons are now being eliminated with the introduction of the binary technology. The costs and technical risks accruing and involved in the production of binaries are far less than those associated with the previous technology; the stockpiling of the binary components is feasible under the conditions of these countries, for example.

These are the reasons why the proliferation of chemical agents of mass destruction must be stopped by the earliest possible conclusion of an International Treaty, mandatory on all countries, on the prohibition of the development, production, stockpiling and use of these weapons and the destruction of their stockpiles.[9]

The arms race in general is an economic madness, but chemical weapons are also of doubtful military value; to the country possessing these weapons they are a time-bomb threatening its own security.

The emotional aspect must be emphasized in public discussion. One need not hesitate about propagating anxiety and apprehension, for there are indeed grounds for real apprehension and real fear in the multiple potential effects of chemical warfare agents on man and his environment. The Russell – Einstein Manifesto (see Appendix 1) is also marked by fear and apprehension, and nobody thought that this was a weak point; on the contrary, everybody realized that the physicists, who are fully aware of the terrible danger of nuclear weapons, had expressed their apprehensions. The same applies to the appeal of the scientists who issued "The Declaration of the Göttingen Eighteen" (see p.124); their knowledge and conscience prompted them to appeal to the public.

We realize that the old form of appeals for disarmament is unlikely to achieve its purpose nowadays. Let us therefore reconsider seriously how to find new ways and means to reach public opinion more effectively in attempts to make people aware of the extent of the dangers involved.

A hopeful example for banning particular weapons is the prohibition of inhumane and indiscriminate weapons. On this topic the *SIPRI Brochure 1981* states [10]

> "The second session of the UN conference on 'inhumane weapons' took place in September-October 1980. A convention on prohibitions or restrictions on the use of certain conventional weapons, and three protocols, were forwarded to the UN General Assembly for commendation. Entry into force requires 20 states to have ratified or acceded.
>
> The one concrete achievement of the first (1979) session of the UN conference had been agreement among all participating states that there should be an outright prohibition of the use of weapons (such as plastic-coated bombs) intended to injure by means of dispersing fragments not detectable in the human body by X-rays. This prohibition was carried forward to the 1980 session where, without further discussion, it was adopted as a protocol.
>
> The second protocol dealt with restrictions and prohibitions on the use of mines, booby traps and 'other devices' (those manually emplaced munitions and devices which are designed to kill, injure or damage and are actuated by remote control or automatically after a lapse of time). The third protocol dealt with prohibitions and restrictions on the use of incendiary weapons.
>
> However, the significance of the new convention and protocols is severely, some would say crucially, limited by the deliberate exclusion of nuclear weapons and other weapons of mass destruction from the negotiations. Another important negative point is that the agreement left the use of incendiary weapons against combatants as unrestricted as before, while even the protection of civilians against incendiary attack was left incomplete.
>
> Much will now turn on the prospects for energetic follow-up of the UN conference to make further advances in the categories of weaponry with which it started to deal. There is now a precise framework within which further advances on this humanitarian front can be made."

The Soviet Union's views on development and prohibition of new weapons technology

What are the problems of new future types and systems of weapons of mass annihilation?

In this field the Soviet Union and its allies have for years waged a struggle against the attitude of the United States and the other NATO-countries which take the view that such weapons cannot be banned as long as they have not become part and parcel of military equipment.

By contrast, the Soviet Union and its allies hold that it would be reasonable and also more economical to interrupt the development of new weapons already in their initial stage and thus prevent any further escalation of the arms race.

The former Soviet general, Mikhail A. Milstein had the following to say on this question on the occasion of a symposium on "Science and Disarmament" organized by the French Institute for International Relations in Paris, in January 1981[11]:

"In the Soviet Union's view, new types and systems of weapons of mass destruction are such as may be created in the future on the basis either of presently known scientific-technical principles, which were not used until now separately or in their totality for the creation of mass destruction weapons, or of scientific-technical principles that may be discovered in the future and that will have properties similar or even stronger in their destructive or injurious effects than the known types of mass destruction weapons.

In other words, this is a weapon based on qualitatively new principles of action.

It is important to determine the criteria, the basic categories of classification principles, according to which it will be possible to specify one or another mass destruction weapon as a new one. The Soviet delegation at the Disarmament Committee proposed the following three criteria:

a. Objects of action
b. Methods of action
c. Effects of action

Proceeding from these criteria (classification features), the novelty of a weapon is determined by the novelty either of the object of action, the method of action or the effects of action...

The Soviet delegation suggested such a list by pointing in the first place to four possible trends in the development of new mass destruction weapons:

1. Radiological weapons of non-explosive type, whose action is based on radioactive materials.

2. Radiation weapons based on the use of charged or neutral particles for affecting biological objects (close to such a weapon is, in particular, the neutron bomb, a greater part of its energy is released in the form of ionizing radiation – fast neutrons).

3. Infrasound weapons using acoustic emission for affecting biological

objects. Infrasound is known to possess at certain frequencies (7 hertz) the so-called psychotropic effect, in which the behaviour of huge masses of people becomes uncontrollable.

4. Radiofrequency weapons. The point at issue is radiofrequency (electromagnetic) emissions of very low levels impairing the human brain, the nervous and cardio-vascular systems and others. Various radio-engineering devices which are available to industrialized countries can be regarded as a potential technical base for the creation in future of such mass destruction weapons.

Understandably, this list can be amplified. Experts in various countries point to the possibility of developing and producing other dangerous types of mass destruction weapons as a result of use for military purposes not only of individual discoveries in various fields of knowledge, but also a systematic use of achievements in the field of natural sciences. Mention is made among them of weapons capable of affecting people of a certain ethnic group, reproduction of progeny, causing (including by covert action) a sharp drop in agricultural output, etc.

...."The first thing that would be needed under such circumstances would be to discontinue the quantitative and qualitative growth of armaments completely. Of special importance could be the conclusion of an agreement prohibiting research into and the development of new types of weapons of mass destruction and new systems of such weapons."

Nothing needs to be added to the above considerations. We must do away with a new round in the spiral of rearmament, before it hurls us down into the abyss which could mean the end of mankind on our planet.

The idea is not to wage war with "intelligent weapons" but rather to wage an action for peace in the interest of intelligent people who want to remain inhabitants of the Earth for another thousand years.

References

1. *Study on the Relationship between Disarmament and Development,* Report of the Secretary-General, United Nations' Doc. A/36/356 (A81). See also World Federation of Scientific Workers, *Ending the Arms Race – the Role of the Scientist.* London, 1977.
2. R. Burt, *New Weapons Technologies – Debate and Directions.* Adelphi Papers No. 126, the International Institute for Strategic Studies, London, 1976.
3. P.F. Walker, Precision-guided Weapons. *Scientific American,* vol.245, No.2, 1981, p.20-29
4. J.P. Perry-Robinson, Binary nerve-gas weapons,: *Chemical Disarmament: New Weapons for Old.* Stockholm International Peace Research Institute (SIPRI), 1975, p.21-74.
5. K. Lohs & R. Trapp, Die Einführung chemischer Binarwaffen in den USA und die Abrüstung im Bereich chemischer Waffen *Deutsche*

Außenpolitik, (Berlin) vol.26, No.10, 1981, p.58-68.

6. *Delayed Toxic Effects of Chemical Warfare Agents*. Stockholm International Peace Research Institute (SIPRI), 1975.

7. K. Lohs and A.H. Westing, Umweltkrieg oder Abrüstung, *Wissenschaft und Fortschritt*, vol.32, No.2, 1982, pp.64-68.

8. *International Herald Tribune*, 26 January 1982.

9. *Chemical Weapons: Destruction and Conversion*. Stockholm International Peace Research Institute (SIPRI). 1980

10. *Armaments or Disarmament*. SIPRI – Brochure 1981, Stockholm International Peace Research Institute (SIPRI), Stockholm 1981. p.26

11. M. Milstein. Science, technology and arms build-up, *Science and Disarmament*. International Colloquium, Institut français des relations internationales, Paris, January 1981.

Chapter 3. The race in military technology

Marek Thee

Technology in command

It is a truism that the arms race today is driven by a technological momentum. In a sense, this observation reflects a structural historical regularity: the quality of arms and, to a great extent, the level of armaments in each period of history usually mirror the degree of technological performance and development of society. Today, the dynamics of world armaments is propelled by the contemporary technological revolution and the potentials inherent in the application of nuclear power. One of the main characteristics of the contemporary arms race is its science-based fixation on an intensive technological thrust.

The explosion in military technology is felt far beyond purely military affairs. The whole structure of international relations is affected. The moment new weapon systems enter the production line and become available, they start to figure high in the political decision-making process. They tend to become a determining factor in the shaping of strategy and policy. They lose the properties of a technical tool and become a political and national security asset to be exploited as an instrument of policy and diplomacy. Policy is prompted and corrupted by the availability of new weapon systems. In a way, technology usurps a commanding position and policy becomes subordinated to the technological drive[1].

This state of affairs is well exemplified by the collapse of the SALT process and the East-West clash about the deployment in Europe of long and intermediate range nuclear weapons. Quite apart from events in the international political sphere, at the root of the collapse of SALT was the emergence and operationalization of new weapon delivery systems of higher accuracy and sophistication, such as cruise missiles or mobile interchangeable ballistic missiles. These weapon systems opened up new strategic options and thereby changed the course of policy. The appearance on the political-military market of new weapon systems actuates their deployment and stimulates their incorporation into the political-strategic game.

True, new weapon systems are not exclusively the product of technological inspiration. There is a mutual stimulation between military aspirations for ever better arms and the autonomous momentum of military R&D. However, the fact remains that it is new military gadgets which lend wings to novel strategies/policies. They impregnate the mind of the strategists/politicians, who themselves are in pursuit of more impressive instruments for the power game. New weapon systems tend generally to act as catalysts for new political and strategic departures. They actually arrogate to themselves a political function.

This is clearly visible in the evolution of deterrence theories/strategies. Advances in the efficiency and operationalization of nuclear weapons animated the process of degeneration of deterrence postures from defensive to war fighting strategies. They marked the way from the "unacceptable damage" and the "mutual assured destruction" doctrines (dissuading deterrence) to war-fighting counterforce/countervailing strategies, as reflected in the Presidential Directive 59 (extended deterrence)[2]. The availability of more perfect technology, and the parallel evolution of new strategic concepts, led both to the deployment of the SS-20 missiles in Eastern Europe and to the decision of NATO in December 1979 about the deployment plans of Pershing II and cruise missiles in Western Europe[3]. Like heroes in search of a role, these new weapon systems were at hand, perfectly suited for the European war theatre[4].

In view of the fact that the United States and the Soviet Union share no common border, that they really never have been engaged in war against each other and need not, in principle, encroach on each other's living space, the Soviet-American confrontation should not be viewed as being caused exclusively by real political and economic contradictions; to a large extent it is the outcome of a clash between two war machines driven by the autonomous momentum of technology.

From a historical point of view, this is a new phenomenon. Though there always existed a structural interrelationship between military technology and the exercise of power, it was policy which was invariably in command while technology served only as a medium for discharging authority, including organized violence and warfare. According to the classical formula of Clausewitz – generally accepted in East and West – war was a continuation of politics by other means. Politics was the prevailing factor. It may have gone wrong in war or may have abdicated to mean violence of war. Yet, as a rule, politics was seen as the independent while technology as the dependent variable. With the explosion of modern military technology after the Second World War politics tends to lose its autonomy, yielding ever more to dictates of technology. Politics is increasingly subordinated to the role of presiding over the administration of technology without being in a position to control fully its germination, mushrooming growth and impelling force.

It is within the crucial context of autonomous technology and its impact on society and international relations that the role of the scientists in the arms race and disarmament has to be visualized. This requires a proper perspective on the present position of the scientist in society, his working conditions and the nature of the contemporary scientific endeavour, with specific reference to the huge empire of military R&D. The very fact that military R&D, East and West, employs today an army of about 500 000 qualified natural and engineering scientists of various disciplines is indicative of the magnitude of the problems and of the radical structural changes, quantitative and qualitative, which occurred in the position of the scientific technological community in relation to past historical periods.

The intrinsic dynamics of military R&D

The transformation of the scientific pursuit in the military domain into a mammoth technological effort rigorously institutionalized in the military R&D establishment has enormous consequences for society and the momentum of the arms race.

The societal effects range from the waste of immense human and material resources for destructive purposes to the corruption of science, the perversion of human priorities and the neglect of urgent developmental needs of humanity. Given the fact that military R&D absorbs approximately 10 – 15 per cent of global military expenditures (i.e. 55–80 billion US $ annually), it follows that it actually appropriates one third to one half of all the world's resources allocated to research and development, civil and military[5]*.

---

*Exact figures for military R&D are subject of debate. The United Nations *Study on the Relationship Between Disarmament and Development*[6], comments as follows:
It should be recalled that the 1972 study, *Disarmament and Development* gives the share of military research and development as 40 per cent of expenditures ($25 billion out of $60 billion). As this figure or even higher figures, are widely quoted in the public debate, it might be of some importance to stress the fact that the most recent estimates point to a share of resources used for military research and development of the order of 20 – 25 per cent as regards both manpower and expenditure. Still, however, the absolute magnitude of expenditures for military research and development is extremely large and it remains by far the largest single objective of scientific inquiry and technological development. If a more accurate accounting were possible, the figures presented above would almost certainly appear conservative. For example, much of the expenditure on space activities in the United States and the Soviet Union has direct or strongly indirect military utility and is undoubtedly primarily for this purpose. More than $10,000 million is spent on "non-military" space activities each year by these countries and others. (para. 150).
American budget figures for military R&D in recent years show a constant rise above the parallel increases in military expenditures. Allocations for military R&D amount to US $16 609 million in 1981, 20 058 million in 1982, and 24 257 million in 1983 (planned). To these figures one could add the National Aeronautics and Space Administration (NASA) budget which amounts to US $5 522 million in 1981, 5 981 million in 1982 and 6 612 million in 1983 (planned). Together, the Defence Budget's military R&D and the budget of NASA amount to 12-13 per cent of military expenditures (*Aviation Week & Space & Technology*, 15 February 1982).

In this way, penetrating almost all disciplines of hard and soft sciences, it assumes a commanding position in global research and development arrogating a strong influence on the direction of scientific endeavour not only in the military but also in the civilian domain. Priorities are decided not from the angle of human development but from the angle of military requirements. The much propagandized spin-off effects of military R&D for civilian purposes, as experience has shown, are negligible in comparison with the huge investments absorbed by the military pursuit[7]. In balance, the social, economic, political and cultural ravages caused by military R&D are overwhelming. It is difficult to overestimate the societal losses.

Most tangible is the evil impact of military R&D on the dynamics of the arms race. Even without deeper insight it should be obvious that the unrelenting effort of half a million highly specialized physical and engineering scientists working persistently to improve existing weapon systems and invent new ones must have a powerful effect on the armaments pull. A closer look at the way military R&D is operating fully confirms this assumption. Some features in the management and functioning of military R&D stand out in this respect.

Especially conspicuous is the competitive drive in which the very quantitative impact acquires qualitative salience. A structured competition exists between numerous branches and sections of military R&D: laboratories and research centres affiliated to different services of the armed forces, university institutes, various specialized research establishments, industrial enterprises etc. Either by competing on parallel projects or through a creative meeting of different technologies, the cumulative incremental result is a constant flow of new breakthrough weapons[8]. Competition on a national scale is heightened by international rivalry, both acquiring specific stringency by the dictate of secrecy imposed on military R&D. In fact, lacking precise information about the advances of the adversary, the rule is to rely on worst case assumptions which presuppose that the other side has made and will continue to make similar technical progress if it is not ahead in new discoveries. The outcome is a process of self-stimulation: one's own achievements serve to impel the competitive drive. Obviously, such a massive research and development effort in conditions of structured competition acts to invigorate the arms race independently of political planning. The ingenuity of military R&D tends to interfere destructively with the political process.

There are also other structural features of military R&D which sustain and buttress the arms race. Of key significance is the dependence of military R&D on the long lead-times required for the process of invention, development, testing and production of new weapon systems. Such a gestation period takes on the average 10-15 years. This invests military R&D with constancy and permanency. It is a stabilizing factor. Once a decision for the development of a new weapon system has been taken, it has to run for years without regard for possible changes in the political climate on the results of arms control negotiations. Given bureaucratic inertia, corporate pressures and internal political implications, governments can rarely withdraw from previously approved projects. Thus, on the one hand, long gestation periods tend to project military planning far into the future, and, on the other hand, to encourage early decisions on new weapon systems so as to pre-empt the adversary. The result is a perpetuation and intensification of the arms race. As a corollary, military technology tends to usurp a superior position in the decision-making process.

Another compelling characteristic in the operation of military R&D is the so-called follow-on imperative and growth propensity. In addition to the constancy and permanency invested in military R&D through long gestation periods, the follow-on imperative stimulates its perpetual growth and expansion. As a crucial and vital link in military preparedness and national security, military R&D enjoys privileges. It is by definition an institution which requires continuous improvement of its exploits and perfection of its work. Each project requires an infinite follow-up to improve constantly the product. No qualified human resources can be dismissed and new talents are always in demand. Moreover, a basic tenet of military R&D is to follow-up any project in offence with counter devices in defence, in a continuous chain-reaction of upward cycles alternatively interlocking offence and defence. This tends to reinforce the action-reaction pattern of armaments on the international scene, adding another pull to the self-stimulating dynamics of military R&D. One of the outcomes is over-reaction – a drive out of proportion to real challenges. There is also a general tendency for the militarists (hawks) on both sides to co-operate in reinforcing each other's influence over the "doves" in their own society (see p.24).

The institutional set-up and mode of operation of military R&D have a strong destablizing effect on international relations. Each new discovery in offence and defence, by producing advantages to one side, tends to destabilize any perceived balance of forces. In a way, even considering the strategic balancing game between the major powers, the prime function of military R&D is ceaseless reproduction of destabilization. It does not enhance security but makes all nations, great and small, ever more vulnerable to new weapon systems.

Finally, when addressing issues of the functioning and impact of military R&D, one has to stress its place and role in the socio-political structure of society. Military R&D is an organic part of the powerful competitive alliance, East and West, of the military, the military industry and state bureaucracy (the military-industrial-bureaucratic-technological complex). Military R&D is well shielded, sustained and bolstered by this complex as one of its most sensitive links. This also has organizational consequences. The scientific staff is subjected to stringent discipline and control. Purely organizational measures are reinforced by economic attractions and political arguments. As a result, scientists and engineers employed by military R&D have shown astounding resistance to appeals calling their attention to social and moral responsibility. The challenge is all the greater to try to bring military R&D under some social and political control, and to halt its devastating impact on the arms race and society.

Strategies for change

If any conclusions can be drawn from the above brief analysis, it is that the problems before us are mainly of a socio-political structural nature, and long-term strategies are called for to bring about change. The persistent plea for, and invocation of, ethical and moral values on an individual basis, has to be accompanied by attempts to build up restraints and socio-political barriers against the misuse of science for military purposes by action in four domains:

1. arms control measures focused on the operation of military R&D;
2. disarmament education aimed at both scientists and the public at large as launched by Unesco[9];
3. organizational steps to free scientists from state and corporate manipulation and to reassert their autonomy and independence as suggested by the Unesco recommendation on the status of scientific researchers (see Appendix 2)
4. co-operation of the "doves" across international borders.

To bring military R&D under some social and political control that will halt its intrinsic dynamics is a tall order. However, step by step intervention by common agreement of the great powers and other governments is possible[10]. It is feasible to impose control on the most sensitive stage in the development of new weapon systems, especially strategic nuclear weapons, i.e. the testing stage. The key issue in this respect today is the conclusion of a Comprehensive Test Ban treaty, now under negotiation by the United States, the Soviet Union and the United Kingdom, which would halt all nuclear weapon testing. As stated in the United Nations expert *Report on a Comprehensive Nuclear Test Ban* (CTB):[11]

> "A comprehensive test ban is regarded as the first and most urgent step towards a cessation of the nuclear arms race, in particular, as regards the qualitative aspect...A compehensive test ban could serve as an important measure of non-proliferation of nuclear weapons, both vertical and horizontal.

A comprehensive test ban would have a major arms limitation impact in that it would make it difficult, if not impossible, for the nuclear-weapon States parties to the treaty to develop new designs of nuclear weapons and would also place constraints on the modification of existing weapon designs."

Experience of the last years has shown little political will among the great powers to accept a water-tight CTB. The need, therefore, arises to mobilize strong public opinion in support of this request. Given its significance, the demand for the conclusion of a CTB should figure high in all actions of the peace movements and organizations concerned with peace, Pugwash included.

Other steps to halt the momentum of military R&D could follow, such as a ban or restrictions on testing of new missile delivery systems, curtailing of resources devoted to military R&D, internationalization of control measures by the setting up of an International Satellite Surveillance and Verification System. A conscious strategy of suffocation of military R&D is a real possibility. More international discussion among scientists, and activities of a Pugwash-like character, are called for.

References

1. Lord Zuckerman: "Alchemists of the arms race", *New Scientist*, 21 January 1982.
2. Marek Thee: "The Doctrine of Nuclear Deterrence, Impact on Contemporary International Relations", in Yoshikazu Sakamoto (Ed.): *Strategic Doctrines and Their Alternatives*, Paris: Unesco (forthcoming).
3. Sverre Lodgaard: "Eurostrategic Weapons and Euronuclear Strategies", *Bulletin of Peace Proposals*, Vol. 12, No. 4, 1981.
4. Gregory Treverton: "Nuclear Weapons in Europe", *Adelphi Papers*, No. 168, Summer 1980.
5. Randal Forsberg, *Resources Devoted to Military Research and Development*, Stockholm, SIPRI, 1972; and Colin Norman, *Knowledge and Power: The Global Research and Development Budget,* Worldwatch Paper 312, July 1979.
6. *Study on the Relationship Between Disarmament and Development*, Report by the UN Secretary-General, Doc.A/36/356, 5 October 1981, para. 149.
7. Seymour Melman: "Twelve Propositions on Productivity and War Economy", *Armed Forces and Society*, Vol. 1, No. 4, 1975; also S. Melman: "Inflation and Unemployment as Products of War Economy", *Bulletin of Peace Proposals*, Vol. 9, No. 4, 1978.
8. Kosta Tsipis: "The Building Blocks of Weapon Development", *The Bulletin of Atomic Scientists,* April 1977; also Herbert F. York and G. Allen Greb: "Strategic Reconnaissance", *Bulletin of the Atomic Scientists*, April 1977.

9. Stephen Marks, *et al.*: Disarmament Education, Special issue of the *Bulletin of Peace Proposals*, Vol. 11, No. 3, 1980.

10. Harvey Brooks: "The Military Innovation System and the Qualitative Arms Race", *Daedalus*, Summer 1975: also Owen Wilkes: "Military R&D: Problems of Arms Control", *Bulletin of Peace Proposals*, Vol. 9, No. 1, 1978.

11. *Comprehensive Nuclear Test Ban*, Report of the Secretary-General, 16 April 1980, CD/86, para 154.

Chapter 4. Dynamics of the arms race: a Third World view

Essam Galal

Introduction

More and more of the developing countries, often referred to as the Third World, are inclined to view themselves as the victims of an escalating arms race, led by a handful of industrialized countries. However it may be described, the global armament phenomenon remains heavily concentrated. For over three and a half decades since the Second World War, the two major military powers the United States and the U.S.S.R. together with their allies in NATO and the Warsaw Pact have continued to account for virtually all the global expenditure on the military R&D, almost 85 per cent of the global military spending, more than 90 per cent of the world-wide military production and roughly 95 per cent of the international exports of military hardware.

By contrast, in 1981 between 14 to 16 per cent of global military spending and not more than 7 to 8 per cent of world-wide military production was spread among over 130 developing countries, their total number having increased three-fold since the Second World War. Almost every newly independent country has incurred some form of military spending and for most of them, making some military allocations became a reflex act after gaining a sovereign status. The reciprocal compulsions it has generated between those developing countries which have some historically rooted animosities, or some outstanding geographical frontier disputes, and the military competition which has resulted from it have by now become a familiar feature of the tension-ridden Third World.

The military competition among several of the developing countries and the arms race among a few industrialized powers do not, however, belong to the same category of inherent dynamics which govern the world-wide arms race. Nowhere is the difference between them more striking than in the relative shares of each in the global military R&D and military production. Collectively all the Third World countries combined do not incur even a barely calculable fraction of the world-wide military

R&D expenditures; individually, not more than 12 to 16 out of the over 130 developing countries possess any significant armament production facilities. Their procurement of military hardware, almost entirely from the industrialized world, however, has continued to increase both in volume and sophistication. This factor, more than any other, has inextricably linked the military competition among the developing countries with the dynamics of the arms race of the industrialized world.

Involvement of the Third World in the arms race

Virtually all the military conflicts in the developing countries have been fought with imported weaponry and in more than two-thirds of the over 120 conflicts, either one or the other industrialized exporters of military hardware has been reported to have viewed its eventual outcome as of some relevance to the geopolitical dimensions of its strategic rivalry with its own global adversary. An intricate chain of listening posts, naval facilities, military bases, and implicit or explicit understandings for direct and indirect military support by the exporting to the importing country have produced a complicated set of changing supplier-client relationships in the area of international arms transfers. Clients left in political or economic orphanage by one supplier have been readily picked up by another; even in regions where the origins of several of the conflict situations had little to do with the strategic rivalry of the major adversaries in the global arms race, the subsequent military build-ups have conformed more to the assessments of the military needs of the supplier than of the client. A most striking example of this is the Middle East, which as a region alone accounts for more weapon imports than all the other developing countries put together. A detailed description of the geo-strategic importance of the Middle East, besides its obvious feature as the largest known reserve base of oil which, incidentally, is an almost irreplaceable source of petroleum for the military industry, falls outside the scope of this paper. What is relevant in the present context is its illustrative significance to demonstrate the inherent dangers of a global situation whereby the dynamics of a heavily concentrated arms race is increasingly spread over the developing countries.

The dynamics of the arms race involves much more than a sum total of the military spending of the individual countries and an up-dated list of its numerical participants. The purposes it serves, the forces which drive it, and the forms in which it manifests itself, have been widely analysed in such a way as to allow each of the major participants in the arms race to present a benign image of its own military build-up while attributing aggressive intentions to its adversary. In this broad sense, the arms race has increasingly become a world-wide phenomenon; and although its intensity differs markedly between regions, no major region and few countries have stayed out of the arms race. As pointed out by some of the United Nations studies on the subject, the term arms race is not appropriate to describe the gathering momentum for the process of expanding and improving military forces. This process may intensify the wider arms race, particularly in regions where countries are exposed to political, military and other kinds of pressures, where the rivalries of the other states lead to involvement or interference, where territories are under foreign occupation and where countries feel their sovereignty and independence to be directly threatened[1]. Essentially, however, the phenomenon of the arms race involves simultaneous increases in military outlays of two or more nations whose foreign and defence policies are heavily interdependent; the military outlays of countries having little contact or no salient interest in each other cannot be appropriately described as an arms race.

"The primary engine of the world-wide arms race is constituted by the qualitative arms race among the largest military Powers. This is due chiefly to the virtual monopoly of these powers in the development of advanced military technology, to their overwhelmingly large share of world production and world exports of advanced weaponry, and to the global character of their interests, politically and militarily.... All significant developments in armaments originate here and spread from here to the rest of the world, with greater or lesser time lags. For many types of conventional weaponry these time lags seem to have diminished in recent years. Meanwhile, as these weapons are being assimilated in the countries at the periphery of the arms race, new generations are under development at the centre to supersede them, preparing the ground for a new round of transfer and emulation. Outside of this small number of producing countries, arms races or competitions are substantially and often wholly dependent on external supplies of arms, technicians and instructors[2]."

Military power and national security

For the developing countries, the dynamics of the arms race, as described above, implies a close relationship between military power and national security. The familiar dilemma about whether the major arms participants are insecure because they are armed, or armed because they are insecure, continues to persist. The fact is that the heavy concentration of military power among the industrialized countries has so far been paralleled by the absence of open military confrontation among them. The notion that military power deters conflict cannot be easily dismissed as long as the major arms race participants do not bring about some meaningful reductions of their military power, particularly in the field of nuclear arsenals. The risk of horizontal nuclear proliferation among the developing countries will continue unabated as long as there is no nuclear disarmament among the major military powers. As pointed out by the United Nations Study on Nuclear Weapons:[3]

> "If there is no progress towards nuclear disarmament the nuclear arms race will go on. Some States may then claim it justifiable to try to acquire a nuclear capability to deter massive attacks against their civilian populations as well as to defend themselves in a conventional military conflict.
>
> It is considered likely by many that the system of security which is inherent in the strategic relationship between the super-Powers based as it is on a nuclear "balance of terror", has discouraged them for over three decades from initiating military conflict directly with each other. It is also assumed that it has prevented regional conflicts in which either might be involved to escalate to global nuclear conflict. This has not, however, prevented either super-Power from major involvement in large-scale conventional military conflicts on a sub-global level. It is even suggested that confidence in the efficacy of the mutual strategic deterrence at the global level may have had the effect of diminishing inhibitions about super-Power involvement in certain regional conflicts.
>
> To live in a world with nuclear weapons also means that certain innate elements of the nuclear arms race endanger international peace and security. Periods may come when one or the other, and sometimes both, of the super-Powers become less confident about their state of national security. This could occur when one considers that the other has acquired a competitive edge in strategic nuclear capability. It is almost axiomatic that the level of international security is adversely affected when a super-Power becomes uncertain about its own security. In general, the state of international security would thus come to vary with the ups and downs of the nuclear arms race. It is indeed a fact that the dynamic of the nuclear arms race has caused an increase in the level of nuclear capability at which the deterrence balance is perceived to be established by the two super-Powers.
>
> The super-Powers' reliance on nuclear weapons for their security confers legitimacy on these weapons as instruments of power. The efforts to encourage states to accept binding multilateral commitments to forgo nuclear weapons will therefore be hindered unless the nuclear-weapon States themselves demonstrate a readiness to take meaningful measures towards the elimination of nuclear weapons. Acquisition of nuclear weapons by more states is, however, likely to undermine international security."

In their anxiety to contain nuclear proliferation among the developing countries, some of the major nuclear powers have followed a policy of encouraging nuclear abstinence by supporting conventional military build-ups of a potential nuclear power. In some cases, this has actually resulted in improving the military power of a developing country involved in an adversary relationship with a hostile neighbour; this situation comes close to either putting a premium on the announcement of an intention to acquire the nuclear capability or superimposing a higher level of military build-up between both adversaries. Neither conforms to the clearly defined position taken in the First Special Session on Disarmament (UNSSOD I) which in its final document had clearly stated: "Enduring international peace and security cannot be built on the accumulation of weaponry by military alliances nor be sustained by a precarious balance of deterrence or doctrines of strategic superiority."[4]

A super-imposition of a higher level of military build-up among the developing countries involved in conflict situations will not promote the cause of either international security or disarmament. Unless, of course, the pursuit of international security continues to be preoccupied, as it has been since the two World Wars, with the prevention of another war in the European theatre, and the search for disarmament remains obsessed, as it is now, with the American-Soviet arms control negotiations, which also serve the purpose of communicating politico-economic threats, assessing military capabilities and adjusting strategic priorities. The either/or proposition between international security and disarmament does not preclude the desirability of making the two contingent upon each other. From a purely strategic viewpoint, however, the proposition that international security will promote disarmament, and the other way around, has not been proven by the experience of the industrialized countries. The East-West negotiations on European security, culminating in the Helsinki Accords of 1975, were neither preceded nor followed by European disarmament. If anything, these negotiations – and their eventual outcome – have been accompanied by a constant build-up of East-West military strength of mutually recognized deterrent capabilities, notably in the nuclear field. The acquisition of some level of nuclear conventional deterrence between and among the various adversaries in the Third World may or may not result in a series of accords similar to that of Helsinki outside Europe. In any case these would not further the prospects for disarmament in the Third World any more than has been the case so far in Europe.

A fundamental difference between the security concerns of Europe and the Third World lies in the specificity and urgency of their respective threat perceptions. The East-West threat perceptions related to each other reflect security concerns about avoiding or fighting a war which has never been actually fought in the past. Such a war is also highly unlikely to occur in the near future, unless both the East and West enter a joint pact for simultaneous suicide and murder. The threat perceptions of the Third World, which came to be identified and described as such only after the two World Wars, emanate from specific security crises actually experienced or directly witnessed. Virtually all the local wars fought since the Second World War have actually occurred in Asia, Africa and Latin America. Even when an industrialized power was militarily involved in a local war, as in the Congo, Vietnam or Chad, the actual fighting took place on the territories of the Third World. Europe has seldom been a theatre of war since the Second World War and the strategic doctrines accompanying this phenomenon do not provide a viable option to bring about a similar no-war situation in the Third World.

Strategic doctrines and the Third World

European notions of strategy have not changed substantially since Clausewitz defined it as "an approach to war which links the outcome of a number of military engagements" and described its object as "the achievement of a favourable overall position in which your opponent has no remaining courses of action open to him reasonably likely to reverse the course of war". The notions of a grand strategy, developed since Clausewitz's time, have expanded the original concept to include factors other than military strategy and a time span covering both war and peace. Paul Nitze's analysis of the European strategy for the 1980's, for example, starts with a definition of grand strategy in which "all factors bearing on the evolving situation – including economic, political and psychological factors as well as military – are taken into account over long periods of time, including times both of peace and war". Both the East and the West have evolved strategic doctrines based upon this grand strategy which determines their respective views of the security issues in the Third World. The establishment of a politico-military détente in Europe has not changed their strategic objectives in the rest of the world.

The achievement of an overall favourable position, the knowledge of an identifiable and constant opponent, and the capability to employ a whole range of political, economic and military power constitute the key elements of the prevailing strategic doctrines which the Third World has not endorsed in order to overcome its security concerns. The Third World has not yet reached a favourable overall position comparable to the politico-territorial *status quo* cemented in Europe by the Helsinki Accord; both the political order and the territorial frontiers are still the subject of unsettled claims within and among the Third World countries. The Third World also has no identifiable single opponent comparable to the chief adversary perceived in the East-West framework; most of the Third World countries have their own adversaries and few among them are inclined to delegate their strategic responsibilities to the overall leadership of a single power comparable to the United States and the Soviet Union in their respective alliance systems. The experience of the Organization of American States in the Inter-American alliance system does not provide an exception, because even in Latin America the latest indications are of intra-regional fragmentation challenging the hemispheric reliance on the United States.

Above all, few among the Third World countries have the economic and military resources comparable to those employed by East and West in pursuit of their grand strategies. Even those who possess such resources are constantly under pressure from the competing claims of national security and developmental concerns. The challenge of providing socio-economic content to political freedom, in the initial stages of nation-building, has been exacerbated by the series of security crises faced by most of the Third World countries. As the euphoria of national independence has given way to a rising discontent of unfulfilled socio-economic expectations, under-development or mal-development by itself has become a source of insecurity. Ethnic, tribal or communal frictions within nation-states have been aggravated by real or perceived denial in the process of economic development and the resulting political instability within these countries has largely obliterated the thin line dividing the internal from external threats to national security.

The only strategic objective shared by the Third World is national survival as independent nation-states. The only strategy endorsed by them in the pursuit of this objective is an attempt to gain maximum advantage from resources that are insufficient to provide for meeting the twin challenges of national security and development. Their national security concerns, by and large, revolve around their territorial frontiers except in cases where these frontiers still conform to a colonial or racial pattern. Their developmental needs reflect a clear distinction between economic growth and development: the former describing goods and services, and the latter pertaining to the quality of life in general. The sheer abundance of human or natural resources in a particular Third World country does not detract from the overall resource insufficiency, particularly when the competing claims of national security and development are taken into account.

The irrelevance of the prevailing strategic doctrines among the industrialized world for the Third World security issues is reflected in the conspicuous absence of a strategic component in the non-aligned movement which, by definition, stipulates a judgement of East-West issues on the merits of a specific situation. Operating at different levels of economic development, enjoying varied degrees of social homogeneity and political legitimacy, having military power and capability, and confronting different adversaries in their respective threat perceptions, the major element of commonality binding the increasing membership of the non-aligned movement is the stated aspiration to stay outside the arena of East-West differences.

Many of the East-West dominated security arrangements with the Third World countries were clearly entered into with different sets of strategic objectives. The East-West framework viewed these arrangments as a co-optation of junior partners outside Europe: the Third World countries joined them in the expectation of receiving additional leverage in their conflicts with actual or perceived adversaries. Since the threats perceived by the Third World not only materialized earlier but also originated in situations different from those dominating the East-West issues, most of these arrangements proved either inadequate or irrelevant to deal with the crises in the Third World. Iran opted out of the United States security umbrella after discovering that its role as a junior partner, to be the Eastern bulwark of the Western alliance system, did not equip it to deal with the phenomenon of Islamic fundamentalism which to a certain degree was also a reaction to the Shah's preponderant reliance upon a massive military build-up to demonstrate his national and regional ambitions. The strategic objectives assigned to CENTO did not converge with those of its individual members: neither Pakistan, nor Iran, nor Turkey got out of it the expected politico-strategic advantages and the alliance withered away. SEATO had another quiet burial as one after another of its members realized that the alliance was either unwilling or incapable of putting its collective weight behind the crises actually confronting its individual members.

A growing tendency among the developing countries to set up domestic armament production centres can in part be seen as a demonstration of extreme reluctance to get involved in the politico-military competition of their arms suppliers. Even if the purely financial costs of importing weaponry appear lower than those of producing them domestically, the overall terms of transfer may involve politico-military costs which few developing countries can afford to sustain without serious consequences. These imply dependence on supportive equipment and personnel, and the risk of becoming an actual theatre of war in a possible confrontation over threats which may be alien and even irrelevant to the importing country's own security. In this context, it is extremely important that the conflict-situations among the developing countries be urgently resolved in accordance with the principle of "undiminished security of all States" stated unequivocally in the final document of UNSSOD I.

The urgency of this task cannot be overstated because these conflict situations not only constitute a major factor in the military spending of the developing countries, but also provide easy targets for the principal arms exporters from the industrialized world in pursuit of their politico-military rivalry. It is here that a basic difference of approach can be seen between the security concerns of a majority of the states and those of the major military powers, particularly the two described as "Super Powers'. The former overwhelmingly share a rather narrow definition of national security; a direct or indirect threat to their national frontiers or their right to self-determination and national independence. On the other hand, the two major military powers continue to define their national security in terms that project their perceived interests far beyond their borders, leading to measures of intervention, neocolonialism and the risk of the division of the world into spheres of interest which is at wide variance with the principles of equality of sovereign states and non-interference in the affairs of others. The Third World interest in a narrower definition of national security is more in consonance with both the letter and the spirit of the Final Document of the UNSSOD I which in more than thirty references to national security broadly used the term in relation to direct threats of aggression across the geographical frontiers of sovereign states.

Implications of the dynamics of the arms race

While differing from the major military powers in their respective national security concerns and, hence, the enormity of the military effort needed to meet them, the developing countries share the near universal concern about two of the most serious implications of the dynamics of the arms race: its unimaginably deadly, destructive potential and its incalculably colossal wastage and misallocation of the world's far from infinite resources. Irrespective of whether they are actually used or not, the continuous production, stockpiling, and deployment of nuclear arsenals is irreversibly affecting the global human and natural environment. The human (labour), natural (fuel and non-fuel minerals), and material (capital and technology) resources consumed by the world-wide military activities are severely narrowing the socio-economic options both at the national and international levels.

There is no target strong enough to resist the intense effects of nuclear weapons nor a meaningful defence against a determined nuclear attack. Figures and rough estimates of the human and physical devastation likely to result from a limited or partial use of these weapons may be given, but there exists a virtually comprehensible limit beyond which such figures have no meaning except a categorical imperative that a nuclear war must never happen:

– the total number of existing nuclear warhead may well be in excess of 40 000. The explosive yield of an average warhead ranges from 100 tons to more than 20 million tons of TNT and in principle there is no upper limit to the explosive yield which may be attained;

– a single Poseidon submarine with its 16 MIRVed missiles can deliver warheads to 160 separate targets; these warheads have a total explosive yield of 6.4 Mt., a larger explosive power than that of all the munitions fired in the Second World War; still this megatonnage is of the order of one or a few thousandths of the megatonnage in either the United States or the Soviet strategic arsenal;

– the largest nuclear warhead ever tested released an energy approximately 4000 times that of the bomb used over Hiroshima.[5]

A total nuclear war or an all-out nuclear exchange would be tantamount to the highest level of human madness because those surviving it would be envying the dead in terms of the socio-economic and political climate they would inherit. Even the most medically advanced among the industrialized countries do not have the facilities to treat more than 200 patients of a nuclear attack in a day during normal conditions. The situation can only be imagined if along with human beings, the physical and material equipment, including hospitals, is destroyed during a nuclear attack. For the developing countries, the effects of a nuclear war would be incalculably more disastrous because few among them possess even the rudimentary elements of civil defence, for a conventional war, let alone facilities to treat any survivors of a nuclear holocaust.

In purely financial terms, the global military expenditure in 1981:
– amounted to roughly $120 for every man, woman and child on earth;
– was comparable to the combined GNP of all the countries in Africa and Latin America;
– exceeded the annual income of roughly two billion people in the world's poorest countries;
– was more than twenty-five times larger than the developmental assistance provided by the industrialized to the developing countries.[6]

Approximately $110 billion, or roughly one-fifth of the total global military expenditure in 1981, was going into improving the existing stockpiles of nuclear weapons. Less than one tenth of this would have been ample to finance a world-wide programme of research and development to discover new and renewable sources of energy, e.g. wind energy, oil shale, tar sands, ocean energy, draught animal power, peat, biomass, solar energy, etc.
– a mere $1 billion would go a long way in initiating global efforts on nuclear waste disposal;
– only $5 billion would be adequate to meet the costs of a world-wide programme for overcoming pollution;
– only $4 billion would suffice to eradicate hunger through direct food aid to the world's poorest children;
– a bare $1 billion additional allocation to the WHO's budget would enable it to provide world-wide child immunization against six diseases: measles, poliomyelitis, tuberculosis, diptheria, whooping cough and tetanus. At present only 10 per cent of the 80 million children born per year in the developing countries are immunized against these and 10 may die every minute in the absence of immunization;[7]

As compared to $13 billion in 1960, the world expenditure on military R&D was estimated to be well over $35 billion in 1981:
– the world expenditure in military R&D accounted for roughly one-fourth of the entire world investment in R&D for all other purposes:
– military R&D alone claimed expenditures roughly equal to the combined R&D investments for energy, transportation, communication, health, agriculture, and pollution control;
– the average expenditure differential between civilian and military R&D is growing wider: R&D programmes for some of the most sophisticated weapons systems are sometimes twenty times more research intensive as compared with investments in the civilian sector. One single weapons programme, the MX missile system, was allocated $1.5 billion in R&D in 1981;
– it is estimated that not more than 20 per cent of the results of the military R&D can be used in any notable way for civilian purposes.[7]

Much too often in the past, the developing countries have been viewed as the major beneficiaries of diarmament because it was hoped that the diversion of even a fraction of the resources currently claimed by world-wide military activities would go a long way in providing for a bulk of the basic unmet needs of the poorest sections in these countries. A recent United Nations study on the relationship between disarmament and development has virtually overturned this argument by suggesting that any additional resource diversions to developmental channels will be an indirect investment in détente and, therefore, to the confidence-building measures urgently required to halt and reverse the arms race.

From the point of view of the Third World, this line of reasoning not only merits being quoted as the conclusion of this chapter, but also needs to be taken up as a possible means of follow-up action by the UNSSOD II:[6]

"The development of a more stable South capable of sustaining its independence through a better economic performance is likely to reduce the areas of political conflicts among the East and West and put détente on a more stable basis than it has been during the last few years of its constant re-examination. Viewed in this context, any direct additional investments in the development of developing countries may become an indirect contribution to détente. Greater flows of external assistance to the developing countries will further the prospects for development but relating this process to military restraint among the major military spenders is likely to create a new political climate which by itself may become a catalyst for military restraint. The amount of financial resources released for development through disarmament measures will be a major benefit for development but the awareness that it is a conscious attempt at viewing development as an integral part of détente will be a major bonus for East-West relations."[8]

References

1. *Economic and Social Consequences of the Arms Race and of Military Expenditures.* United Nations Publication. Sales No. E.78.IX.1, paragraph 15.
2. *Ibid.* paragraph 17.
3. *Comprehensive Study on Nuclear Weapons,* Report of the U.N. Secretary General A/35/392, September 1980, Paras 398-401.
4. *Final Document, Special Session of the General Assembly on Disarmament, 1978.* United Nations, Department of Public Information, DPI/679, February 1981. paragraph 13.
5. *Comprehensive Study on Nuclear Weapons, op. cit.,* paragraph 9.
6. *Study on the Relationship between Disarmament and Development,* United Nations, 1981, A/36/356. paras 102-104.
7. Estimates provided by the Centre for Disarmament, United Nations, New York, 1982.
8. *Study on the Relationship between Disarmament and Development, op.cit.* paragraph 241.

PART II
Role of scientists in the arms race

Chapter 5. The dilemma of scientists in the nuclear age

Engelbert Broda

Introduction

In April 1981, the Austrian group of the international Pugwash Conferences on Science and World Affairs, in an Open Letter, drew the attention of the Federal Chancellor, Bruno Kreisky, to the extent of the disaster of a nuclear war, if it were to break out. The Open Letter was signed by 330 Austrian University professors. Some of the data in it may be of general interest.

As pointed out in a document[1] of the Office of Technology Assessment (O.T.A.) of the United States Congress, one single large nuclear weapon would be sufficient to blot out a town like Detroit or Leningrad and kill 3 million people. The explosive power of each of the biggest weapons known (60 megatons TNT* equivalent) is about that of dynamite with a weight of 10 Cheops pyramids. Some fifty thousand nuclear weapons in various sizes are now believed to be in the arsenals. If their total explosive power were divided up equally, one Hiroshima bomb could be exploded somewhere on Earth every second (!) day and night, for two weeks, before the arsenals were exhausted.

Moreover, it is widely feared that, with the increasing number and precision of nuclear weapons and progress in anti-submarine technology, a "first strike" against the adversary may become feasible within the next few years. The temptation to adopt a "launch on warning" policy may then well become overwhelming. Ultimately this would mean the complete exclusion of humans from the decision process of the country that sees itself as the defender. As soon as the sensors "think" they have detected an enemy attack, the computer so-to-speak presses the red button for the massive counter-attack, and brings civilization in the target country to an end. Another danger is the increased likelihood of a preventive war.

This situation would not have arisen without the determined efforts of

*TNT is the chemical explosive widely used in the two World Wars.

scientists, and it would not continue to worsen without their ceaseless endeavour. The technologists, in turn, build upon the original ideas of the scientists. The nuclear and other weapons of mass destruction are firmly based on the bold thoughts and solid achievements of many of the most competent scientists of the world. They are directly in the service of their government or employed by firms on contract with governments. Interestingly, the leading weapons scientists and technologists were all men.

Einstein and the Bomb

Not all weapon scientists were and are evil. On the contrary, among the men who invented and perfected weapons we find many who were concerned with progress and the fate of mankind. In prenuclear times, Paul Langevin, with his work on sonar (submarine detection) during the First World War, may serve as an example. Well-meaning and responsible men like Leo Szilard and Harold Urey were among the pioneers in the work on the atomic bomb. However, the most striking case was that of Albert Einstein.

It is well known that all his life, from 1914 onwards, Einstein[2] gave much time, thought and effort to social problems, and that world peace was always a major concern for him. Between the two World Wars he was an absolute pacifist. Yet in 1939 he was persuaded by Leo Szilard[3] to urge President Roosevelt to start work on the military, i.e. destructive, applications of nuclear energy. True, contrary to what has been said, he did not ask for the construction of weapons, let alone for their actual use[4], but it must have been clear to Einstein that nuclear weapons were inevitable as soon as the research work urged by him had led to recognition of their feasibility and efficiency.

Before we return to Einstein's dilemma, attention should be drawn to one general point. Historical experience shows that the introduction of any new weapon, provided its value is confirmed, constitutes an irreversible step. The evil spirits cannot be put back into Pandora's box. Thus, the consequences of a scientist's action inexorably persist and develop even after the original reason for the action has vanished. In Einstein's specific case the bomb was used against Japan in 1945 after it had turned out that a nuclear threat by Germany or her allies, the original justification, did not exist. The Nazis' astonishing failure in this field has been well described and discussed by Samuel Goudsmit[5]. According to him many nuclear scientists in Germany wanted their weapons project to be successful; but this conclusion has been contested by some of the scientists involved.

Because of Einstein's great sympathy for Japan[6], dating from his visit there in 1922 when he was welcomed by hundreds of thousands of people, the dreadful death of so many men, women and children in Hiroshima and Nagasaki must have been particularly bitter to him. It would not even be true to say that nuclear bombs would have been dropped on Japan in any case, Einstein letter or not. The acceleration of the development of nuclear weapons, due to Szilard's efforts and Einstein's letter, was probably sufficient to get the bombs ready in time before the surrender of Japan, which in any case would have occurred in 1945. So Einstein had to shoulder considerable co-responsibility[7]. Later he bitterly regretted his action[2]. This did not change the fact that nuclear weapons continued to proliferate after the war, long after the end of the Nazi empire, and still do so. In fact proliferation has been speeding up.

Scientists content with work on weapons

For most experts, scientists and technologists, who are inventing and improving weapons, an Einsteinian dilemma simply does not exist. They are happy in their work, in which they are supported, honoured and well paid. They do not doubt that they are doing the right thing. They are either convinced that their products are needed for the good in the world, i.e. that it is their own side, and only their side, that is in the right, or they take the position that it is Parliament and Government (both elected by the people, provided elections exist) who have to decide. As long as these bodies say "yes" and provide the means, it is not a matter for the weapons expert to question their wisdom.

On the basis of his incomparable experience, Herbert York[8,9], has, in his awesome book *The Race to Oblivion*, described the situation in a gripping way:

"The various individual promoters of the arms race are stimulated sometimes by patriotic zeal, sometimes by a desire to go along with the gang, sometimes by crass opportunism, and sometimes by simple fear of the unknown. They are inspired by ingenious and clever ideas, challenged by bold statements of real and imaginary military requirements, stimulated to match or exceed technological progress by the other side or even by a rival military service here at home, and victimized by rumours and phony intelligence. Some have been lured by the siren call of rapid advancement, personal recognition and unlimited opportunity, and some have been bought by promises of capital gains. Some have sought out and even made up problems to fit the solution they have spent much of their lives discovering and developing. A few have used the arms to achieve other, hidden objectives.

Nearly all such individuals have had a deep long-term involvement in the arms race. They derive either their incomes, their profits, or their consultant fees from it. But much more important than money as a motivating force are the individuals' own psychic and spiritual needs; the majority of the key individual promoters of the arms race derive a very large part of their self-esteem from their participation in what they believe to be an essential – even a holy – cause."

Life in Los Alamos

More specific is the example of the scientists of Los Alamos. We are not arguing here whether their deathdealing work was justified, or even necessary. The fact is that the majority of scientists and their wives enjoyed themselves hugely in their fascinating job in excellent and stimulating company. Many books of reminiscences have appeared where the spirit of Los Alamos is recalled with delight, including the book by Laura Fermi[10]. Aage Bohr[11] also was deeply impressed with the "pioneer character of the undertaking", the "unique intellectual atmosphere" and "the magnificent natural surroundings". We now quote from a review with the promising title "Intense Living in Secret Cities", of a recent collection of lectures[12]. In this review, by Jane Wilson[13] we read:

"Los Alamos was an adventure, and some sense of its excitement shines in these lectures ... It was such intense living ... impression that their labours might save civilization ... Los Alamos was the home of heroes – and very young heroes, at that. For him (Richard Feynman) and many another young person collaboration and friendship with older, established scientists like Fermi or Bethe was a delight. The land itself was enchanted; it had beautiful scenery and exotic inhabitants. Bernice Brode and Elsie McMillan speak fondly of their relations with the Indian women of the Santa Clara and San Ildefonso pueblos. The work was challenging ... Above all there was a high sense of purpose."

To add to the flavour, the readers of the review are treated to a cheerful picture of a Sunday outing with Fermi, Bethe, Rossi, Segrè and others.

Perhaps we should stop for a moment to consider the fact that in some miraculous way it almost seems as if there had been no causal connection between the cheerful life at Los Alamos and the cruel death, through blast, fire and radiation, of hundreds of thousands of people far away[14,15]. (A horrifying concrete account[16] is contained in a manuscript by a doctor, Shuntaro Hida, who survived at the periphery of Hiroshima. He had to deal with large numbers of victims.) Konrad Lorenz[17] emphasized how small are human inhibitions against committing crimes (or making wars) against humans one does not see. Long ago, the English novelist Arnold Bennett[18] wrote a tale about human insensitivity to suffering that is not noticed directly. Who would refrain from becoming rich if the price were merely the death of an unknown person in China? Clearly such insensitivity applies not only to one person far away, but also to millions.

A recent television film sponsored by the American government showed an intercontinental rocket silo in the Middle West. One of the soldiers, whose task it would be on Day X to turn the key for the release of the rocket, was interviewed. He was in his early twenties and may have been a farmer's boy. He was not unpleasant. Asked about his feeling, he shrugged his shoulders and said that he just wanted to do his job well. Of course, he was not told what the target of his private rocket is, i.e. what exactly his job would involve. He added that he preferred not to know; he might feel sorry for the people in the target town.

So it depends on the turning of a key, by an unknowing farmer's boy from Texas (or from the Volga), or on the turning of several keys by several such boys in conjunction, whether a town, maybe in Europe, is changed instantly into a heap of burning, radioactive rubble, a town that may have been built by thirty generations of engineers, architects and artists and may house millions of peaceful people.

To return to recent history, few members of the lively and thriving community of Los Alamos pondered the fact that the American government had not given any pledge about the use or non-use of nuclear weapons. Leo Szilard was, of course, one of the noble exceptions. He did care, he organized petitions, and he made desperate attempts to prevent the use of bombs against Japan. Again he enlisted Einstein's help, but this time the attempt failed[3]. Einstein could no longer influence the government.

Nuclear surrender in the Second World War?

We return now to Einstein's dilemma in 1939. He was an extreme case – a totally incorruptible man. He would not have enjoyed the Los Alamos atmosphere even if he had been invited to participate – which he was not. General Leslie Groves, Robert Oppenheimer, and the other men in power wisely refrained from doing so. Yet, in the light of what was known at the time, could he have acted differently than he did, through his first letter? Was it not necessary to counteract the threat of nuclear arms in the hands of the Nazi criminals? Would Einstein not have seen himself as an unwilling accomplice of Hitler in his murderous onslaught on the world, and more particularly on the defenceless Jews, who soon afterwards were marched to the gas chambers in the East, if he had withheld Szilard's information from President Roosevelt? The situation of lesser scientists than Einstein, who likewise wanted to be effective against Nazi barbarism, was not different in principle from his, even though they could not influence events to a similar extent. The views and actions of the Soviet nuclear scientists during the war are interestingly described by Igor Golovin[19].

Nevertheless, the question must be asked: *Would it not, in spite of everything said, have been right during the war to refuse the participation in the development of nuclear weapons?* It would be easy to say "yes" – i.e. that total and absolute refusal would have been correct – in hindsight, presupposing our knowledge that Hitler would have no nuclear weapons. But this could not be known in 1939. And what if the scientists of the anti-Nazi alliance had, in spite of nuclear bombs in German arsenals, nevertheless insisted on the non-construction of nuclear weapons? It could be argued that Hitler, in one sided possession of nuclear weapons, might have forced the world to surrender, but that sooner or later, in one way or another, freedom would have re-emerged. Provided the nuclear refusal could have been upheld, there would then have been a world without nuclear weapons. This world might have given more hope for survival than our present world, where total annihilation of human civilization in the near future is a very real possibility. This hypothetical line of thought might have led, in present terms, to a slogan like "better brown than dead" (brown was the colour of the Nazi party).

What is the answer to this crucial question? Probably the question cannot meaningfully be asked. Sensibly one cannot assume for 1939, or any other date, a knowledge of the future that just did not exist. Could one take a post-Hitler world for granted in which international tensions would reach unprecedented heights and in which the improvement of American-Soviet relations, undertaken by Roosevelt since 1934, would be totally reversed, for whatever reasons? This is one of the grounds, probably strong enough in itself, why no sufficient support for a policy of total refusal, implying the possibility of nuclear surrender, could have been found among scientists in 1939. In any case, a surrender idea would have been inacceptable to the huge majority of the people who would have suffered from it.

The intervention of Niels Bohr

It is interesting to compare Einstein's attitude with that of another tower of intellectual and moral strength. Niels Bohr learned about the Manhattan project only in 1943, when he was enrolled. To judge from his son Aage's report[11], he did not hesitate to take part, and it is not evident that he gave much thought to the use of the weapons in the Second World War. However, at an early date he began to worry about an arms race between the victorious allies after the war. The action he took is described in chapter 7 (see p.102).

In his famous Open Letter to the United Nations in June, 1950,[20] Bohr still desperately argued for international collaboration. But now he put the accent on his claim that complete openness in respect of all national facts would guarantee international security. The serious problem that in an antagonistic world complete openness favours the stronger side was hardly touched by Bohr, who seems to have overlooked the vulnerability of small powers. To give a somewhat extreme, but clear example: during the Vietnam War, the Americans could safely tell the world where they made their explosives but the Vietnamese could not.

The idea that mere openness in military and weapons matters is a way to salvation may lead to bizarre consequences. Thus, a full recipe how to make a hydrogen bomb was prepared to be published in 1979, apparently with the best intentions, by a freelance journalist in a periodical meant to be progressive. The American Government at first tried to prevent publication, but later gave up. The case for the periodical was supported by physicists of standing. The text of the article is freely available now[21].

A general scientists' strike?

We have thus to face the fact now that the nuclear armaments are here and represent a danger far beyond any power of human imagination[22]. Let it not be said that the sheer size of the danger is so enormous that no further significant addition can be made. Not only is the total power of the weapons being increased, but more kinds of weapons are being developed, as for instance, the neutron bomb which lowers the nuclear threshold. Other "progress" leads to an increase of the chances of a successful first strike against the nuclear weapons of the adversary. The development of cruise missiles, of intermediate range rockets, and of means for anti-submarine warfare are examples which make the adoption of a "launch on warning" policy more likely.

So the dilemma is still with us, with scientists and technologists (and all mankind). Indeed, because of the enormous size and power of the nuclear establishment, the dilemma is more acute than ever. What should be done? Laymen often ask whether a worldwide strike of weapon scientists (and technologists?) would be possible. In the light of experience, the answer must unfortunately be "no". The large majority of our colleagues in weapons work are tied to it by the mechanisms experienced specifically in Los Alamos and described more generally, mainly in respect to later periods, by Herbert York[8,9]. For this reason alone a scientists' strike is an empty illusion. Even if the scientists' community consisted of incorruptible Einsteins, the bona-fide beliefs of so many scientists would make common action impossible. Too deep is the conviction of one's own country's justification everywhere.

We must tell our lay friends that scientists are, for better or worse, just humans, even though they have more factual knowledge about modern warfare than others. Scientists are superior neither in socio-political insight nor in moral strength. When scientists devote themselves to the common good, we must cheer, as we do with other humans, and help them, but a reversal of the terrible world situation through the united action of all scientists is out of the question.

No defeatist attitude is suggested. There are many scientists indeed whose conscience has led them, or will lead them, to a consideration or reconsideration of their place in life. In the case of scientists engaged in war work it is not only rational analysis that produces second thoughts. It is also deeply unsatisfactory to devote one's life to the perfection of means of destruction. In normal, though not all, people the natural instincts are perverted by such activity. Thus, there is an emotional as well as a rational component in the resistance against war work.

Many examples of eminent scientists who combined scientific insight and a critical attitude with conscience and social concern come to mind. In addition to Langevin, Einstein, Bohr, Szilard, and Urey, already mentioned, let us recall men and women like Pierre and Marie Curie, Frédéric and Irene Joliot, Linus Pauling. Bertrand Russell, Piotr Kapitza, Vladimir Engelgardt. Not all these scientists were working in the nuclear field, but they all bravely stood up against the wrong, and worked for a better world.

The effect of activities of such leaders for truth, peace and progress can be large indeed. While scientists, inside or outside military work, will not act as a monolithic block, many scientists can be influenced by respected colleagues with wider views, and made to think critically. Let us hope that this is especially true for younger scientists. These socially-active scientific leaders also played, and some are still playing, an important part in the birth and the growth of organizations of scientists that devote themselves to world progress and peace rather than to the mere representation of their professional interests.

Scientists addressing the people

Pugwash[23] (see p.132) is an important example showing that socially inspired, essentially peace-directed, activities of scientists can extend far beyond the laboratories. They can affect national and international life. In all countries some social currents seek to improve international relations and maintain peace. (Peace, it may be added, on a more secure basis than that of the alleged equilibrium of terror, an equilibrium easily upset by new technical, political or even financial factors). These currents often include large numbers of devoted high-minded and self-sacrificing women and men, but generally they are short of expert advice. This can be provided by people in Pugwash or in other groupings of scientists for peace.

As examples let us take trade unions or religious organizations. In Austria, for instance, the unions are closely connected with the Socialist (Social Democratic) Party, and the leading force in religious life is the Roman Catholic Church, but it does not matter that in other countries the situation may be different in these particular respects. The political parties themselves are also to be considered in this connection. Often such organizations include large parts of the active populations in the countries, but few of the members or supporters have the needed scientific qualification. Hence again and again such organizations either fall victims to wrong views on matters where science is relevant, or their attention is not drawn in adequate time to matters where the organization ought to take a stand. Thus, the failure to respond correctly to need is often not the result of negligence, even less of bad faith, but of ignorance. The most important need, of course, is that of the struggle against the nuclear war threat.

This is the field where concerned scientists in our nuclear age can intervene. They should speak out in public and invite the large organizations to make use of their services. With determination, a positive response will be obtained. In fact, experience shows that after some time a real expert, who also has the skill to express himself clearly and be understood by lay persons, will run into great difficulties in finding the time to provide all the services needed. Conversely, strong mass movements will not fail to awaken more scientists and make them realize their duties. In many ways, scientists ought to learn from the common people.

Some concerned scientists have also found that the mass media can be induced to print, broadcast or display their views – not only in the form of short pieces of information, but also in the form of major contributions. This applies even to media, say, popular newspapers, that one looks at with suspicion. Of course, there are extremes where it would not work. But by and large, even in media that do not normally attract scientifically-minded people, editors who have sufficient sense of responsibility and decency to print the concerned scientists' views can be found. Or they might even consider such action as a clever piece of editorial policy. All this is based on the supposition that the scientist has learned to express himself clearly and easily. It is his duty to do so.

Military work permitted?

A few words about the contents of the scientists' message. We take it for granted that he will search for peace; he will try to act against aggressive tendencies, against the perilous policy of strength, and for détente, disarmament and co-existence leading to co-operation and reconciliation. Now by tradition and habit most people are tempted to argue their own country's political line. On the whole, however, this should be left to others. The essential thing is precisely to explain the other person's point of view. The scientist ought to present the technical constraints on each side; often it will be found that there is a rational kernel in the "adversary's" argument. It requires little wisdom to know this, but we must act accordingly. Especially in respect to the nuclear threat, the need of everybody's security, not only of one's own country, must be recognized. The people at large should be shown why "adversaries" must insist on certain points, or reject certain actions of others if they are not to surrender. Only through negotiations on such a basis, preferably supplemented by unilateral actions in expectation of reciprocation, can improvements be obtained.

Finally, the question of rules for the individual professional behaviour of scientists engaged in military work should be addressed. Should one tell all such individuals to get out as quickly as possible and to turn to peaceful occupations? No doubt a move from war work to peace work would command great sympathy among concerned scientists, especially if sacrifices in standard of life, in possibilities of advancement, in prestige, etc. are involved, as will often be the case.

Yet, to one's deep regret it may not be advisable to make it a general slogan for scientists to abandon immediately military research work in all circumstances. Situations still exist where such work, unfortunately, must be considered as morally legitimate. Consider the example of some small country, perhaps a country in the Third World, that only recently gained its freedom and that has reason to feel threatened by a major power, maybe its former master. Could one tell the (few) scientists of such a country to stay away from defence? Take the case of a chemist in Vietnam at the time of the war who could hardly have been expected to stop making and improving on explosives. Legitimate work may also, in certain circumstances, serve defence against nuclear threats, and therefore it may involve the study of nuclear weapons systems. For instance, work for the improvement of the survival chances of submarines needed for retaliation, and therefore for deterrence, may be justified at the present moment.

Admittedly, it could be taken as sheer hypocrisy when scientists on military work preach disarmament and peace. A lot of tact and understanding is required. The military-industrial complex and the hawks will exploit real or seeming inconsistencies.

Criteria for decisions

It certainly would make life easier and solve our dilemma if hard and fast rules could be given to a concerned and responsible scientist, who wants to act for peace, as to what is allowed and what is not allowed. If only there were a superior moral authority which could lay down such rules! But general rules do not exist. On the contrary, each scientist must in the light of the knowledge available determine for himself what should be done, and what not. Here again the situation of scientists is not really fundamentally different from that of other persons. But the effects may be more far-reaching.

These last considerations should not be interpreted as a plea for easy relativism or for irresponsible permissiveness. The problems of the scientists are desperately serious. The action or inaction of each individual can have the gravest consequences, for evil or good. Thus, the problems must be pondered in real depth by the scientists. Consultation with their fellows and organizations is also required. In our age, people do not act in isolation. The judgement cannot be that of the famous lonely lighthouse keeper, mentioned and envied by Einstein.

On the positive side, scientists ought to urge work on possible paths to disarmament and also on its techniques. For instance, assuming international agreement for the destruction of nuclear weapons being achieved, we would not even know how to do it. Dump them on the sea bottom? Explode them underground? Convert the material to nuclear fuel? Dilute the uranium-235 with uranium-238? And what about plutonium? Certainly these problems can be solved, but much study will be needed to find the solution.

Prevention of nuclear war is the common task of all mankind. This need transcends all contradictions that otherwise exist. There is no challenge whatsoever that would justify the first use of nuclear weapons.

Finally, a brief view on the idea of world government, so dear to Einstein, though this is not the place for a discussion in detail. World Government will be a necessity. The thought is absurd that our Earth will remain divided in antagonistic states in the future. Yet we must not underestimate the tremendous difficulties. For instance, will each one of the 600 million Indians have as much say in world government as each one of 6 million Swiss? Will there be an equal right to vote for all? In any case, enmity, force and oppression do not lead to world government. It can be approached only through decrease of tension, removal of distrust and barriers, abolition of the threat of nuclear war, through rapprochement and collaboration. These are the objectives to aim at now.

References

1. Office of Technology Assessment, Congress of the United States, *The Effects of Nuclear War*, Croom Helm, London, 1980.
2. O. Nathan and H. Norden, *Einstein on Peace*, Simon and Schuster, New York, 1960.
3. S.R. Weart and G.W. Szilard, (eds.), *The Collected Works of Leo Szilard*, vol.2, His Version of the Facts, MIT Press, Cambridge, Mass., 1978.
4. E. Broda, Der Wissenschafter zwischen Erkenntnis und Verantwortung, *Physikalische Blätter*, vol. 36, p.84 1980.
5. S.A. Goudsmit, *Alsos*, Sigma Press, London, 1947.
6. B. Hoffmann and H. Dukas, *Albert Einstein, Creator and Rebel*, Hart-Davis McGibbon, London, 1973.
7. F. Herneck, Einstein und die Atombombe, Vortr. Schrift. No.51, *Archenhold-Stenwarte*, Berlin-Treptow, 1951.
8. H. York, *The Race to Oblivion*, Simon and Schuster, New York, 1962.
9. H. York, *The Advisors – Oppenheimer, Teller and the Superbomb*, Freeman, San Francisco, 1976.
10. Laura Fermi, *Atoms in the Family*, Chicago University Press, Chicago 1955.
11. A. Bohr, *The War Years and the Prospects raised by the Atomic Weapons* in S. Rozental (ed.) *Neils Bohr, his Life and Work as seen by his Friends and Colleagues*, North Holland, Amsterdam 1967.
12. L. Badash, J.O. Hirschfelder and H.P. Broida, (eds.), *Reminiscences of Los Alamos*, Reidel, Dordrecht, 1980.
13. J.S. Wilson, Intense Living in Secret Cities, *Physics Today 34* No. 7, 57, 1981.
14. S. Glasstone and P.J. Dolan, *The Effects of Nuclear Weapons*, 3rd edition, US Dept. of Defense, Washington, 1977.
15. The Committee For the Compilation of Materials on Damage Caused by the Atomic Bombs in Hiroshima and Nagasaki, *Hiroshima and Nagasaki*, Iwanami Shoten Publishers, Tokyo 1981.
16. Shuntaro Hida, *Under the Mushroom-Shaped Cloud in Hiroshima*. Manuscript. Author's address: 390 Segaskai Urawa Saitama, Japan.
17. K. Lorenz, *Das sogenannte Bösse*, Deutscher Taschenbuch-Verlag, Munich, 1954.
18. A. Bennett, *The Murder of the Mandarin*, in: *The Grim Smile of the Five Towns*, Penguin, Harmondsworth and New York, 1946, p.67.
19. I.N. Golovin, *I.V. Kurchatov*, Atomizdat, Moscow, 1967 (in Russian).
20. Niels Bohr, For An Open World, *Bulletin of the Atomic Scientists*, vol. VI, July 1950, p.213.
21. A. de Volpi, G.E. Marsh, T.A. Postol and G.S. Stanford, *Born Secret: The H-Bomb, The Progressive Case and National Security*, Pergamon, Oxford, 1981.
22. E. Broda, *Technology, Effects and Doctrines of Nuclear Warfare*. Manuscript 1981. A slightly older German version appeared in the monthly *Neues Forum*, Vienna, in September 1981.
23. J. Rotblat, *Scientists in the Quest for Peace: A History of the Pugwash Conferences*, MIT Press, Cambridge, Mass., 1972; The Fourth Pugwash Quinquennium, 1972-1977, *Pugwash-Newsletter*, Special Issue, London, 1977.

Chapter 6. Scientists as advisers to governments

Herbert York and Allen Greb

Introduction

The Second World War was a watershed period for scientists. The technological community had been mobilized before during times of crises, but never to the extent and depth it was called upon after 1940. Scientists and engineers, moreover, did not simply respond to the requests of government authorities for advice. Instead they became full partners in the policy-making process. Not only did they invent and build new weapons, they actively promoted them and participated in deciding when and even how these new instruments should be used.

Scientists became deeply embedded in the policy process during the war period because the technologies they developed in effect redefined the very nature of warfare and national security. Often they had initially to convince a reluctant political-military leadership of the validity of their ideas. Once convinced, however, this leadership provided massive support for several types of military research and development (R&D) projects and actively recruited scientists to direct them. "Never again would or could a government relegate the scientist to a secondary position", Robert Gilpin writes. "Scientific research had become a major element in national power."[1]

Officials found it necessary, and scientists found it useful, to institutionalize formally the government-science relationship through the creation of special organizational and management apparatus. In the United States, this "organization of science for war,"[2] as one author puts it, took the form of a few interlocking boards and committees headed by a small group of the country's best scientists. The triumvirate of Vannevar Bush, Karl T. Compton, and James B. Conant stood at the pinnacle of the wartime scientific effort. Bush, a Massachusetts Institute of Technology professor of electrical engineering up to 1940, directed the new Office of Scientific Research and Development (OSRD), which provided direct scientific advice to President Franklin Roosevelt, and chaired the Joint

New Weapons and Equipment Board (JNWEB). All three were members of the National Defense Research Committee (NDRC), the parent, and after 1941, an important advisory body of the OSRD.[3]

This process was not unique to the United States. As political leaders on both sides gradually realized the integral connection between technological innovation and military power, they too created machinery to foster government-science interaction. The United Kingdom, for example, set up a complex administrative structure to conduct war research which became closely tied to the American effort. In the Soviet Union, Joseph Stalin appointed S.V. Kaftanov a "plenipotentiary" for science *(upolnomochennyi GKO po voprosam nauki)* and established a special Scientific-Technical Council to direct wartime research for the State Defence Committee. Although much less effective in execution, the two major Axis nations also established bodies similar to America's OSRD: the *Reichsforschungsrat* in Germany and the Board of Technology in Japan.[4] In all of these countries, scientists proposed and officials approved the R&D programmes in such revolutionary new weapons systems as radar, jet aircraft, rocketry, and, most dramatic and portentous of all, nuclear weapons.

The atom bomb projects

The development of the atom bomb is perhaps the quintessential example of a technological advance stimulating and promoting the government-science relationship. In the 1930s nuclear physics research was international in scope, with scientists from many different countries working to unlock the secrets of the atom. Information among this select group flowed easily during this decade. As one historian comments, "Theoretical and experimental results were communicated quickly ... and a discovery in one laboratory spurred further work in the others."[5] In the United States and the United Kingdom this initial work led eventually to the establishment of a full scale co-operative nuclear weapons programme during the Second World War. Only one other country, the Soviet Union, managed to start a viable nuclear project during the war, although German, French, and Japanese physicists also initiated very modest top secret nuclear research efforts with the interest and support of their governments.

Significantly in each of these cases, scientists, not military men, recognized the military potential of atomic energy, and brought it to the attention of their respective political leaders. In France, the Nobel Prize Laureate physicist Frédéric Joliot-Curie, who had helped to confirm the possibility of a chain reaction during the 1930s, convinced authorities to fund a small-scale atomic project. Joliot's group had actually worked out plans for a viable reactor when defeat and occupation at the hands of the Germans suspended work in 1940. German and Japanese physicists interested in developing the bomb also initiated tenuous associations with their governments, but their programmes could not compete for funds with conventional weapons projects.

The atom bomb project in the United States

Circumstances were different in the United States, where economic resources and the isolation of the country made an atom bomb project a realistic objective. Even there, however, physicists had to cajole reluctant military and political leaders into undertaking such a programme. Thus in 1939, after unsuccessful efforts to interest the American military in atomic weapons, the émigré scientists Leo Szilard and Eugene Wigner raised the uranium question directly with President Roosevelt through a letter signed by Albert Einstein.[6] On November 6, 1941, after extensive consultation with British scientists who had been working on the bomb under a project code named the Maud Committee, OSRD Director Bush approved a report to Roosevelt which set into motion America's nuclear weapons programme. Designated the Manhattan District Project in 1942, the programme gathered together a remarkable complex of experts, laboratories, and production facilities in a very short time[6].

Less than a year after the initial organization, project leaders established the Los Alamos Scientific Laboratory (LASL) as their primary research centre. Located in a remote part of New Mexico for security reasons, LASL operated through a United States' Army contract with the University of California. Its first director was J. Robert Oppenheimer, a theoretical physicist on the faculty at the Berkeley campus. During its first year, LASL attracted an unprecedented concentration of the most brilliant nuclear physicists and other scientists in the United States. Many refugee scientists from Nazi-occupied Europe, and many who had worked on the atomic bomb in Britain and France, joined the American team at Los Alamos and other project centres. Together they produced a great outburst of intellectual energy culminating in a test explosion on July 16, 1945, and the two explosions over Hiroshima and Nagasaki on August 6 and 9, 1945[7].

The atom bomb project in the USSR

The pattern, but not the magnitude, of Soviet nuclear weapons development was essentially the same during the war period. Again the problem moved from the scientific community to the government, ultimately occupying a central place in state affairs and involving scientists in critical policy decisions. On October 12, 1941, Piotr Kapitza, a leader in Soviet physics, spoke of the military importance of atomic energy at an international "anti-Fascist" meeting in Moscow. A short time later, another physicist working on the problem, G.N. Flerov, wrote directly to Stalin imploring that it was "essential not to lose any time in building the uranium bomb".[8] The State Defence Committee subsequently set up a programme under the leadership of Academician Igor V. Kurchatov.

Unlike the Manhattan Project, which tapped the expertise of literally thousands of scientist-technologists, the Soviet effort initially relied on only a small coterie of prominent physicists. Because of more immediate demands placed on the war machine, Kurchatov directed a staff that numbered no more than fifty people before 1945. The programme began in earnest only after the Hiroshima and Nagasaki explosions. At a meeting in mid-August 1945, Stalin issued a cryptic order to Kurchatov and to the Commissar of Munitions, Boris Vannikov:

> "A single demand of you, comrades, provide us with atomic weapons in the shortest possible time. You know that Hiroshima has shaken the whole world. The equilibrium has been destroyed /*ravnovesie narushilos'*/. Provide the bomb – it will remove a great danger from us."[9]

With full government backing, Kurchatov and his colleagues proceeded to put together a nuclear device in approximately the same time span as the American project scientists. They produced a chain reaction on December 25, 1946; put a production reactor into operation in 1948; and exploded the first Soviet atomic bomb on August 29, 1949. The Soviet historian V.M. Khaitsman captures the mood of extreme urgency that surrounded this effort for both the scientist participants and their political superiors:

> "Investigations of nuclear problems were conducted at the highest pitch. Scientists understood the importance of achieving completion of the Soviet atomic project; they knew its significance in ensuring the safety of the Soviet Union. The necessity to create an equal atomic weapon prior to the time when its mass production would be developed in the USA dictated the fast tempo of the work."[10]

Scientists in the decision-making process

Just as the atomic energy and other wartime weapons projects brought scientists into the government fold at an unprecedented rate, rapid technological changes throughout the postwar period have kept them in the forefront of the decision-making process. Scientists and engineers have continued to interact fully with state authorities, playing the role of policy initiator as well as adviser. Following a brief period of demobilization and uncertainty immediately after the war, science advisory organizations and institutions have continued to develop and proliferate. These mechanisms have taken a number of different forms in different countries, including permanent agencies, committees, and laboratories at all levels of government bureaucracy; university, industry, and privately operated research institutes; and special *ad hoc* groups of experts. As this scientific-government network has grown in size and influence, personal contacts, associations, and alliances between scientists and the political establishment have played a major part in promoting a free flow of ideas and breaking down normal bureaucratic-organizational barriers.

All of this is not to say that science advice has been uniformly wise and productive. The scientific community is not monolithic in its views, and scientists have not presented a united voice to governments on technological matters. Some participants have urged the full exploitation of all scientific-military discoveries. Edward Teller, the father of the hydrogen bomb, is a prominent example of this group, as was Wernher von Braun, who developed large rockets both in Germany and the United States. Each of these men testified before numerous congressional committees; each gave advice to presidents, secretaries of defence, and other officials; and each mounted extensive public campaigns in support of their views.

Other scientists have been less willing to pursue all military applications of modern technology; they see a need for control and restraint as well as development in the weapons acquisition process. Their goal, in Gilpin's words, has been "to prevent a technical advance which would outstrip man's political ability to control it."[11] Robert Oppenheimer, for example, oversaw the development of the atomic bomb but opposed a "crash" programme to develop the hydrogen bomb. Others in this school include several former chief advisers to American presidents – James R. Killian, George Kistiakowsky, and Jerome Wiesner – who have become strong nuclear arms control proponents; Lord Zuckerman, whose career has followed a similar path in the United Kingdom; and Andrei Sakharov, who played a key role in the Soviet hydrogen bomb programme, but later expressed great public concern over the nuclear arms race.

Science – government relationship in the United States

One of the best ways to explore the growth of the post-war science–government relationship is to follow carefully its course in a particular country. We have chosen the United States as a case study, both because we are most familiar with it and because patterns there apply (in lesser and greater degrees) to nearly all advanced technological societies and many less developed states today. Science advisory apparatus within the United States has gone through an evolutionary process since the Second World War, punctuated by instances of major programmatic change brought on by perceived technological challenges of the Soviet bloc. Specifically, events such as the first Soviet atomic explosion, the Korean War, the launch of Sputnik, and the development in the USSR of an H-bomb and intercontinental missiles, stimulated organizational and programmatic responses which continue to influence and shape American defence and national security policy.

The Pentagon has been a focal point for many of these changes. During the formative stages of the Cold War, between 1945 and 1950, government officials attempted to consolidate technical advice through the creation of the Joint Research and Development Board (JRDB) in June 1946, and its successor the Research and Development Board (RDB) a year later. Designed to take over the functions of the OSRD and JNWEB, the charters of the new boards emphasized the management concepts of co-ordination, integration, and avoidance of duplication. But the complex system of part time committees, composed of "civilian experts" and military officers, set up to do the work of the boards proved unequal to the task. As Isidor Rabi complained at the time, the RDB's "very organization makes it impossible for it to do a good job because the committees and panels consist largely of people who serve part time and are not in the position to analyse the problems and see the whole picture".[12]

The RDB, however, did have important indirect effects on the future course of military R&D. Many of the board's civilian scientists, for example, served on other more influential bodies and used the RDB to exchange information and ideas. Moreover, although they had no budgetary authority or any real control over programmes, scientist members nonetheless gained experience in the public policy arena and received a valuable education in national security matters.

The Eisenhower period

The opportunity to use this education came sooner than expected. On January 21, 1953, the Republican administration of Dwight D. Eisenhower moved into power in Washington convinced that modern technology and science was not being fully exploited in the interests of national security. The Korean War and other East–West confrontations did much to contribute to this belief. Suddenly the cold war had turned hot, the communist danger appeared more unified, and the technological danger it posed more imminent. Civilian technologists and members of the scientific community (many veterans of the Second World War R&D programmes) began to re-evaluate independently the state of American military preparedness as a result. The new administration welcomed this development and sought to mobilize the scientists' efforts within the government.

Defense Department changes were incorporated under Reorganization Plan No.6 of 1953. The plan abolished the RDB and replaced it with two assistant secretaries of defence, one for research and development (ASD/R&D) and one for applications engineering (ASD/AE). Scientist-engineers occupied both posts and the ASD/R&D became a particularly important cog in defence decision-making, under the leadership of Donald Quarles. Quarles had been a part of the R&D operation for many years, being both a member and chairman of the RDB's Committee on Electronics. From March 1952 until he took the new R&D position in September 1953, he was president of Sandia Corporation, a laboratory subsidiary of Western Electric responsible for the ordnance design of nuclear weapons. In 1955 Quarles became secretary of the air force and in 1957 he took over as deputy secretary of defence, a post he held until his sudden death in 1959.

During his six years in the Pentagon, a period of exceptionally rapid change and flux, Quarles greatly influenced both the content and the style of defence R&D. Although unassuming and somewhat reticent, he was a good judge of people and had a superior intellect. Above all, he excelled in his ability to distinguish technological sense from nonsense. He was not afraid to say "no" to programmes and ideas whose main, often sole, virtue was their glamour, novelty, or technological virtuosity.

The post-Sputnik period

The last significant series of rearrangements in the Pentagon's technology-management apparatus occurred in 1957-1958, triggered by the Soviet Sputnik launch of October 4, 1957. Except perhaps for its weight, Sputnik did not come as a major surprise to most American government scientists, the White House, or the defence establishment. These groups were well aware of Soviet progress in the development of the types of rockets needed to launch a satellite. The event, however, produced a great shock wave among the general public, the press, and a Democratic Congress, that the Eisenhower administration failed to anticipate. Moreover, as one political analyst wrote, Sputnik "represented more than a psychological setback ...; it highlighted the technical potential of Soviet rockets and suggested that the USSR might be moving even more rapidly than anticipated toward an operational ICBM capability".[13] Officials again viewed this as a technological challenge which demanded a technological reply.

In the Pentagon, the reply came in the form of major new legislation, the Defense Reorganization Act of 1958, which abolished the office and the position of ASD/R&D, created the office of the director of defence research and engineering (DDR&E), and gave the new post more authority and wider scope. In brief, while the assistant-secretary had been limited to an advisory and co-ordinating capacity, the DDR&E had direct authority to approve, disapprove, or modify all defence R&D programmes. Key special programmes, such as ballistic missiles (under a separate director or "missile czar" at that time) and satellites (run as a so-called top secret "black programme"), now came under the DDR&E's jurisdiction and his formal status was made equal to that of the service secretaries. Physicists have always directed this important office: Herbert York (1958-1961), Harold Brown (1961-1965), John S. Foster, Jr. (1965-1973), Malcolm Currie (1973-1977), and William Perry (1977-1981).

During this same post-Sputnik period, the secretary of defence also created a new technological action unit within the department, the Advanced Research Projects Agency (ARPA). He did so at the urging of President Eisenhower, who wanted an apparatus to cut through the usual service red tape associated with various special weapons projects. York also served as the first chief scientist of this agency before moving up to the office of DDR&E.

Each of the military services, too, found it necessary to enlist the aid of science advisers in increasing numbers during the postwar years. The Government's emphasis on maintaining qualitative technological superiority encouraged the close collaboration of military officials with certain members of the scientific community. Unfinished projects had to be continued and, more important, new technological opportunities had to be identified and exploited. In the case of the air force, in fact, a small number of scientists actually defined and set the tone of R&D for most of the 1950s and 1960s.

New organizational structures

As usual, the new technological demands required the creation of new organizations and organizational forms. The two most important of these in the air force were the Science Advisory Board (AFSAB) and the RAND Corporation. The AFSAB was the direct outgrowth of the collaboration of two remarkable men, General H.H. Arnold and Theodore von Karman. General Arnold was chief of staff of the army air force during the war; von Karman was a distinguished professor of aeronautics at the California Institute of Technology. In September 1944, Arnold contacted von

Karman and asked him to organize a long range postwar planning effort designed to keep the air force at the leading edge of technology. The formal charge, dated November 7, 1944, read in part:

"I believe the security of the United States... will continue to rest in part in developments instituted by our educational and professional scientists. I am anxious that Air Forces postwar and next-war research and development programs be placed on a sound and continuing basis. In addition, I am desirous that these programs be in such form and contain such well thought out, long range thinking that, in addition to guaranteeing the security of our nation and serving as a guide for the next 10–20 years period, that the recommended programs can be used as a basis for adequate Congressional appropriations."[14]

One result of this request was a very thorough report called "Toward New Horizons," issued in December 1945. Written by von Karman and a team of his scientific colleagues, the report consisted of thirty-three volumes, each covering a topic of special interest. Because of its comprehensiveness and because of the influence of its authors, specific observations and recommendations from "Toward New Horizons" reverberated through air force thinking for years to come.

The other major result of Arnold's request was the establishment of the SAB with von Karman as its first chairman. The SAB still operates today and provides a particularly effective means of keeping lines of communication open among air force officials, industrial contractors, and the general scientific public. Significantly, many civilians who have had overall authority over air force technology programmes served at one time on the SAB or its staff. In this way the board, like each of the other services' high level advisory panels,* has played a key educational function for future science policymakers, generating advice and ideas which in effect were later received and implemented by persons who had formulated them in the first place. Since the 1950s, and Sputnik, the top level civilians in each of the services' R&D structure have consistently been scientists and engineers with management experience. Military R&D officers, moreover, typically have had advanced academic training in technology, as well as management techniques.

Think-tanks

Like the high level scientific advisory committee, the other new military organizational form – the independent not-for-profit, research advisory corporation, or so-called "think-tank" – also dates from the earliest postwar period. A wartime group of scientists which conducted

---

*The office of Naval Research and the Naval Research Advisory Committee, for the navy; the Operations Research Office, for the army. The Defense Department itself has its own separate scientific advisory group, the Defense Science Board, which assists both the secretary and the DDR&E.

operations analysis for Secretary of War Henry Stimson originated the idea of creating a permanent body to study the problem of technology and national defence. Headed by Edward Bowles of MIT, the group examined various ways to keep at least a substantial cadre of specialists working on high intensity, high quality R&D programmes after the war. First, Project RAND (a division of Douglas Aircraft), and since 1948 the autonomous RAND Corporation, were the result. Over the years, RAND has had a strong influence on the government's R&D policy and programmes, both directly through its reports and briefings (e.g. on military satellites and ICBMs), and indirectly through its people, many of whom have gone on to become important officials within the defence structure.[15]

The army and navy, as well as the Defense Department itself, have developed their own operations analysis groups. The most interesting of these, the Institute for Defense Analyses (IDA) has worked closely with the secretary of defence and the Joint Chiefs of Staff since 1956. Originally a unique consortium of universities put together by James Killian, IDA today is a free-standing not-for-profit corporation like RAND. The Center for Naval Analysis performs a similar role for the navy as does the Research Analysis Corporation for the army.

Scientific advisers to the President

In the aftermath of Korea, many scientists and technologists believed they could be most effectively mobilized outside the direct control of the military. Ideally, they hoped to set up some new structure similar to the OSRD and NDRC with its apex in the White House. As early as August 1948, RDB Chairman Vannevar Bush asked Irvin Stewart, former deputy director of the OSRD, to examine the "general question of mobilization of the civilian scientific effort in the event... of an emergency".[16] In December 1949 (after the first Soviet atomic test), the committee organized by Stewart submitted a report to the RDB which called, in effect, for a new OSRD reporting directly to the President.

Apparently Korea constituted the kind of "emergency" Bush had had in mind. A new report, by William T. Golden of the Budget Bureau, and submitted to President Truman on December 18, 1950, recommended "the prompt appointment of an outstanding scientific leader as Scientific Adviser to the President".[17] Acting on this and the Stewart report, the following April Truman established a Scientific Advisory Committee, reporting not to him directly but to the White House Office of Defense Mobilization (SAC/ODM). He named Oliver Buckley, recently retired president of Bell Laboratories, as the first SAC/ODM chairman. The rest of the original membership of the committee was an especially august group, including National Academy of Sciences President Detlev W. Bronk, RDB Chairman William Webster, National Science Foundation Director Alan Waterman, and long time government advisers Lee DuBridge, James Conant, James Killian, and J. Robert Oppenheimer.

Despite the prestige of its members and its central position in the bureaucracy, the SAC/ODM did little during the Truman years. Buckley was ill most of the time and, in any case, he did not believe the committee should initiate policy. Consequently, the SAC/ODM merely kept abreast of the technical military developments in the United States, standing ready to advise the President on scientific mobilization, should a new emergency arise. It was not until the Eisenhower years, in particular following Sputnik, that the White House science advisory apparatus began to grow in size and status and assume a new character.

In the wake of the Soviet achievement, Eisenhower established a new full-time position, the special assistant for science and technology, and reconstituted the SAC/ODM as the President's Science Advisory Committee (PSAC) reporting directly to him. Significantly, the body of science advisers brought into the government in this way were, for the most part, not committed to nuclear weapons development as the sole basis of national security. In PSAC, one analyst asserts, "Eisenhower found a group of brilliant and thoughtful men to whom he could turn for alternative advice to that provided him by the AEC and the Pentagon".[18]

The first two special assistants in this new era, James Killian of MIT and George Kistiakowsky of Harvard, fit this description well. (Both have written fascinating accounts of their tenures as science advisers[19]). So, too, did several distinguished individuals who served on PSAC, such as the eminent atomic physicists Hans Bethe and Isidor Rabi. Each of these scientists endevoured to understand both the technological and political aspects of defence policy, and each developed close working relationships with Eisenhower and other high level officials (including the new DDR&E, Herbert York). During the late 1950s, PSAC scientists reviewed almost every important high technology programme of the Defense Department and the AEC. Few ideas or programmes that did not have their full approval got very far within the bureaucracy.

For the first time, moreover, science advisers generated a real movement within the government towards arms control and disarmament, acting as an important counterbalance to the Pentagon, the AEC, and such scientists as Teller and Ernest O. Lawrence. Killian, Kistiakowsky, Bethe, Rabi and other PSAC members became especially interested in the nuclear test ban problem. They provided Eisenhower with technical and political advice which led directly to the 1958-1961 test moratorium, and indirectly to the 1963 Limited Test Ban Treaty. They also played an active role in the establishment of the Arms Control and Disarmament Agency (ACDA) under the Department of State. Organized in late 1961, ACDA grew during the Johnson years to become the first permanent agency to study arms control issues in Washington.[20] (see p.145).

Several scientific "overlords", to use the phrase of Lord Zuckerman,[21] have followed Killian and Kistiakowsky: Jerome Wiesner, Donald Hornig, Lee DuBridge, Edward David, Guyford Stever, Frank Press, and, at present, George Keyworth. None, however (except perhaps Wiesner), have enjoyed the special influence of their predecessors. Competition from other offices and failure to deal with special problems, have led to a gradual decline in this particular science-government link. PSAC itself, abolished by Nixon in 1973, has been replaced (since 1976) by the much smaller and weaker Office of Science and Technology Policy (OSTP).[22]

The scientific-technological community has also contributed its expertise and advice on defence and national security matters through a number of less permanent organizations – special commissions and task forces, autonomous *ad hoc* study panels or committees, and independent political pressure groups. In some cases, the national leadership has turned to scientific experts to direct special reviews of strategic and defence policies. Several of these studies have had a far reaching impact on the direction of overall national security affairs. In other instances, scientists themselves have taken the initiative to organize and push forward their ideas before the government. Rather than being directly involved with military R&D, these "public scientists", as they might be called, have often been concerned with the larger issue of how to control the technological arms spiral. Like PSAC and ACDA, they have frequently served as a moderating force in the weapons acquisition process.

Two particularly influential studies stand out as examples of the government-initiated type: the report of the Strategic Missile Evaluation Committee (SMEC), or Teapot Committee, of February 1954; and that of the Technological Capabilities Panel (TCP), or Surprise Attack Panel, of February 1955. Established by the secretary of defence to review the nation's incipient missile programme, the top level unit known as SMEC collected together a very special group of scientist-engineers, including Trevor Gardner, John von Neumann, George Kistiakowsky, Simon Ramo, Dean Wooldridge, Charles C. Lauritsen, and Jerome Wiesner. Gardner, who had joined the air force staff in 1953, chaired the study. The recommendations made by him and his colleagues, many of whom would later hold high government positions, led directly to the development of the first US strategic missile system.[23] Gardner, one contemporary wrote, was the real "catalyst" in the US ICBM programme. "He worked at this task with a ferocity that astonished his associates, and a sense of urgency that baffled less technically perceptive officials."[24]

The TCP had a similarly outstanding cast of participants and produced an equally influential report. The director was the ubiquitous James Killian of MIT, and the deputy director was James B. Fisk of the Bell Telephone Laboratories. Both Killian and Fisk were also members of the SAC/ODM.

The study itself, requested directly by President Eisenhower in part because of his concerns about a surprise Soviet attack, made several recommendations which became a permanent part of American strategic defence policy. It endorsed the ICBM programmes just then getting underway; it urged development of the IRBM, including a sea-based version; and it promoted intelligence gathering through both reconnaisance aircraft and satellites.[25] By clearly and firmly endorsing these ideas and proposals, the Killian panel was able to break the bureaucratic log jam typically associated with new systems, accelerating their R&D timetables by several years.

Activities of independent scientists

Public scientific activity has taken a variety of forms with varying degrees of success. Groups like the Federation of American Scientists (FAS) and the *Bulletin of the Atomic Scientists*, for example, became deeply involved in the postwar debate over both the domestic and international control of atomic energy. The FAS and BAS continue today as major fora for the dissemination of scientists' views on government policy[26] (see pp.117 and 118).

Other public scientists have been very active on an individual basis. During the 1950s, Linus Pauling led a strong scientists protest against nuclear weapons testing, which enlisted such prominent men as Albert Schweitzer and one-time nuclear proponent Albert Einstein. Leo Szilard was another scientist who after the Second World War devoted his public life to controlling the weapons he had done so much to create. Szilard died in 1964, but one of his students, Bernard Feld, has continued the quest for nuclear disarmament particularly through his contributions to the international Pugwash Movement. Still others have adopted the cause of arms control and disarmament after serving in the military-defence establishment. From their positions in the universities, private enterprise, and elsewhere, Wiesner, York, Killian, and Kistiakowsky, to name a few, have promoted such arms control measures as a comprehensive test ban and strategic arms limitation treaties, and opposed such weapons systems as the anti-ballistic missile and the multiple independently-targetable re-entry vehicle (MIRV).

Conclusion

It is not difficult to extrapolate from this long and varied American government-science interface to the rest of the world. In the Soviet Union, for example, scientists since the 1950s have coalesced into a "potentially powerful sub-elite," to use the words of one political analyst.[27] Indeed, all of the scientific roles we have spelled out in the American case have very close analogues in the Soviet system. In the United Kingdom, the government has a well-established Scientific Civil Service. Other countries have set up specific scientific ministerial portfolios. Even such supranational bodies as the Common Market and NATO have science officials as part of their permanent organizational structures. "Without any badge of authority conferred on them either by democratic decision or by autocratic diktat, without any coherent concern for political values or goals," Lord Zuckerman concludes, "scientists and engineers (have) become the begetters of new social demand and the architects of new economic and social situations...."[28]

In the South and East, too, the government–science relationship has grown remarkably during the post Second World War era, again largely the consequence of the nuclear revolution and sometimes under the guise of the "peaceful atom". In India, for example, which exploded a so-called peaceful nuclear device in 1974, the founder of the atomic programme, Homi Bhabha, paved the way for a mercuric rise of scientific influence in state affairs. For Bhabha, who received his physics training in Western universities, nuclear energy offered the means to bring his country into the modern technological world and at the same time ensure its independence and security. Aided by the Indian political-economic elite, in particular by Prime Minister Jawaharal Nehru who shared an uncompromising faith in technology, Bhabha established and administered the Indian Atomic Energy Commission from 1948 until his death in 1966. Despite grave problems, this body and its scientists and technologists continue to command an unprecedented level of autonomy, money, and prestige within the Indian government bureaucracy today. Two other Western educated physicists who in the late 1950s began the Chinese nuclear programme, Qian San-qiang and Wang Gan-chang, and the Nobel physicist Abdus Salam of Pakistan, have given the scientific communities of their nations a similar strong foothold in the decision-making apparatus.

Where is this world-wide revolution in the government-science interface, as several scholars have called it,[29] taking us? Are we becoming "the captive of a scientific-technological elite,"[30] as President Eisenhower warned the American public in 1961? Or does the possibility exist for scientists and engineers to direct public policy into more useful and worthwhile channels? Certainly if we look to the American example, the prospects appear mixed. As we have seen, the dominant theme in the interaction of science and government in that country since 1945 has been the development of ever more complex and more sophisticated weapons systems. Significantly, the principal high level inside group which competed against this trend, PSAC, did not survive the 1970s and no comparable body has taken its place.

France provides a similar lesson. After the war, Frédéric Joliot-Curie sought to revitalize the French nuclear project under the umbrella of Charles de Gaulle's provisional government. Shortly after assuming control of the new state Commisariat à l'Energie Atomique (CEA) in 1946, Joliot managed to get work started on a research reactor. But within a few years, he became embroiled in controversy over the CEA's programme objectives and his personal ties to the French communist party. Specifically, he began to protest loudly against the development of nuclear weapons as opposed to nuclear energy. His reputation as the nation's most famous scientist notwithstanding, Joliot's protests resulted only in his dismissal from the CEA; its takeover by the pro-bomb forces of "Les X," military trained engineers of the Ecole Polytechnique; and the subsequent development of an independent French nuclear arsenal, *la force de frappe*.[31]

Many scientists interested in moderating the arms race and in promoting disarmament, however, remain active on lesser committees and agencies within the American, French, and other government infrastructures, including even such conservative bastions as the Defense Science Board in the United States. In addition, the body of public scientists concerned about the dangers of nuclear weapons and nuclear war continues to grow. In such contexts of international organizations as Pugwash and the United Nations, they persist in acting as yet another check and balance on the world-wide military R&D structure.

References

1. Robert Gilpin, *American Scientists and Nuclear Weapons Policy*, Princeton University Press, Princeton, N.J. 1962, p.10.
2. James Phinney Baxter III, *Scientists Against Time*, MIT Press, Cambridge, Mass.: 1968, p.7.
3. *Ibid.*, pp. 119-35.
4. David Holloway, Entering the Nuclear Arms Race: The Soviet Decision to Build the Atomic Bomb, 1939-45, *Social Studies of Science*, vol. 11, 1981, p.171; Baxter, *Scientists Against Time*, pp.8-12.
5. D. Holloway, *op.cit.*, p.162.
6. The Einstein letter is available in Spencer R. Weart and Gertrud Weiss Szilard, eds., *Leo Szilard: His Version of the Facts, Selected Recollections and Correspondence*, MIT Press, Cambridge, Mass., 1978, pp.94-96. On the early US nuclear programme, see Henry D. Smyth, *Atomic Energy for Military Purposes*, Princeton University Press, Princeton, N.J. 1945; Richard G. Hewlett and Oscar E. Anderson, Jr., *A History of the United States Atomic Energy Commission: The New World, 1939-45*, Pennsylvania

State University Press, University Park, Pa.; 1962, and Anthony Cave Brown and Charles B. MacDonald, eds., *The Secret History of the Atomic Bomb*; Dell Publishing Co., New York, 1977.

7. Alice K. Smith, Los Alamos: Focus of an Age, *Bulletin of the Atomic Scientists*, vol. 26 (June 1970), pp.15-20.

8. Herbert F. York, *The Advisors: Oppenheimer, Teller, and the Superbomb*, W.H. Freeman, San Francisco, 1976, pp.30-31.

9. A. Lavrent'yeva in "Stroiteli novogo mira (Builders of a New World)," *Vmireknig* (In the World of Books), No.9, p.4, as quoted in Holloway, "Entering the Nuclear Arms Race," p.183. On the Soviet nuclear programme see Arnold Kramish, *Atomic Energy in the Soviet Union*, Stanford University Press, Stanford Ca, 1959; I.N. Golovin, *I.V. Kurchatov*, 3rd ed.: Atomizdat, Moscow; 1978; P.T. Astashenkov, *Akademik I.V., Kurchatov*, Moscow, 1971; and York, *op cit.*, pp.29-40.

10. V.M. Khaitsman, *The USSR and the Problem of Disarmament, 1945–1959*, Nauka, Moscow; 1970, p.94.

11. R. Gilpin, *op. cit.,* p.99.

12. I.I Rabi, The Organization of Scientific Research for Defense, American Academy of Political Science, *Proceedings*, vol.24 (May 1951), p.360.

13. Jerome H. Kahan, *Security in the Nuclear Age: Developing US Strategic Arms Policy*, The Brookings Institution, Washington, D.C. 1975, p.39.

14. General H.H. Arnold to Theodore von Karman, Nov. 7, 1944, Mixed Files, Air Force Space and Missiles Systems Office, Los Angeles, California.

15. Bruce L.R. Smith, *The RAND Corporation: Case Study of a Nonprofit Advisory Corporation*, Harvard University Press, Cambridge, Mass. 1966.

16. Vannevar Bush to Irvin Stewart, Aug. 13, 1948, US President's Science Advisory Committee (PSAC) Records, Washington, D.C.

17. William T. Golden Memorandum to President Truman, "Mobilizing Science for War: A Scientific Adviser to the President", Washington Bureau of the Budget (Dec. 18, 1950), PSAC Records.

18. R. Gilpin, *op. cit.,* p.177.

19. James R. Killian, Jr., *Sputnik, Scientists, and Eisenhower: A Memoir of the First Special Assistant to the President for Science and Technology* MIT Press, Cambridge, Mass., 1977. George B. Kistiakowsky, *A Scientist at the White House: The Private Diary of President Eisenhower's Special Assistant for Science and Technology*, Harvard University Press, Cambridge, Mass., 1976.

20. Duncan L. Clarke, *Politics of Arms Control: The Role and Effectiveness of the US Arms Control and Disarmament Agency*, Free Press, New York, 1979, pp.13, 69-71.

21. Solly Zuckerman, *Science Advisers, Scientific Advisers and Nuclear Weapons*, The Menard Press, London, 1980.

22. William T. Golden, ed., *Science Advice to the President*, Pergamon Press, New York, 1980); Daniel S. Greenberg, "The Fall and Rise of the White House Science Office," *Chronicle of Higher Education*, Sept. 7, 1976; George Keyworth (interview), "Science and the Reagan Administration," *SIPIscope*, 9(May-June 1981), pp.1-5.

23. "Recommendations of the Strategic Missiles Evaluation Committee" (Feb. 10, 1954), Office of Air Force History, Department of the Air Force, Washington, D.C.

24. Robert Hotz, "The Lonely Warrior," *Aviation Week and Space Technology*, 79 (Oct. 14, 1963), p.21.

25. *The Report to the President by the Technological Capabilities Panel of the*

Science Advisory Committee (2 vols., Feb. 14, 1955) I, pp.16, 24-25, 38, 44; II, pp.63-66, Gordon Gray Papers, Eisenhower Library, Abilene. Kansas.

26. R. Gilpin, *op. cit.,* pp.27-28; Alice Kimball Smith, *A Peril and a Hope: The Scientists' Movement in America, 1945-1947* University of Chicago Press, Chicago, 1965, pp.203-97, 510-11.

27. Christer Jonsson, *Soviet Bargaining Behaviour: The Nuclear Test Ban Case* Columbia University Press, New York, 1979, p.141. See also Arthur J. Alexander, *Decision-Making in Soviet Weapons Procurement,* Adelphi Papers No.147 and 148 (Winter 1978/79), pp.13-14, 35-42.

28. Solly Zuckerman, *op. cit.*

29. Robert C. Wood, Scientists and Politics: The Rise of an Apolitical Elite in Robert Gilpin and Christopher Wright, eds., *Scientists and National Policy Making* Columbia University Press, New York, 1964 pp. 41-72; Harvey M.Sapolsky, "Science Policy in American State Government" in Thomas J. Kuehn and Alan L. Porter, eds., *Science, Technology, and National Policy* Cornell University Press, Ithaca, 1981, pp.367-68.

30. *Public Papers of the President, 1960-1961*, Washington, D.C.: Government Printing Office, 1961, p.1038.

31. Peter Pringle and James Spigelman, *The Nuclear Barons*, Holt, Rinehart and Winston. New York, 1981, pp.125-135.

Chapter 7: Scientists in opposition to the arms race

Vasily Emelyanov

Introduction

Although the term arms race can be applied to all types of armaments, we are primarily concerned with the ongoing race in nuclear weapons which – if not checked – may end up in an unprecedented catastrophe.

At the very beginning of the 20th century, after the discovery of radioactivity, it became clear to many scientists that mankind was entering a new era, with the prospect of a fundamental discovery which would open the way to the practical utilization of the enormous store of energy inside the atom. Scientists began to think about the consequences of this discovery in terms of the great benefits it could bring to mankind, because progressively thinking scientists engage in science not merely for the sake of science, or for their own glory, but with the notion that the scientific achievements would be applied to further the development of human civilization. Genuine scientists never entertain Herostratus-like ideas.

At the same time, attempts to deprave science and bend it to the interests of a state, as had happened during Hitler's fascist regime, are strongly resisted by the scientific community. In that particular episode an appeal was made to the scientists of the world to break off relations with the German scientists who collaborated with the Hitler regime.

Yet, the first practical application of the discovery of nuclear energy was its release as an explosive which devastated two Japanese cities. This shameful outcome of scientific endeavours, the development of weapons of mass destruction, has continued ever since and became enormously amplified by the nuclear arms race. The argument has been advanced that these arms are needed to contain aggression. Such an argument reminds one of the behaviour of a primitive human creature who, in order to kill a mosquito on the forehead of another fellow creature, smites the forehead with an axe!

Many of the scientists who participated in the research work that has led to the production of the first atom bomb soon realized the folly of this type of argument, and the grave danger to mankind from the existence of nuclear arms. They, and their followers, took up a strong stand against this development, and openly voiced their opposition to the nuclear arms race. Some scientists expressed this in individual efforts, others in collective measures.

Individual scientists against the arms race

Niels Bohr

Probably the first scientist to recognize the danger of a nuclear arms race and to express vigorously his opposition to it was Niels Bohr, one of the founders of modern physics. After escaping from Nazi-occupied Denmark, he went to the United States in 1943 and spent some time at the Los Alamos Laboratory as a senior consultant.

Earlier, and more than any other person living at that time, Bohr realized the tremendous social and political implications of the discovery of nuclear energy and of the development of nuclear weapons. He saw these events as a portentous landmark in the history of mankind, after which the world will never be the same again. He was convinced that if mankind were to survive and continue in the aftermath of that discovery, entirely new approaches would be necessary to world problems. In particular, he predicted with prophetic vision, the dire consequences of a race in nuclear arms between East and West. Among the radical measures which he felt were essential to prevent such an arms race, he advocated the sharing of the secret of the atom bomb with the Soviet Union. His specific proposal was that the Soviet leaders be told about the atom bomb *before* it was used, that the potentialities of the discovery of nuclear energy be explained to them, with an offer of sharing them, on condition that they would agree to a system of joint management and control of nuclear energy in all its aspects.

The basic principle of Bohr's philosophy was openness in science. He realized that secrets in science cannot be kept for any length of time, that Soviet scientists would in any case soon discover the secrets of the atom bomb, and that therefore there was very little to be lost by sharing the secrets.

Bohr's ideas were conveyed to President Roosevelt who appeared to be greatly impressed by them. He advised Bohr to put his case to Winston Churchill. Bohr came to London in May 1944 for an interview with Churchill, but this interview ended in failure, with Churchill completely rejecting Bohr's proposals.

Bohr followed up his ideas in 1950 with an "open letter' to the United Nations, which included the text of his 1944 memorandum to President Roosevelt[1]. Addressing himself "to the organization, founded for the purpose of furthering cooperation between nations on all problems of common concern" he speaks of "the terrifying prospect of a future competition between nations about a weapon of such formidable character", and he warned that "permanent grave dangers to world security would ensue unless measures to prevent abuse of the new formidable means of destruction could be universally agreed upon and carried out". Alas, Bohr's advise was not heeded, and the arms race started with a series of tests of different types of nuclear weapons.

Albert Schweitzer

The issue of nuclear tests was later taken up by the philosopher and physician, Albert Schweitzer, who called for an end to the arms race and, in particular, for the cessation of tests of nuclear weapons. In his "Declaration of Conscience", issued in 1957 [2], he explains the nature of the radiations emitted at the explosion of nuclear weapons and their harmful effect on health.

"To fail to consider its importance and its consequences would be a folly for which humanity would have to pay a terrible price. We are committing a folly in thoughtlessness. It must not happen that we do not pull ourselves together before it is too late. We must muster the insight, the seriousness, and the courage to leave folly and to face reality".

And he concludes in a highly emotional way:

"The end of further experiments with atom bombs would be like the early sunrays of hope which suffering humanity is longing for".

Linus Pauling

One of the most active in the campaign against nuclear tests, and most successful in raising the conscience of the scientific community, was Linus Pauling, Nobel Prize Laureate in Chemistry and Peace. In January 1958 he placed in the hands of Dag Hammärskjöld, the Secretary-General of the United Nations, a petition from 9235 scientists (later increased to over 11000) from 49 countries. The signatories included many Nobel Prize Laureates, as well as other eminent scientists of the world. The following is the text of the petition[3]:

"We, the scientists whose names are signed below, urge that an international agreement to stop the testing of nuclear bombs be made now.
Each nuclear bomb test spreads an added burden of radioactive elements over every part of the world. Each added amount of radiation causes damage to the health of human beings all over the world and causes damage to the pool of

103

human germ plasm such as to lead to an increase in the number of seriously defective children that will be born in future generations.

So long as these weapons are in the hands of only three powers an agreement for their control is feasible. If testing continues, and the possession of these weapons spreads to additional governments, the danger of out-break of a cataclysmic nuclear war through the reckless action of some irresponsible national leader will be greatly increased.

An international agreement to stop the testing of nuclear bombs now could serve as a first step toward a more general disarmament and the ultimate effective abolition of nuclear weapons, averting the possibility of nuclear war that would be a catastrophe to all humanity.

We have in common with our fellow men a deep concern for the welfare of all human beings. As scientists we have knowledge of the dangers involved and therefore a special responsibility to make those dangers known. We deem it imperative that immediate action be taken to effect an international agreement to stop the testing of all nuclear weapons."

Bertrand Russell

The individual who more than anyone else inspired the scientific community, as well as the general public, to take action against the arms race was the British philosopher and mathematician Lord Russell. He is rightly considered to be the founder of the Pugwash Movement, (see p.132). for it was his speech "Man's Peril", broadcast in 1954, that formed the basis for the Russell-Einstein Manifesto (see Appendix 1). He was also the founder of the Campaign for Nuclear Disarmament and of other action groups whose protests he led personally. One of his concerns about the ongoing nuclear arms race was the danger of a pre-emptive war against the Soviet Union which the military of the United States might urge. In the preface to a book by Fred Cook, *The Warfare State*, he had the following to say:[4]

> "*The Warfare State* is one of the most important and also one of the most terrifying documents that I have ever read. His thesis is that the 'military-industrial complex' has become so powerful in the United States that it dominates the Government and is, at the same time, so insane that it is quite ready to advocate what is called a 'pre-emptive' war against the Soviet State. The evidence which he adduces is massive and unanswerable except by plain abuse.
> There was a time when American authorities assured us that they would not initiate a nuclear war. This time is past. It may be that the President and the State Department still cling desperately to the hope that they can prevent a pre-emptive war, but fresh evidence to the contrary continues to pile up. ...It is obvious that the determined men who control the armed forces of the United States can, at any moment, create an incident which will appear to be proof of Russian aggression and will be met by full-scale nuclear retaliation... ...There is only one way of reversing the trend towards pre-emptive war. It is to make the truth known to the American public. This is a difficult task."

The necessity to tell the public the true facts about the danger and consequences of a nuclear war is as valid today as it was in 1962. We shall return to this later.

Groups of scientists against the arms race

The Movements of scientists against the arms race are described in chapter 8; here we shall quote a few specific proposals made by several groups of scientists.

The Franck Committee

Even before the bombs were dropped on Hiroshima and Nagasaki, Bohr's initiative was taken up by a committee of scientists under the chairmanship of James Franck (see p.116). In their report to the American Secretary of State for War, they wrote[5]:

> "...in the past, scientists could disclaim direct responsibility for the use to which mankind had put their disinterested discoveries. We feel compelled to take a more active stand now because the success which we have achieved in the development of nuclear power is fraught with infinitely greater dangers than were all the inventions of the past".

and they conclude:

> "...Unless an effective international control of nuclear explosives is instituted, a race for nuclear armaments is certain to ensue following the first revelation of our possession of nuclear weapons to the world."

Despite this reasoned appeal, the bombs were used to destroy the Japanese cities.

The Pugwash Conferences

The First Pugwash Conference, held in July 1957, concluded with a statement stressing the dangers to mankind of a nuclear arms race and emphasizing the social responsibility which scientists bear on this issue. The Soviet scientists who took part in this Conference, on returning to Moscow, presented a report to the USSR Academy of Sciences and put forward a motion to support the conclusions of the Pugwash Conference: "We, Soviet scientists, express our full readiness to support the efforts of the scientists from other countries in discussing any suggestions about the prevention of a nuclear war and aiming to ensure peace and quiet for the entire mankind." The motion was adopted and signed by 198 members of the Academy of Sciences and of other Soviet academies.

The Third Pugwash Conference was held in Kitzbühel and Vienna in 1958. It occupies a significant place in the fight of the scientists against the arms race by the adoption of the Vienna Declaration, which is considered as the tenet of the Pugwash Movement, and was subsequently endorsed by several thousand scientists from all over the world[6]. The Declaration emphasizes that in the age of weapons of mass destruction, the risk of local conflicts growing into major wars is too great to be acceptable; therefore, mankind must set itself the task of eliminating all wars, including local wars. While calling for the cessation of tests of all nuclear weapons, whether they are classified as "dirty' or "clean", the Declaration points out that the main problem is to reduce the danger of a nuclear war by halting the arms race. The armaments race is the result of distrust btween states; it also contributes to this mistrust. Any step that mitigates the arms race, and leads to even small reductions in armaments and armed forces, on an equitable basis and subject to necessary control, is therefore desirable. The Declaration ends by stressing the special responsibility of scientists.

> "In the eyes of the people of many countries, science has become associated with the development of weapons. Scientists are either admired for their contribution to national security, or damned for having brought mankind into jeopardy by their invention of weapons of mass destruction. The increasing material support which science now enjoys in many countries is mainly due to its importance, direct or indirect, to the military strength of the nation and to its degree of success in the arms race. This diverts science from its true purpose, which is to increase human knowledge, and to promote man's mastery over the forces of nature for the benefit of all.
> We deplore the conditions which lead to this situation, and appeal to all peoples and their governments to establish conditions of lasting and stable peace."

World Federation of Scientific Workers

Another organization of scientists concerned with these issues is the World Federation of Scientific Workers (see p.126). A Symposium held in October 1980 in Varna came to the unanimous conclusion that an important precondition for socio-economic development and for the reconstruction of economic relations in the interests of all peoples was the easing of international tensions. The participants of the Symposium supported the various activities launched during the recent months for the preservation of peace, and endorsed the appeal of the "World Parliament of the Peoples for Peace" to live in peace and understanding[7]. In November 1980, the Bureau of the WFSW issued a declaration drawing attention to the fact that mankind has entered a period of tension of historic importance:[8]

106

"...Today the greatest danger lies in the efforts now being made to prepare new strategies based on the thesis of a controllable and even winnable nuclear war: to this end public opinion has to be persuaded that a nuclear war would not necessarily lead to a global catastrophe...Scientific workers should insist that real security cannot be achieved through the accumulation of weapons and the acceleration of military preparations. Attempts to achieve military superiority are senseless and dangerous: they can only lead the arms race to a level where controls are no longer possible... The WFSW Bureau calls on scientific workers and their organizations to lead a campaign of explanation of the dangers of the arms race and its consequences and on the need to end the race before it engulfs us.

There is only one way forward, through negotiations based on the principles of equality and mutual security. For this reason we call for constant pressure on governments:

  – that all the steps already made towards the limitation of arms, including SALT II, should be ratified and developed;
  – that negotiations on the limitation and the banning of all weapons systems, including those on medium-range nuclear weapons and modernization systems in Europe should be renewed and taken to successful conclusions;
  – that confidence between States, which has contributed to progress in the field of international détente, be re-established and reinforced;
  – that every country should have the right to choose its political status and its forms of development."

The Groningen Conference, "Nuclear War in Europe"

The danger of a nuclear war in Europe has acquired a new dimension after the NATO decision to introduce long-range theatre weapons (Pershing II and cruise missiles) in Europe, and the announcement by President Reagan to produce and stockpile neutron bombs to be available for deployment in Europe within a few hours. This danger was given expression at an international conference on "Nuclear War in Europe" held in April 1981, in the Netherlands. A number of speakers from Europe and America, many of them veterans in the various scientists' movements, discussed the ways a nuclear war might start in Europe, how it might be fought, what would be its results, and what can be done to prevent it[9]:

The Third World War is likely to be fought in Europe just as the First and Second World Wars were. There is a growing feeling that we are moving inexorably towards nuclear war in Europe. The NATO nations are urged to acquire more accurate nuclear weapons, but there is no evidence that these new weapons will make Europe more secure. Even if the war in Europe were limited to the use of tactical nuclear weapons the result would be hundreds of Hiroshima's on the very heart of Europe. There is nothing humane about the neutron bomb; in the conflict in Europe, thousands of these weapons may be used, covering large areas with lethal levels of radiation.

An essential first step toward lessening the risk of nuclear war is a freeze on testing, production and deployment of nuclear weapons, of missiles, and of new aircraft designed to deliver nuclear weapons. Some measures could be taken by unilateral action, e.g. the denuclearization of individual countries in Europe. But a more radical solution would be a nuclear-free zone in Europe stretching from Poland to Portugal.

Finally, the need was emphasized to set up an authoritative international committee of scientists, as proposed by President Brezhnev (see p.110), to warn nations of the deadly consequences to mankind of a nuclear war.

The Bucharest Symposium "Scientists and Peace"

The fundamental issues of peace and war at the present time, and the attitudes of scientists towards them, were the subject of a Symposium held in Bucharest on 4-5 September 1981, under the patronage of the President of Romania Nicolae Ceausescu. It was attended by 68 scientists from 32 countries. The Symposium received an inspiring message from President Ceausescu, in which he emphasized the high duty of scientists and the role they can play in ensuring that the acquisitions of man's genius should help mankind and not lead to its destruction.

At the end of the debates, the participants adopted an appeal to scholars, intellectuals, and all people, to join their efforts and co-operate more closely to defend peace.

> "Our age has seen not only the tremendous advancement of science and technology, evinced by great discoveries that have influenced all the domains of human life, but also anachronistic actions running counter to mankind's interests, using science and technology for destructive purposes that are harmful to the people's peace and liberty. This is a time when humanity is faced by particularly complex problems; there is a renewed, impetuous arms race, military budgets have arisen to unprecedented levels, new means of mass destruction are produced and improved, all of which seriously aggravate the international situation, being an ever heavier burden to the peoples, increasing the danger of conflagrations that can destroy life on the whole planet, the very civilization created over the millennia."

> "We are deeply convinced that, by rallying our forces, by intensifying our co-operation, science will become a true weapon of life so that all peoples may make an enhanced contribution to the world patrimony of knowledge, so that peace, security and collaboration may triumph on our planet."

The Appeal also adopted the idea contained in President Ceausescu's message about setting up an International Committee "Scientists and Peace", which – among other objectives – would ensure that opinions of scientists will be heard in all forums which debate questions of disarmament, peace, security and international cooperation (see also p.111).

What the advocates of the arms race say

In the struggle against the arms race it is important to know the arguments used by those who want the arms race to continue and promote the concept of a limited nuclear war. The basic differences between the "hawks" and the "doves" in relation to arms control measures were described earlier (see p.24). Here we shall emphasize some specific arguments, and the views of scientists in favour of the arms race.

The argument for the need of weapons to fight in a limited nuclear war runs on a medical analogy: Why does one not describe as killers the surgeons who, to save the life of an ill person, are forced to carry out surgical operations to amputate an arm, a leg, or to remove a diseased kidney, although this inflicts suffering on the patient? At present the whole of mankind is ill, and to save it one has to take recourse to operations, but instead of a scalpel one has to use weapons. This problem calls on the scientists to increase the accuracy of missiles so that the removal of the diseased part of mankind will not affect the sound part. Another serious requirement of the scientists is to produce a weapon which would not contaminate the locality in which such surgical operations are carried out, so that the healthy part of mankind could develop unharmed.

Scientists who put forward this type of argument insist on the necessity to develop and manufacture new weapons. They subscribe to the concept of a limited nuclear war and believe that nuclear warfare can stay limited.

At a conference "Nuclear War and its International Implications", held in Erice, Italy, in August 1981, one such scientist called on the West to step up its nuclear force. He urged the production of missiles fired with small nuclear warheads, which would be sophisticated and manageable, and able to destroy in the air heavier and less manouverable long-range missiles. "If a friendly country is involved, even with conventional weapons, then we must use nuclear bombs with the consent of the invaded ally. The neutron bomb, for example, is so precise it would cause only limited damage"[10].

An international committee of scientists

The fact that so much misleading information about nuclear weapons is provided by scientists who influence the military, shows the urgent necessity for the scientific community to take steps to provide data about the consequences of a nuclear war. Such data should come from a body of scientists commanding respect and confidence in all parts of the world.

This is the basis for the idea put forward by President Brezhnev in his Report to the 26th Congress of the Communist Party in February 1981[11]. Among the several new ideas to remove the threat of war he proposed that:

"a competent international committee should be set up which would demonstrate the vital necessity of preventing a nuclear catastrophe. The committee could be composed of the most eminent scientists of different countries. The whole world should be informed of the conclusions they draw."

In this speech Leonid Brezhnev gave a clear account of the posture of the Soviet Union in relation to the arms race and the increased danger of nuclear war:

"Today the state of world affairs requires new, additional efforts to remove the threat of war and buttress international security. Permit me to put before the Congress a number of ideas directed to this end.

In recent years, as you know, flash points of military conduct, often threatening to grow into a major conflagration, flared up now in one and now in another region of the world. Experience has shown that it is not easy to extinguish them. It would be far better to take preventive measures, to forestall their emergence."

A specific suggestion in the Report relates to a moratorium on the deployment of medium-range nuclear weapons in Europe:

"Now about the nuclear-missile weapons in Europe. An ever more dangerous stockpiling of them is in train. A kind of vicious circle has arisen, with the actions of one side precipitating countermeasures by the other. How to break this chain?

We suggest coming to terms that a moratorium should now be set on the deployment in Europe of new medium-range nuclear missile weapons of the NATO countries and the Soviet Union, that it, to freeze the existing quantitative and qualitative level of these weapons, naturally including the United States forward-based nuclear weapons in this region. The moratorium could enter into force at once the moment negotiations begin on this score, and could operate until a permanent treaty is concluded on limiting or, still better, reducing such nuclear weapons in Europe. In making this proposal, we expect the two sides to stop all preparations for the deployment of respective additional weapons, including United States Pershing II missiles and land-based strategic cruise missiles."

An appeal to world scientists in support of President Brezhnev's proposal was made by the Presidents of Academies of Science in the Socialists countries, when they met in Bulgaria in October 1981. The text of the Appeal is attached to this chapter (p.111).

These appeals must be taken up by the whole of the scientific community and efforts should be intensified to implement them; these steps are vital if a global catastrophe is to be avoided.

References

1. N. Bohr, For an Open World, *Bulletin of the Atomic Scientists* vol. VI, July 1950, p.213.
2. A. Schweitzer in *No more war*, by Linus Pauling, Gollancz, London, 1958, p.225.
3. *The Scientists' Petition to the United Nations*, in *No more war* by Linus Pauling, Gollancz, London, 1958, p.160.
4. F.J. Cook, *The Warfare State*, Macmillan, New York, 1962, p.VIII.
5. A Report to the Secretary of War ... June 1945, *Bulletin of the Atomic Scientists*, vol. I, May 1946, p.2.
6. J. Rotblat, *Scientist in the Quest for Peace: A History of the Pugwash Conferences*, MIT Press, Cambridge, Mass, 1972.
7. *Scientific World*, vol. XXV, No. 1, 1981, p.19.
8. *Scientific World*, vol. XXIV, No. 4, 1980, p.24.
9. *Pravda*, April 26, 1981.
10. *The Daily Telegraph*, London, 18 August 1981.
11. *Komunist*, No. 4, March 1981.

TO THE SCIENTISTS OF THE WORLD

We, the representatives of the Bulgarian Academy of Sciences, the Hungarian Academy of Sciences, the National Centre of Scientific Research and the Committee for Social Sciences of the Socialist Republic of Vietnam, the Academy of Sciences of the German Democratic Republic, the Academy of Sciences of the Republic of Cuba, the Academy of Sciences of the People's Republic of Mongolia, the Polish Academy of Sciences, the Academy of the Socialist Republic of Romania, the Academy of Sciences of the Union of Soviet Socialist Republics, and the Czechoslovak Academy of Sciences, having met at a regular session in Sofia, on behalf of all the scientists of our countries express deep anxiety over the dangerous development of international affairs.

Man is meant not to destroy, but to create! Unfortunately, the aggressive circles, the enemies of the peaceful coexistence of the states, attempt to undermine the policy of international détente, intensify the arms race, aggravate the existing and create new hotbeds for armed conflicts in the various regions of the world. Particularly dangerous are the plans for the deployment of medium-range nuclear missiles in Western Europe and in certain regions of Asia, and the decision for the production of neutron weapons.

Scientists cannot fail to see the scale of the threat for mankind, created by the deterioration of the international situation. The nature of contemporary weapons is such that any war can grow into a global nuclear conflict, which will jeopardize the very existence of civilization and human environment.

We are aware that every state is interested in ensuring its safety. In the nuclear age, however, this cannot be achieved by counting on military superiority or on victory in a nuclear war. Real safety is the safety of the entire world community, equal safety for all states, established on the basis of international agreements and accords for the limitation and reduction of armaments, for the banning and

111

elimination of weapons of mass destruction. It is necessary to think of the safety of all humanity because otherwise nobody will feel safe.

We are convinced that there is no fatally inevitable war in our times. But peace is not a blessing that is automatically granted. Peace is seriously threatened nowadays. Peace must be actively safeguarded and defended.

In the defence of peace the voice of scientists can and must resound with particular force: they clearly see the vast possibilities for the present and the coming generations to solve many vital problems humanity is faced with. They are also aware of the disastrous consequences of a nuclear war, if it is allowed to break out.

Scientists must actively oppose the policy of confrontation, the arms race, and return to the cold war times. Scientists cannot fail to be aware that without an equitable dialogue and business-like negotiations it is impossible to solve the international problems of the contemporary world, however acute and complex they may be.

That is why we call on the scientists of the whole world to come forward in defence of universal human values, peace for all and social progress, against the arms race, for holding a constructive dialogue between states to settle all international issues by negotiations only, and for strengthening and continuing the policy of détente and peace. We warmly support the idea of setting up an international committee of scientists which would have its authoritative say in connection with the threat of a nuclear war and its disastrous consequences and would point to the vital necessity of its prevention.

We welcome and support the initiatives of international scientific forums and of individual groups of scientists for rallying the efforts of scientists in the defence of peace.

Only with the joint efforts of all peace-loving forces can the peace of our planet be preserved and strengthened. It is a question now of the fate of all the peoples and the survival of mankind!

A. Balevski (Bulgaria); K. Polinski (Hungary); Tran Dai Nghia (Vietnam); W. Scheller (GDR); Han Boyng Hi (Democratic People's Republic of Korea); J. Altschuler (Cuba); B. Shirendev (Mongolia); A. Gieysztor (Poland); I. Anton (Romania); A.P. Aleksandrov (USSR); and B. Kvasil (Czechoslovakia).

PART III
Movements of scientists against the arms race

Chapter 8. Movements of scientists against the arms race

Joseph Rotblat

Introduction

As individuals, scientists often participated in anti-war movements and sometimes took leading roles in these movements. Thus, Albert Einstein was a co-founder, in 1914, of the "Bund Neues Vaterland" in Germany[1], an organization which – apart from the direct aim to bring the First World War to an end – had also a long-term objective: the establishment of an international system which would make future wars impossible. However, the setting up of anti-war movements of scientists themselves did not occur until much later. Actually, the first of these movements started off as trade unions of scientists, and their aim was to improve and defend the professional status and financial interests of scientists. An example is the British Association of Scientific Workers (AScW), which started in 1919 under the name "National Union of Scientific Workers"[2]. In the course of time political goals were added to the aims of these organizations, including anti-war objectives. But it was not until the end of the Second World War, and the horrors of Hiroshima and Nagasaki, that movements of scientists specifically concerned with disarmament, and seeking ways to prevent a nuclear arms race, began to emerge, first at national levels and subsequently as international movements.

A. NATIONAL MOVEMENTS

In different countries national movements of scientists started at different times, under different circumstances and with different incentives. Some embraced large numbers of the scientific community, others consisted of a few devoted individuals. In some countries the movements played a significant role in shaping national policies, exerting an influence not necessarily correlated with the numerical strength of the organization. Some of these organizations continue their existence up to the present, while others faded away. Some of the national movements were instrumental in setting up international movements, while in other countries the reverse occurred: national groups started as branches of an international movement.

The importance of this sociological phenomenon calls for a detailed analysis of the development and significance of all these organizations, but constraint of space makes it necessary to select only a few of them for this review.

The United States

Eight weeks before the atom bomb was dropped on Hiroshima, scientists working on the Manhattan Project formally voiced their concern about the intended use of the atom bomb and the grave implications of such use. This concern was expressed in a report of a Committee set up by the Chicago branch of the Project and is known as the Franck Report, from the name of the chairman of the Committee. The report was largely the work of Eugene Rabinowitch, one of the 7 members of the Committee, of which the most active and trenchant was Leo Szilard. The immediate recommendation of the Franck Report was that the destructive power of the bomb should be conveyed to the Japanese in a demonstration explosion, and not in its use against the civilian population, which – it was stressed – could bring grave and incalculable consequences. The Report went on to consider the long-term implications of the discovery of nuclear energy. It pointed out that other nations were certain to acquire nuclear weapons within a few years, and that the inevitably ensuing arms race would dominate and poison the world climate ever after. The release of nuclear energy was the strongest single argument for the establishment of a World Authority, but until such a supra-national body was set up, international control of nuclear weapons would be an essential preliminary step. In order to make such control feasible it might even be advisable to renounce temporarily the large-scale production of fissile materials for industrial purposes[3].

Although the immediate recommendation was not accepted by the United States Government, the other issues raised in the Franck report became the basis for scientists' programmes of action in the following years, and were echoed in official proposals, such as the Baruch Plan (see p.120).

The Franck Report was submitted to the American Government, but since nuclear energy was still an official secret, the Report instantly became a classified document and as such could not be used to canvass support among scientists in the other laboratories of the Manhattan Project. But when the Second World War came to an end – with the detonation of atom bombs on Hiroshima and Nagasaki – and the discovery of nuclear energy became public knowledge, the scientists felt free to express their views, and their grave concern became obvious forthwith. Associations of scientists were promptly set up in several laboratories of the Manhattan Project, i.e. in Oak Ridge, Los Alamos, Chicago and New York. By the end of October 1945 these associations, together with a few other groups, became amalgamated in a new body, the Federation of Atomic Scientists.

The immediate task of the Federation was to fight a proposed legislative measure, the May-Johnson Bill, which would have perpetuated the role of the military in the future management of nuclear energy. The Federation mounted a very vigorous campaign in the Press and the lobbies of Congress: the first concerted effort by scientists to influence decision makers. From the perspective of time it is doubtful whether it was justified to spend so much energy on a domestic issue, instead of tackling the perilous international implications so eloquently expressed in the Franck Report. But the memories of the restrictive practices, and often unnecessary secrecy rules imposed by the military, were still fresh in the minds of the scientists who feared that a continuation of the military regime would stifle all future developments. Anyhow, the campaign succeeded in replacing the Bill by the McMahon Act, in which the control of all nuclear energy matters, peaceful and military, was vested in a civilian authority. Thus the first political campaign conducted by scientists was successful.

The Federation of American Scientists (FAS)

Although problems specific to nuclear energy, such as its international control, greatly occupied the minds of the members of the Federation of Atomic Scientists, there was a growing feeling in the scientific community that not only 'atomic' but all scientists should be concerned with these issues. Many groups of scientists, often centered round one laboratory, sprang up, all interested in the same problem: the role of scientists in shaping the new world, born by their efforts. Eventually these groups, together with the Federation of Atomic Scientists, amalgamated in the Federation of American Scientists, officially set up in January 1946.

Among the aims of the FAS were: to urge the United States to initiate and perpetuate an effective and workable system of world control of nuclear energy based on full co-operation among all nations; to strengthen international co-operation among scientists; to study the implications of scientific developments which may involve hazards to enduring peace and the safety of mankind[4]. Arising from these aims, one of the most important early actions of the FAS was concerned with the international control of nuclear energy. Its views were incorporated in the Acheson-Lilienthal Report which was the basis of the Baruch Plan.

At the time of its foundation in 1946 the FAS had over 3000 members. But the initial flash of enthusiasm soon faded, and for a time the existence of the Federation became somewhat precarious, with the membership falling to about one thousand and financial difficulties restricting the scope of its activities. However, even though working at a low key, the FAS continued to influence scientific opinion in the United States. In recent years, under the vigorous directorship of Jeremy Stone, the FAS not only consolidated itself but begun to grow again. By 1981, the membership was about 5000, a large proportion of them physicists, but with a majority from other natural and social sciences, as well as engineering. A measure of the prestigious nature of the FAS is the fact that about a half of all living American Nobel Prize Laureates are its members.

Traditionally, the FAS is concerned with lobbying the Senate with proposals to contain the arms race. More recently it has become concerned also with encouraging increased energy efficiency. The FAS describes itself as "a unique, non-profit civic organization, licensed to lobby in the public interest...(which) has functioned as a conscience of the scientific community for more than a quarter century"[5]. Although in this role of the conscience of scientists the FAS takes up many issues, including civil liberties and freedom of scientists, its monthly publication "F.A.S. Public Interest Report" (formerly the FAS Newsletter) is mainly concerned with problems of the nuclear arms race.

The Bulletin of the Atomic Scientists

The Bulletin is one of the most important media for debate on problems of the arms race and the role of scientists in it. Although not a movement of scientists by itself, this periodical has stimulated the thinking of scientists and energized the movements of scientists not only in the United States but all over the world.

It started in December 1945 as *The Bulletin of Atomic Scientists of Chicago* and was the creation of two scientists: Hyman H. Goldsmith and Eugene Rabinowitch. After the former died in 1949, Rabinowitch became editor-in-chief and continued in this post, and as the main driving force of the Bulletin, until his death in 1973.

The chief aim of the Bulletin is to educate the scientific community and the public at large on all matters relating to the impact of science on the community, particularly to make them aware of the perils of a nuclear war. In the early years – and to a large extent even now – the Bulletin was the main source of information on these issues for newspaper columnists and other writers. But apart from this educational role the Bulletin was the voice of scientific opinion, and through its editorials and articles was expressing the conscience of scientists in the atomic age in all aspects of the relationship between science and society. After 36 years of continuous publication – with Bernard Feld now as editor-in-chief – the Bulletin is one of the most esteemed of American journals and looked at as a watch-dog over the policies of the United States and other countries in matters affecting the security of mankind. The 'doomsday-clock' depicted on the cover of the Bulletin, showing how many minutes are left to midnight (a nuclear holocaust), has become a barometer of the political climate, and every change of the minute-hand (since 1981 it stands at four minutes to midnight) is commented upon in journals and other media all over the world.

Emergency Committee of Atomic Scientists

The financing of the activities of the FAS and the Bulletin was initially provided chiefly by the Emergency Committee of Atomic Scientists, a fund-raising and policy-making agency for several organizations of American scientists. Its chairman was Albert Einstein and the members included Hans Bethe, Linus Pauling, Leo Szilard, Harold Urey and Victor Weisskopf. The magic of Einstein's name assured a successful fund-raising campaign. At its first meeting in 1945 the Emergency Committee summarized its policy as follows[6]:

"These facts are accepted by all scientists:
1. Atomic bombs can now be made cheaply and in large numbers. They will become more destructive.
2. There is no military defense against the atomic bomb and none is to be expected.
3. Other nations can rediscover our secret process by themselves.
4. Preparedness against atomic war is futile, and if attempted will ruin the structure of our social order.
5. If war breaks out, atomic bombs will be used and they will surely destroy our civilization.
6. There is no solution to this problem except international control of atomic energy and, ultimately, the elimination of war.
The programme of the committee is to see that these truths became known to the public. The democratic determination of this nation's policy on atomic energy must ultimately rest on the understanding of is citizens."

After 36 years these statements are still valid; in a somewhat modified form they are often repeated in statements from scientists' movements (e.g. Pugwash).

Initially, the Emergency Committee endorsed Einstein's view that the only solution to the problems created by the development of nuclear weapons was a world government, but later a divergence of opinion emerged on this issue. Gradually, the Emergency Committee lost its impetus and was dissolved in 1951.

The Baruch Plan

As already intimated the most important outcome of the heated debates among scientists in the immediate post-war era was a document which became known as the Baruch Plan.

The early concern of scientists in the United States about the international implications of the discovery of nuclear energy and the peril of a nuclear arms race – prophetically expounded by Niels Bohr in 1944[7] – led to many discussions among scientists about the ways and means to control the awesome consequences of a nuclear arms race. The debates between groups of scientists and governmental bodies culminated in the 'Acheson-Lilienthal Report'[8], so called after the names of the two leaders of the discussants. The proposals aimed at ensuring that nuclear energy would be used for peaceful purposes only. For this reason the Report recommended the creation of an International Atomic Development Authority to which should be entrusted all phases of the development and use of nuclear energy, starting with the raw materials, and including managerial control or ownership of all activities potentially dangerous to world security, as well as power to control, inspect and licence all nuclear activities. Nuclear weapons would be renounced and, after an adequate control system had been agreed upon, the manufacture of nuclear weapons would cease and existing bombs would be disposed of.

It was the intention that the Acheson-Lilienthal Report be presented to the Atomic Energy Commission of the United Nations as an official United States document. But, in the event, the official document was somewhat different. Bernard Baruch, who was appointed by President Truman as his representative at the United Nations, made a number of modifications. The Baruch Plan[9] – introduced in June 1946 – contained additional measures, particularly the abolition of the veto in the Security Council on punishment for violations of the agreement. At a time when the United States had a monopoly on all nuclear matters, the acceptance of this clause was obviously doubtful. Although Baruch introduced his Plan with the stirring words "We are here to make a choice between the quick and the dead", this rhetoric was not enough to assuage the apprehension of the Soviet Union that the whole plan was a means of preventing the development of a nuclear industry in other countries, leaving the monopoly of nuclear weapons to the United States.

A comprehensive plan, based on the Baruch proposals, was approved

120

by the United Nations in November 1948, but for the reasons stated it was never implemented. It is conceivable that the original proposals from the scientists, without the severe restrictions imposed by Baruch, might have been more acceptable, but the political climate was not ripe for such a radical scheme. If the proposals had been made in 1949, *after* the Soviet Union tested its first nuclear weapon, or – better still – if the secrets of the atom bomb had been shared with the USSR *before* the bomb was used, as proposed by Niels Bohr, the chances of avoiding a nuclear arms race might have been much better.

The United Kingdom

Like their American colleagues, many of the British scientists who worked on the Manhattan Project were deeply worried about the implications for the future of the use that had been made of the atom bomb. After returning to the United Kingdom they began to talk about these matters to other scientists, and it soon became clear that there was a need for an organized body of scientists to be concerned with the new situation following the discovery of nuclear energy.

The Association of Scientific Workers, (see p.115) which by that time had a membership of some 15 000, and had set up a committee on atomic energy, offered itself as such a body. However, most of the scientists involved were not happy about this offer. The AScW was a trade union, and it was felt that nuclear energy matters would figure only marginally among its activities; the left wing image of the AScW was also a detracting factor. For these reasons it was thought that an independent organization would be preferable, and this was set up in March 1946 as the Atomic Scientists Association (ASA).

The aims of the Association were:

1. To bring before the public of this country the true facts about Atomic Energy and is implications.

2. To investigate and make proposals regarding the international control of Atomic Energy whenever the political situation makes this appropriate.

3. To help to shape the policy of this country in all matters relating to Atomic Energy.

Full membership was restricted to scientists with specialized knowledge of nuclear energy so that the Association could speak on this subject as a body of experts; but there was also a class of Associate Members. Nearly 200 scientists joined as full members, and at the height of its activities the total membership was about a thousand.

In the initial period, the second of the aims of the ASA, i.e. the international control of atomic energy, was considered to be the most urgent task; the Provisional Committee charged with the formation of the ASA prepared a memorandum on this subject [10], and submitted it to the UN Atomic Energy Commission. Not surprisingly – since members of the British team on the Manhattan Project discussed these issues with their American colleagues before returning home – the solutions with which the Committee came up were very similar to those in the Acheson-Lilienthal Report. After the failure of the Baruch Plan, with the decision in 1948 to adjourn the UNAEC, the Committee of the ASA issued another statement that, while continuing its belief in some form of international control as the most desirable ultimate solution of the problem of atomic weapons, it did not consider that any good purpose would be served by pressing for it now[11]. This was the last official statement of the ASA on this issue; under the pressure from the 'establishment' (see below) it was decided that the Committee should not continue to speak for its members on this topic.

This left the ASA with the first and third of its aims. The educational aspect was pursued with much vigour. The most important activity of the ASA was the 'Atom Train', a travelling exhibition containing a number of models, many of them in working order, aiming at emphasizing the two faces of nuclear energy, the good (peaceful uses) and the evil (military uses). The exhibition was mounted in railway carriages and during 1947/48 it travelled the length and breadth of the United Kingdom, visiting many cities. The attendance was extremely good and, together with the 'Atomic Energy Weeks' held in conjunction with the exhibition, the audience ran into hundreds of thousands. The guide book to the exhibition, veritably a popular text-book on nuclear energy prepared by the ASA Council, sold over 50 000 copies, probably the largest sale in the United Kingdom of a book on this subject.

After the end of the tour, the exhibition was loaned to Unesco and it was on show in Beirut during the third session of the General Conference of Unesco in December 1948. It then visited several other countries in the Middle East, and later in Scandinavia.

The third aim, of helping to shape British policy on atomic energy matters, was largely fulfilled through articles and discussions in the ASA publication 'Atomic Scientists News', later renamed 'Atomic Scientists Journal'. Although far behind the standard and readership of the Bulletin of the Atomic Scientists, it fulfilled a similar purpose of providing information and stimulating public debate.

Keeping in mind the aim of helping to shape the policy of the United Kingdom, it was felt that the ASA should be seen as a highly respectable organization. This image was acquired by having a long list of Vice-Presidents, which included the most eminent scientists in the country as well as government scientific advisers and leaders of the nuclear energy authorities. This impressive slate of Vice-Presidents turned out to be a millstone round the neck of the ASA; it stifled discussion and eventually led to its demise. Some of the Vice-Presidents were fierce hawks and advocated the speedy acquisition of nuclear weapons by the United Kingdom; they did not like any criticism of such policy, and prevented the ASA from making pronouncements on this subject. And even scientific fact-finding was dampened if it was not in line with government policy. In 1957, the Radiation-Hazards Committee of the ASA issued a public statement, approved by Council, about the hazard of strontium-90 from tests of nuclear weapons[12]. At that time the British Government was in favour of continuing tests and tried to minimize their hazards. The ASA statement brought the wrath of the Establishment on the Council, with a request from the Vice-Presidents that in future no public statement would be issued without their approval. Many members of the Association saw this as a suffocation of the activities of the ASA; it practically brought all work to a halt. With the foundation of the Pugwash Movement, in which members of the ASA took a decisive part, the need for the Association has greatly diminished and the ASA was formally dissolved in 1959. Many ASA members later joined the British National Pugwash Group.

The lesson of this experience, of the price to be paid for 'respectability', was not lost when the Pugwash Movement came across similar situations.

Other countries

In a number of other countries the social concern of scientists was a motivation for their joining movements of scientists, but in most cases the national movements sprang up, or became consolidated, as branches of international movements. Thus, in the Soviet Union and other Socialist countries in Europe, as well as in China, large numbers of scientists belonged to the national affiliated groups of the World Federation of Scientific Workers (WFSW). In France there was a strong group 'Association de Travailleurs Scientifiques', which together with the British AScW was the co-founder of the WFSW. The activities of the latter will be discussed later.

Federation of German Scientists.

In the post-war Federal Republic of Germany there was initially very little activity among scientists on matters relating to the nuclear arms race. But the concern of scientists was aroused when the Federal Government

123

began to make noises in favour of nuclear weapons, for example, the statement by Chancellor Adenauer that nuclear weapons are only a further development of artillery. This has provoked a group of 18 eminent atomic scientists to issue in 1957 a statement that they would not participate in any project concerned with nuclear weapons. The group included: Max Born, Otto Hahn, Werner Heisenberg, and Karl von Weizsäcker, and their statement has become known as "The Declaration of the Göttingen Eighteen"[13].

The Göttingen Declaration evoked a strong echo in the scientific community of the Federal Republic of Germany and many other scientists wanted to be associated with it. In 1959, a number of them decided to set up a new organization called the Vereinigung Deutscher Wissenschaftler (VDW) with the following aims:

> to study the consequences of scientific discoveries and technical developments for the conditions of human life;
>
> to make the public aware of such developments; and
>
> to raise the consciousness of those in research and development, as well as of the general public, of the consequences of scientific and technological innovations.

The VDW has over 300 members; all of them are scientists but the majority are from the social sciences. The VDW is a very active organization, it holds regular meetings, organizes symposia and produces numerous publications. It is also the Federal Republic of Germany's National Group of the Pugwash Movement.

B. INTERNATIONAL MOVEMENTS

The scientific community was always international in character and derived its strength from the close contacts maintained by scientists in many countries. During this century these contacts became institutionalized by the setting up of a number of international unions for different disciplines, under the overall umbrella of the International Council of Scientific Unions. ICSU and its constituent bodies are primarily concerned with research, and aim at ensuring the most efficient organization of scientific resources. However, its objectives are also "to encourage international scientific activity for the benefit of mankind, and so promote the causes of peace and international security throughout the world". In accordance with this the General Committee of ICSU, at its meeting in Dubrovnik in 1981, passed a resolution urging "scientists to do their best to demonstrate to the governments and people of all countries the vital necessity of preventing nuclear warfare".[14] In the early years the meetings of ICSU and of individual unions provided opportunities for informal discussions among scientists and enabled contacts to be made which proved valuable for the international movements concerned with the arms race and disarmament.

These movements began after the end of the Second World War and were triggered by the use of nuclear weapons. The progress of the several national movements of scientists were keenly watched by scientists in other countries. This resulted in correspondence in which the possibility of international co-operation was frequently discussed. As already mentioned, the international conferences convened to discuss purely scientific matters provided an opportunity to raise these matters, particularly between scientists from the East and West at a time when other contacts between the two ideological blocs hardly existed.

As a result of these contacts the idea has grown that international movements of scientists would be a more effective means of achieving the aims of the national movements in relation to the danger of war, particularly nuclear war. The first such movement sprang up between scientists holding somewhat similar political views, as this made it much easier for them to find a common platform, to adopt resolutions, and to launch appeals to the public. It took somewhat longer for the open recognition that the aim of avoiding war and halting the arms race is common to scientists irrespective of their political convictions, and that movements of scientists representing a wide spectrum of political opinion are more likely to be successful.

At the beginning the East-West divide was the main issue, but gradually scientists from the less developed countries, conscious of the threat to their security mainly arising from the alignments with the great powers, began to join the debates on these issues and to take an active part in them. The movements thus became truly international, bringing together scientists from East, West, and the Third World.

In this review only two international movements of scientists will be discussed, the World Federation of Scientific Workers (WFSW) and the Pugwash Conferences on Science and World Affairs. A number of other organizations are concerned with problems of the arms race and disarmament, but they are either not movements of scientists, or they are not truly international in the sense of including scientists from all parts of the world.

It should also be mentioned that scientists are frequently called upon by governments to serve on committees of experts appointed by the United Nations or its specialized agencies; since the scientists then act as representatives of governments, this type of international collaboration does not come into the category of movements as reviewed here.

A special role is played by Unesco, which has concerned itself, at the request of the United Nations and its own General Conference, with the issues of the arms race and disarmaments in a variety of ways (see Chapter

16). Apart from calling on scientists as government representatives, Unesco has from the early years maintained close contact with the WFSW, and sporadically also with Pugwash.

The World Federation of Scientific Workers

The World Federation of Scientific Workers was set up in 1946 following preliminary discussions between the British AScW and the French Association de Travailleurs Scientifiques. The British AScW was the prime mover because of the special conditions in the United Kingdom which produced a particularly lively interest in the promotion of an international organization of scientists. As mentioned earlier, the British AScW had a large membership and was very active during and immediately after the Second World War. Many scientists from Western Europe sought refuge in Britain and became associated with the AScW. This led to the setting up by the AScW of a Foreign Scientists Committee, which often discussed the advantages of forming similar organizations in other countries. When many of these scientists returned to their homelands, the links with the United Kingdom were maintained by the International Relations Committee of the British AScW[15].

The event that led directly to the formation of the WFSW was an international conference on "Science and the Welfare of Mankind" held in London, in February 1946. The desire to create a world federation of scientists came through strongly during the Conference. The British AScW was asked to prepare a draft constitution for such a federation, and to convene an inaugural conference. This too was held in London, in July 1946, under the chairmanship of Patrick Blackett, with the participation of scientists from 14 countries. An Executive Council was set up with Frédéric Joliot-Curie as President. At a meeting of the Executive Council, held in Paris in November 1946, it was decided to set up a central office of the Federation in Paris, which remains the headquarters of the WFSW to this day.

Aims

The aims of the Federation as laid down by its Constitution, are:

a.   To work for the fullest utilization of science in promoting peace and the welfare of mankind, and especially to ensure that science is applied to help solve the urgent problems of the time.

b.   To promote international cooperation in science and technology in particular through close collaboration with Unesco.

c. To encourage the international exchange of scientific knowledge and of scientific workers.

d. To preserve and encourage the freedom and coordination of scientific work both nationally and internationally.

e. To encourage improvements in the teaching of the sciences and to spread the knowledge of science and its social implications among the peoples of all countries.

f. To achieve a closer integration between the natural and social sciences.

g. To improve the professional, social and economic status of scientific workers.

h. To encourage scientific workers to take an active part in public affairs and to make them conscious of, and more responsive to, the progressive forces at work within society[16].

Organizational structure

As is seen from the list of aims, the WFSW includes objectives which are usually associated with trade unions. This is reflected in the structure of the Federation, which has two types of organization affiliated to it: trade unions and independent associations of scientific workers. The great majority of members are in fact in the trade union affiliated organizations, many of them are engineers rather than scientists. In 1981, the scientific worker membership was nearly 300 000, with affiliated organizations in 31 countries. About two thirds of the membership is in the socialist countries.

The supreme governing body of the Federation is the General Assembly, which meets about every three years. Between these meetings, the Executive Council (about 30 members) is responsible for guiding the work of the Federation. The Executive Council, in turn, delegates its powers to a Bureau consisting of the officers; it is run by the Secretary-General. Pierre Biquard held this post from 1947 to 1976.

The Head of the Federation is the President. After Joliot-Curie's retirement in 1957, Cecil Powell took over the Presidency and held it until his death in 1969. He was succeeded by Eric Burhop, a prime mover and the most active member in the field of nuclear disarmament; he was President until his death in 1980.

Political image

Numerically, the World Federation of Scientific Workers is by far the largest organized group of scientists and engineers who are concerned with the social implications of science and technology, striving for the maintenance of peace in the world, and opposed to the misuse of science for war. But its influence on these issues is not commensurate with the numerical strength of its membership.

The main weakness of the WFSW is that by the distribution of its membership and the tenor of its pronouncements it is seen by many scientists in the West as being politically biassed towards the communist ideology. In the early years, this bias frequently led to a division of opinion within the organization. For example, in 1948 the Netherlands Group disaffiliated itself in protest against the link between the WFSW and the World Federation of Trade Unions, the latter being regarded as predominantly a communist body[17]. Under the pressure of the British group, the Federation decided to break the agreement with the WFTU but the link was re-established later.

The perceived left wing image was an obstacle in many ways. Table 1 lists the dates and locations of the General Assemblies held so far. It will be noted that most of them were held in East Europe. This partly reflects the centre of gravity of the membership, and partly the difficulties of having meetings in non-communist countries. For example, the 2nd Assembly was scheduled to be held in Paris, but the French Government refused to grant visas to the delegates from socialist countries. A complementary meeting was therefore arranged in Prague, and the business was conducted in both cities using a telephone link and two messengers commuting between Paris and Prague. The 11th Assembly in London also experienced visa difficulties and the arrival of many delegates was considerably delayed.

Table 1 WFSW General Assemblies

	Date	Place	Topic of symposium
1.	September 1948	Prague	
2.	April 1951	Paris – Prague	
3.	September 1953	Budapest	
4.	September 1955	Berlin (GDR)	
5.	September 1957	Helsinki	The Training of Students in Science and Technology
6.	September 1959	Warsaw	Science in the Development of the Economy and Welfare of Mankind
7.	September 1962	Moscow	Higher Scientific and Technological Education
8.	September 1965	Budapest	The Advancement of Science in Developing Countries and the Role of International Scientific Co-operation
9.	April 1969	Paris	(No Symposium)
10.	September 1973	Varna	The Scientist in Society
11.	September 1976	London	The Interrelation of Current Economic and Social Development with Science and Technology
12.	May 1980	Berlin (GDR)	Higher Training of Scientists and Engineers

Problems of nuclear war and disarmament

Since 1957 International Symposia were held in conjunction with the General Assemblies, and table 1 lists the topics of these symposia. As can be seen they deal with a variety of problems concerning scientists but not with their role in relation to the arms race and disarmament. Nevertheless, these issues were of major interest to the WFSW. The preamble to the Constitution states [18]:

> "Scientists can no longer passively acquiesce in the misuse of science, which not only brings about unnecessary suffering and waste but impedes the advance of science itself. Science can only be fully used for the betterment of mankind in an era of peace and international cooperation, and scientists have, therefore, a responsibility greater than that of the ordinary citizen in maintaining stable political relations between nations... The members of the WFSW (believe) that the only way to prevent mass destruction by the misuse of science is through the elimination of war as an instrument of national policy. War, or the threat of war, can be prevented only if the people of the world understand the causes of war and are able and willing to ensure that those causes are removed. Science properly applied can remove or lessen the poverty, disease and ignorance which in some measure are always among the causes of war."

The development of nuclear weapons and the subsequent nuclear arms race were seen as a challenge which members of the Federation attempted to combat not only by educating themselves and the community at large, but also by influencing public opinion and leaders of nations.

In all these endeavours, the undoubted driving force was Eric Burhop; it was under his guidance, and frequently by his personal input, that the WFSW campaigns, the publications, symposia, public statements and appeals were mounted.

The first major action was against nuclear testing. In 1956 a pamphlet "Unmeasured Hazards" was published in 12 languages, with a circulation of about 120 000; it undoubtedly influenced many scientists in their attitude towards nuclear tests by explaining the hazards, particularly to future generations, from the fall-out radiation. In May 1959, a delegation of senior members of the Federation was received by Nikita Khrushchev and explained to him the attitude of the WFSW to the continued testing of nuclear weapons. The audience was the result of a letter addressed to the heads of Government of France, United Kingdom, United States and USSR. There was no response from any of the Western leaders.

The signing of the Partial Test Ban Treaty in 1963 resulted in a curious division of opinion among the representatives of member organizations of the Federation. The majority took the view that the Treaty should be warmly welcomed because of its immediate effect: a reduction of the radiation hazard, as well as of its long term effect: as a first step towards concrete measures of disarmament. However, others regarded the advantage of the Treaty as illusory and dangerous in that it created a false idea about its accomplishment[19].

A follow up of "Unmeasured Hazards" was a special issue, in 1958, of Scientific World (the official organ of the WFSW) on the dangers of nuclear weapons. It contained 12 articles, written by scientists from 7 countries, describing the effects of nuclear tests as well as the consequences to humanity of the use of nuclear weapons in war. J.D. Bernal, in an analysis of disarmament problems, argued that the technical aspects of nuclear disarmament are quite soluble; the real obstacle is the political division of the world but this could be overcome by the pressure of public opinion. This theme was also taken up by Frédéric Joliot-Curie in an article describing the world-wide movement against the atomic peril. This was one of his last writings: he died before the issue came out.

The most important event in the field of nuclear disarmament was the Symposium on "The Role of Scientists and of their Organizations in the Struggle for Disarmament"[20]. It was held in Moscow, on 15-19 July 1975, and was attended by 425 scientists from 62 countries including representatives from 20 international organizations. It was the largest symposium organized by the WFSW, and perhaps the largest gathering of scientists to discuss the role of scientists in disarmament. The main discussions took place in five Commissions on the following topics:

Commission 1: The social and economic aspects of disarmament; the economic burden of the arms race and the problems of scientific workers;

Commission 2: The interdependence between détente and disarmament; the role of organizations of scientific workers in promoting détente.

Commission 3: The problems of ending the arms race and of eliminating the danger of a nuclear war, the scientists' contribution to the solution of these problems.

Commission 4: The banning of chemical, biological and geophysical weapons; the scientists' responsibilities.

Commission 5: The specific forms of cooperation of scientific workers and their organizations with the broad movement for peace and disarmament.

At the end of the Symposium, a summary of the discussions and the main conclusions of each of the Commissions were presented at plenary sessions. With such a large gathering it would have been unreasonable to expect unanimity on the conclusions, and a number of dissenting opinions were voiced at the last session, but on the whole there was a considerable measure of agreement. All Commissions stressed the important role of scientists and organizations of scientists towards achieving disarmament. This role called not only for a study of the basic problems of peace and disarmament and the dissemination of authentic information on the consequences of a nuclear war, but also for the taking of active parts in social movements which strive to achieve the implementation of concrete measures leading to disarmament and international security. It was emphasized that the efforts of scientists could be most effective only when they are combined with relevant efforts of all the peace forces. In this sense the WFSW identified itself with mass movements against nuclear war.

The Symposium ended with an appeal to scientists of the world to unite their efforts to attain peace and security. This appeal[20] was subsequently sent out to a large number of scientists, asking for their endorsement by collecting signatures of scientists, engineers and technicians in all places where they worked. The proceedings of the Symposium were subsequently published in a booklet "Ending the Arms Race – the Role of the Scientists", which also contains the texts of relevant resolutions of the Executive Council of the WFSW and of the General Assembly of the United Nations.

Achievements in the disarmament field

It is not easy to make a meaningful assessment of the achievements of the WFSW in problems of the arms race and disarmament. As the numerically largest organization of scientists its influence should have been very considerable. But although its objectives specifically included the promotion of peace, the major purpose of the Federation was to protect the professional standing of its members. The great majority of the membership enrolled by virtue of the trade union character of the WFSW, and only few of them were actively concerned with disarmament problems. Furthermore, the political brush, with which the Federation has been tainted since early years of its existence, meant that its pronouncements were viewed with some suspicion by the members of the scientific community outside the Federation, and with a lack of credibility in the Western world. By contrast, the WFSW enjoyed a high prestige in the socialist countries where it had a strong following and its statements were accepted with acclamation. It is doubtful whether the image of the Federation can be changed after all these years. Acknowledging this state of affairs, there is still a great deal of gratitude to be felt to the WFSW, and satisfaction with the limited but excellent efforts in the disarmament field,and with the great influence it exerts at least in some sectors of the scientific community.

The Pugwash Movement (Pugwash Conferences on Science & World Affairs)

Although in relation to the arms race and disarmament the objectives of Pugwash and the WFSW are similar, the two movements differ from each other very considerably in a number of important aspects. Numerically, the Pugwash Movement is minute compared with WFSW – over a period of a quarter of a century only about 2000 scientists have taken a direct part in Pugwash activities – yet Pugwash has acquired a much higher reputation than the WFSW; it is considered as a prestigious and authoritative body, and its pronouncements find wide acceptance in the world. Two reasons for this may be mentioned. The first is that, unlike the WFSW, problems of the arms race and disarmament are the main area of interest in Pugwash; the Movement was in fact set up specifically for this purpose. Although many other issues of concern to the scientific community, and the world at large, have been discussed in the Pugwash forum, the nuclear arms race, the threat it poses to mankind, and the ways to remove it, are always on the top of the Pugwash agenda. The second reason is that recognizing that the main danger arises from the ideological differences in the world, referred to in the Russell-Einstein Manifesto (see Appendix 1) as "the titanic struggle between Communism and anti-Communism", Pugwash insisted from the beginning that the scientists participating in its activities should cover a wide spectrum of political opinion and that there should be no bias towards any of them.

The importance of ensuring that no scientist is denied participation because of his political views or because of diplomatic contingencies was expressed in the principle that Pugwash meetings will be held only in countries which will admit all those invited by Pugwash. Throughout the whole period of the cold war and political upheavals this principle held good, and the first violation occurred in 1981, when the Canadian government refused visas to two Soviet scientists invited to the Conference in Banff.

The insistence on political impartiality did not prevent attempts to smear the Pugwash Movement; for example, in 1960 in the American Senate, Pugwash was labelled by Senator Dodd as a communist organization. Even now Pugwash is branded as such by groups or individuals who dislike any attempt to bring the two sides together, but such views have little following. By the way it conducts its affairs, by the tone, standard and substance of its pronouncements, Pugwash has earned for itself the reputation of an independent, high integrity movement of scientists genuinely concerned with alleviating the dangers to the world community which to some extent have arisen from the work of other scientists.

Origins of Pugwash

There appear to be some misconceptions about the origin of the idea to convene an international conference of scientists. There is a wide-spread but mistaken belief that the idea came from Mr. Cyrus Eaton, a Canadian-American industrialist, who helped to finance a few of the early Pugwash Conferences. Actually, the idea of an international conference was mooted among scientists on a number of occasions, and concrete steps were discussed in letters between the FAS and the ASA in 1954; a study group to prepare for an "International Conference on Science and Society" was set up in that year by the ASA[21].

However, the credit for starting the Pugwash Movement must undoubtedly go to Bertrand Russell, because it was his initiative that set the whole process into motion. Following his famous BBC broadcast "Man's Peril" at Christmas in 1954, he wrote to Albert Einstein with the suggestion that the text of his speech might be used as the basis of a declaration to be endorsed by eminent scientists, and calling on scientsts from many countries, representing different political views, to gather in conference to assess the dangers to mankind that have arisen from the development of weapons of mass destruction and to help in averting that danger. Einstein immediately responded enthusiastically, asking Russell to draft the text which he would sign. As it turned out, Einstein's signature was one of the last acts of his life: it reached Russell after Einstein's death. Russell then set about to secure the signatures of other scientists, mostly Nobel-Prize Laureates. Among these was Frédéric Joliot-Curie, at that time President of the WFSW. Joliot-Curie wanted to make some modifications to the draft and asked Burhop to negotiate them with Russell. Eventually, Pierre Biquard, the Secretary-General of WFSW, had to come to London to finalize the amendments which appear as footnotes to the Manifesto[22].

The text of the Russell – Einstein Manifesto is given in Appendix 1 (see p.301). It was issued in London, at a large Press Conference on 9 July 1955. Russell was anxious to have a nuclear physicist with him, to help in answering technical questions, and he asked Joseph Rotblat, one of the signatories of the Manifesto, to chair the meeting[23]. The Press Conference, attended by representatives of the media from all over the world was a great success and received huge publicity. This in turn brought a flood of letters and cables from individuals and groups endorsing the Manifesto and offering help in bringing the conference about.

It was initially intended to convene the conference in New Delhi, in January 1957, in conjunction with the Indian Science Congress, and following an invitation from Jawaharlal Nehru. But the Suez crisis made the situation rather uncertain and this plan had to be abandoned. The offer was then accepted from Cyrus Eaton to provide travelling expenses and hospitality for the conference, if it were held in Pugwash, Nova Scotia,

Eaton's birth place.

Russell asked Powell, Rotblat and Burhop to help him in the preparatory work of the conference. Burhop offered the services of the London Office of the WFSW, and initially much of the correspondence was handled by that office. However, Russell was unhappy about the involvement of the Federation, and he asked Rotblat to take over. Subsequently, the organizational work of this conference, as well as of many later conferences, was handled from Rotblat's office in the University of London, until the Pugwash Central Office was set up in London in 1968.

Russell was extremely anxious that the conferences should not have any connection with organizations which were considered to be on any given side of the political spectrum; he extended this to individuals who were known to be politically militant. This is the reason why Burhop was not formally involved in the preparations, and why his name does not appear in the list of participants of the First Conference although he was actually present.

The First Pugwash Conference

The first of the series of conferences of scientists, under the aegis of the Russell – Einstein Manifesto, was held in Pugwash, in July 1957. It was a very small gathering; the official number of participants was 22, but they were individuals invited because of their standing in the scientific community and their expertise and interest in the subjects discussed. They came from 10 countries, which included the United States, United Kingdom, France, the USSR, China and Poland. The work was divided among 3 committees, with the following topics:
(1) hazards arising from the use of atomic energy in peace and war; (2) control of nuclear weapons; (3) the social responsibility of scientists.

The possible hazard from the radioactive fall-out from nuclear weapons tests was a major issue at that time, and it was of considerable importance that such an international group of scientists, covering a wide range of political opinion, managed to reach unanimous agreement on the quantitative assessment of the consequences of large-scale testing of nuclear weapons. The committee on the social responsibility of scientists was also unanimous in its findings, which took the form of a statement of common beliefs. The most controversial was the discussion in the committee on the control of nuclear weapons, because this included the whole area of arms limitations and reductions, and the steps needed to achieve general and complete disarmament, topics which were to occupy most of the time of future Pugwash Conferences. But there was unanimous agreement that scientists can and ought to contribute to the debate on these problems, and that further conferences were needed. Thus, the go-ahead was given for the setting up of a Movement of Scientists, which got its full name "The Pugwash Conferences on Science and World Affairs" from the venue of the first meeting.

Organization and nature of Pugwash

The task of organizing future conferences was entrusted to a Continuing Committee of five persons: three from the United Kingdom and one each from the United States and USSR. Except for the Chairman of the Committee, Bertrand Russell, they were all physicists. In the course of time, with the widening of the scope of activities, the governing body of Pugwash – later named the Council – was greatly increased in numbers, in countries of origin, and in scientific disciplines represented. In 1982 the Council consisted of 23 members (apart from the two officers) from 16 countries; less than half of them were physicists and five were from the social sciences.

The titular head of the Movement is the President (Hannes Alfvén during 1970-74; Dorothy Hodgkin since then). The executive officer is the Secretary-General (Rotblat until 1973, Bernard Feld until 1977), later renamed Director-General (Martin Kaplan since 1976).

The main task of the first Continuing Committee was to determine the nature and goals of Pugwash activities. The two principal alternatives were: (a) small private meetings, to study specific problems in depth, aiming at influencing decision-makers; (b) large gatherings aiming at influencing public opinion. Russell was in favour of the second option but later he recognized that such tasks would be better undertaken by mass-movements, such as the Campaign for Nuclear Disarmament, and that Pugwash can fulfil its role better by private meetings. The decision in favour of the first alternative was influenced by the replies to a poll conducted among scientists in the United Kingdom and the United States. Although public meetings, largely of an educational character, are held from time to time in conjunction with Pugwash activities, the meetings themselves are of a private nature, attended only by those invited individually; with a few exceptions the Press is excluded. A summary of the discussions and the recommendations are usually issued by the Council on behalf of the Conference, in the form of a public statement.

In the course of time the scope of Pugwash activities increased very considerably, but the general principles of its operation remained essentially the same: (a) Pugwash is largely an amorphous body, with no constitution, no formal membership, no rigid set of procedure, and the minimum of bureaucratic machinery; (b) all activities are carried out by Pugwash independently, and no joint action is normally undertaken with other organizations; (c) scientists participate in Pugwash activities as individuals, and they do not represent anybody; (d) participation is sought from the East and the West, and also from the Third World; (e) the participants are scientists but this term is taken in its broader meaning of scholars; (f) the debates are conducted in the scientific spirit; in particular, there is no indulgence in propaganda for one side or another.

As already mentioned, despite the strenuous efforts to maintain objectivity, Pugwash was initially viewed with suspicion as a political body with tendencies to the left. It took several years before the Governments in the West accepted that Pugwash was even handed. This has resulted in a reverse threat to the independence of Pugwash: recognizing the importance of the Pugwash debate, the Western Governments attempted to influence it by suggesting names of participants and topics for discussion; but these offers were rejected. The non-involvement of Pugwash in political propaganda was recognized as a great asset in the East also. For both sides the debates in Pugwash are seen of great value in providing an informal but informed channel of communications.

Table 2. Pugwash Conferences

Serial No.	Date	Location	No. of Participants	No. of countries	Theme
1.	July 1957	Pugwash, Canada	22	10	
2.	March-April 1958	Lac Beauport, Canada	22	8	The Dangers of the Present Situation of the Atomic Arms Race, and Ways & Means to Diminish Them
3.	September 1958	Kitzbühel, Austria	70	20	Dangers of the Atomic Age & what Scientists can do about them
4.	June-July 1959	Baden, Austria	25	7	Arms Control & World Security
5.	August 1959	Pugwash, Canada	26	8	Biological & Chemical Warfare
6.	Nov-Dec 1960	Moscow, USSR	75	15	Disarmament & World Security
7.	September 1961	Stowe, USA	41	12	International Cooperation in Pure & Applied Science
8.	September 1961	Stowe, USA	43	11	Disarmament & World Security
9.	August 1962	Cambridge, UK	67	19	Problems of Disarmament & World Security
10.	September 1962	London, UK	*175	36	Scientists & World Affairs
11.	September 1963	Dubrovnik, Yugoslavia	64	24	Current Problems of Disarmament & World Security
12.	Jan-Feb 1964	Udaipur, India	56	25	Current Problems of Disarmament & World Security

13.	September 1964	Karlovy Vary, Czechoslovakia	74	19	Disarmament & Peaceful Collaboration among nations
14.	April 1965	Venice, Italy	68	20	International Cooperation for Science & Disarmament
15.	Dec 1965-Jan 1966	Addis Ababa, Ethiopia	63	31	Science in Aid of Developing Countries
16.	September 1966	Sopot, Poland	69	22	Disarmament & World Security especially in Europe
17.	September 1967	Ronneby, Sweden	*180	44	Scientists & World Affairs
18.	September 1968	Nice, France	81	29	Current Problems of Peace, Security & Development
19.	October 1969	Sochi, USSR	101	29	World Security, Disarmament and Development
20.	September 1970	Fontana, USA	98	31	Peace & International Co-operation: A Programme for the Seventies
21.	August 1971	Sinaia, Romania	97	31	Problems of World Security, Environment, & Development
22.	September 1972	Oxford, UK	*174	43	Scientists & World Affairs
23.	Aug-Sept 1973	Aulanko, Finland	97	29	European Security, Disarmament & other Problems
24.	Aug-Sept 1974	Baden, Austria	117	32	Disarmament, Energy Problems & International Collaboration
25.	January 1976	Madras, India	78	35	Development, Resources & World Security
26.	August 1976	Mühlhausen, GDR	87	28	Disarmament, Security & Development
27.	August 1977	Munich, FRG	*223	47	Peace & Security in a Changing World
28.	September 1978	Varna, Bulgaria	108	33	Global Aspects of Disarmament & Security
29.	July 1979	Mexico City Mexico	121	39	Development & Security
30.	August 1980	Breukelen, Netherlands	117	38	Arms Limitations, Security and Development
31.	Aug-Sept 1981	Banff, Canada	133	40	The Search for Peace in a World in Crisis

*quinquennial conferences

Pugwash activities

The major Pugwash activity is the Annual Conference. Table 2 lists the 31 Conferences held before 1982, with their locations, numbers of participants and themes. As is seen the size of the Conferences has been increasing steadily. (The Conferences marked by an asterisk, which take place every 5 years, are in the nature of a General Assembly of Pugwash, and all former participants are entitled to come to them.) Since the chief form of work is as a debate round a table, the large size necessitates the division of the Conference into a number of Working Groups, each with a different topic; the number of Working Groups is such that each should not have more than about 30 participants.

Topics other than the nuclear arms race and disarmament usually figure on the agenda. In particular, problems of developing countries have been coming up increasingly; at each Conference there is at least one Working Group dealing with some aspects of development. Considerable pressure has been exerted by scientists from the Third World to increase the Pugwash effort in problems of development. Other Pugwashites resisted this tendency, arguing that the initial reason for Pugwash coming into being, i.e. the danger of a nuclear war, is still as great now, if not greater. The compromise reached was that only those problems of development which are linked with security should be debated in Pugwash. Other topics, such as energy, are also treated primarily in the context of world security.

Apart from the Annual Conferences several symposia and workshops are held every year. Each of these is devoted to a specific topic which is studied in depth; their size is such that the participants – who are selected primarily on the basis of their expertise – can sit round a table. The papers presented at some of the Symposia are published as Pugwash monographs, i.e. "Implications of Anti-Ballistic Missile Systems" (1969); "Impact of New Technologies on the Arms Race" (1971); "A New Design Towards Complete Disarmament" (1977); "The Dangers of Nuclear War" (1979); "New Directions in Disarmament" (1981); "New Weapons Systems and Criteria for Evaluating their Dangers" (1982).

Workshops differ from Symposia primarily in that they continue an in-depth examination of the same topic in a number of separate meetings; thus there were 9 workshops on the subject of Chemical Warfare, and 5 on Theatre Nuclear Weapons in Europe.

Other Pugwash activities take the form of even more private meetings, in which advantage is taken of the confidence in each other of Pugwash scientists, to tackle some sensitive issue. Examples are: intercession in crisis situations, such as the Cuban missile crisis, or the Vietnam war; and talks between scientists from countries who, at the time, are involved in hostilities, in regions like South Asia and the Middle East.

The role of Pugwash in nuclear disarmament

Despite the small size of the Movement, and the absence of publicity,

Pugwash has probably played a more significant role in the field of nuclear arms control and disarmament than any other non-governmental organization. The main role was to provide a forum for debate – and sometimes agreement – on specific measures towards stopping or decelerating the nuclear arms race. The opportunities provided at Pugwash meetings for scientists from East and West to talk freely and informally, often lead to ideas which pave the way to official agreement at governmental level. Several examples will be given.

The Partial Test Ban Treaty. As already mentioned, the hazard associated with atmospheric testing of nuclear weapons was the first topic discussed in Pugwash. Having agreed among themselves and then conveyed to Governments the concern about the risks to public health arising from the tests, the next step was to work out the terms of a treaty to ban tests, and the methods of verification of adherence to the treaty. Underground tests presented the main difficulty, since at that time it was generally believed that without on-site inspections it would not be possible to differentiate between a seismic signal due to a natural tremor and one resulting from a test of a nuclear weapon. A way to overcome this obstacle was put forward at a Pugwash conference jointly by American and Soviet scientists; it was the 'black-box' idea, the installation of unmanned automatic seismic detectors in areas of seismic activity. This idea, which was subsequently taken up in an exchange of letters between Kennedy and Khrushchev, removed the pretext that the obstacles were of a technical rather than political nature. A private Pugwash meeting, attended by experts in seismology, helped to clarify the problems involved. This meeting ended with a document, submitted to the governments concerned, concluding that "the clarity now attained in the scientific and technical aspects of the problem provide a sufficient basis for the governments to arrive at an agreement for the conclusion of a test-ban treaty in the near future"[24]. The Partial Test Ban Treaty was indeed signed a few months later, and it is generally believed that the Pugwash meeting substantially helped in reaching the agreement. The fact that it was later followed by an intensive programme of underground tests should not detract from the value of the Treaty which marked a significant turning point in arms control negotiations, quite apart from greatly reducing the radiation hazard to populations.

The Non-Proliferation Treaty (NPT). The so-called "n-th country" problem, i.e. the danger arising from many states acquiring nuclear weapons, nowadays known as horizontal proliferation, was a topic of concern to Pugwash from its earliest meetings, when means were sought to convince governments to undertake not to acquire nuclear weapons. The many problems involved in providing safeguards against the diversion of sensitive materials from programmes of peaceful nuclear energy, and at the same time guaranteeing security against nuclear attacks on states which gave up the option of acquiring nuclear weapons themselves, were discussed at great length. At one stage, when it appeared that the opposition to the proposed treaty may win the day, Pugwash issued one of its rare public statements, calling on scientists to urge their governments to sign the treaty[25]. Despite its many shortcomings, the NPT, which came in force in 1970, is still considered to be one of the few successful control measures which have helped to reduce the danger of horizontal proliferation.

Anti-ballistic missiles (ABM). Pugwash was greatly concerned about the danger of escalating the nuclear arms race by the introduction of anti-ballistic missile systems in the United States and USSR. For several reasons, including the fact that offensive missiles are cheaper than defensive ones, there was the worry that the installation of ABM systems will result in a large increase in the numbers of offensive missiles. The task of Pugwash was to convey to the governments, through the scientists, the fallacy of the ABM strategy. Eventually these efforts of Pugwash were successful, and the SALT I agreement in 1972 put a limit on the number of ABM systems for both sides. The argument against ABM's was so convincing that even the allowed options were not taken up.

These three cases illustrate the type of debate carried out in the Pugwash forum, and the proposals on specific issues which contributed to the conclusion of international treaties. Many more topics which did not have such a successful outcome, were discussed in Pugwash, but they were nevertheless useful in clarifying the issues and preparing the ground for future negotiations.

General and Complete Disarmament (GCD). In the early years the possibility of a treaty on GCD appeared highly promising, and much time was spent in Pugwash on problems connected with such a treaty, e.g. the economic consequences of disarmament, or with the steps leading to it, e.g. minimum deterrent. A time table for the necessary stages to GCD was extensively discussed with a view to reducing the differences between the American and Soviet proposals (the McCloy – Zorin schemes for GCD). When, because of political vicissitudes, these plans were abandoned, the emphasis shifted to step-by-step arms limitation measures. The feasibility of these has been pursued over the years, but the ultimate aim of general and complete disarmament was never abandoned and is frequently put on the agenda.

The arms limitation measures which received much attention included the following:

Comprehensive Test Ban Treaty. An extension of the Partial Test Ban

Treaty to include all underground tests is considered by Pugwash to be technically feasible and politically very desirable. The threshold of 150 kilotons, agreed to in Vladivostok, was thought to be far too high, taking into account that most of the strategic MIRVed missiles carry warheads of much lower yield, quite apart from mini-nukes and neutron bombs.

Ban of flight testing of missiles. A halt to the flight testing of all missiles and other nuclear delivery vehicles, if coupled with a comprehensive test ban treaty, would provide an important limitation on the technological arms race.

Cut-off of production of fissionable materials. Such a cut-off would limit the expansion of nuclear weapon arsenals; it would also reduce the risk of horizontal proliferation as the nuclear power states would then become subject to IAEA safeguards. The cut-off will have to include a ban on the treatment of plutonium from reactors to make it more suitable for weapons; such treatment is being proposed now.

Nuclear-weapon-free zones. The reduction of the danger of a nuclear war, by restricting the areas in which nuclear weapons are allowed to exist, has been discussed by Pugwash from the early years. The possibility is frequently expressed in terms of nuclear-free zones. Two specific cases of such nuclear-free zones have been successfully negotiated: the Tlatelolco Treaty, relating to Latin America, and the Treaty banning military installations in the Antarctic. In a sense, the treaties banning the placement of nuclear weapons on the sea bed and in outer space, come in the same category. However, attempts to apply this concept to areas which are more likely to be war arenas, such as Europe, have so far failed. The Rapacki plan for a nuclear-free zone in Europe was much discussed in the 1960s, but was not acceptable to some nuclear weapon states. Later Pugwash extended the concept into a "World-Wide Nuclear-Weapon-Free Zone", which combines the idea of nuclear-free zones with guarantees of no-first use of nuclear weapons against nations adhering to the treaty. The main difference from the conventional concept of a nuclear-free zone is its non-contiguous nature: any nation in the world can join it; in this sense it goes back to an earlier Pugwash concept of a "non-nuclear club". A draft of a treaty, couched in formal terms, was prepared by Pugwash and presented to the United Nations [26]. Hopefully, it will be taken up by governments one day.

Destabilizing measures: anti-submarine warfare. The danger of a nuclear war is increased by any measure which destabilizes the balance of terror. The introduction of MIRVed warheads was such a development in the nuclear arms race, and Pugwash has consistently – alas unsuccessfully – warned against it. Another destabilizing development would be the ability to detect the location of submarines carrying nuclear weapons. Much effort was spent in Pugwash to point out the dangers of such an eventuality, and governments were implored not to engage in research on anti-submarine warfare.

Misconceptions: counterforce strategy. The technological advances in the nuclear arms race, such as MIRV and great accuracy in hitting military targets, have brought to the fore the counterforce strategy, in place of the MAD (mutual assured destruction) doctrine. Associated with the counterforce strategy is the concept of a limited nuclear war. Pugwash keeps pointing out the fallacy of this concept. It is one of the several common misconceptions which need correcting. Thus, it is a fallacy to believe that nuclear war can be limited in quality or quantity; that civil defence can provide a chance for the survival of the community; that a counterforce strategy can destroy the retaliatory capacity of the other side; and that parity in nuclear weapons is necessary for effective deterrence[27].

SALT. Needless to say, Pugwash has consistently supported all arms limitation negotiations at the official level, such as SALT I and II, even though it was realized – and frequently stressed – that they can make only a slight impact on the arms race. New directions in nuclear arms limitations are always on the Pugwash agenda, even when SALT and other negotiations have broken down, in the hope that consensus reached in the Pugwash forum on various specific plans will one day serve as a blueprint for official negotiations.

The general role of Pugwash

Apart from providing a forum for debate on specific measures towards stopping and reversing the arms race, Pugwash played a more general role, as a channel of communications between East and West. In the early years Pugwash was the only channel for talks at sub-governmental level between informed and influential scientists from both sides. They attended the Pugwash meetings in their individual capacities, without commitments to any other body; this made it possible for them to reach agreement well ahead of official negotiations and sometimes paving the way for such negotiations. In the later years a number of other avenues opened up, but since these were mostly on a more official level they were subject to political influences and likely to be closed in times of crises. This happened, for example, during a period of the Vietnam war or after events in Afghanistan in December 1979 when all official and semi-official talks between the United States and USSR were suspended. At these times, the Pugwash channel remained open; in fact, it was able to make some progress, for instance, in relation to theatre nuclear weapons in Europe, by putting forward the idea of a moratorium, later taken up at governmental levels.

Another general role of Pugwash was to stimulate research, theoretical and practical, on problems of the arms race and disarmament. As a result of their involvement in Pugwash, many scientists felt impelled to think and apply their creative powers to these problems; some went even further and made the study of these problems their main occupation. With its meagre financial resources, and with everybody participating on a spare time basis only, Pugwash was not in a position to conduct the full-time research that the implementation of its own proposals demanded, but it was instrumental in setting up organizations in which such full-time research is carried out. A notable example is SIPRI (see p.152) whose programme is the outcome of a Pugwash response to the initiative of the Swedish Government. A number of other peace research institutes came into being as a result of stimulation by Pugwash.

Pugwash achievements

The last few pages illustrate the type of input made by Pugwash in its attempt to prevent the greatest danger facing mankind at the present time, a nuclear holocaust. How significant was this input? Considering that the nuclear arms race has escalated beyond belief and shows no signs of abating, and that the danger of a nuclear war is now generally considered greater than ever before, one might conclude that the Pugwash effort was a failure. On the other hand, the situation might have been far worse, and a nuclear conflict might have already occurred, if it were not for the few disarmament measures and international agreements which acted as brakes on an accelerating arms race. While these are conjectures, there is one undisputable fact: nuclear weapons have not been used in combat since 1945. How much credit should go to Pugwash for the avoidance of a nuclear war so far? It is impossible to give a quantitative answer to this question. With a highly complex problem, in which so many diverse factors interact, one cannot measure the influence exerted by any single element. However, it is generally accepted – and attested by leading statesmen – that Pugwash was an important force in bringing better understanding between East and West in matters relating to the nuclear menace, particularly in educating decision-makers about the folly of any side expecting a victory in a nuclear war.

Surely, at a time when a very high proportion of the scientific manpower is engaged in military research and development, when it is alleged that scientists are the instigators, and dictate the pace, of the nuclear arms race, it is of the utmost importance to realize that a group of scientists voluntarily give their time, talent and thought in the reverse direction, to stop the nuclear madness. Not only does Pugwash serve to restore the tarnished image of scientists, but it is a shining example of the devotion of scientists to positive values, of their desire to be of service to the community in seeking a safe and peaceful world, and the fulfilment of their social responsibilities.

C. PEACE RESEARCH INSTITUTES

Introduction

Although the institutes concerned with peace research do not come under the category of "Movements of Scientists Against the Arms Race", many scientists working in those institutes carry out studies which help to understand the causes of conflict and war, and in this way they contribute to the efforts aimed at eliminating the arms race and creating conditions of peace in the world. Some of the institutes also provide factual material which aids scientists' movements against the arms race.

The basic philosophy of peace research is described in chapter 13, and as will be shown, the definition of peace research is open to wide interpretation and the scope goes well beyond the subject of this book. This section describes the history and current activities of some of the institutes, with emphasis on problems related to the arms race and disarmament.

Directory of peace research institutions

There exists a great variety of organizations which are described as peace research institutions. Unesco publishes a directory of these organizations every few years. The last edition[28], published in 1981, contains 313 entries, of which 49 are described as international or regional peace research institutions, and 264 as national institutions in 44 countries. It is not easy to recognize the criterion for distinguishing between international and national institutes. Thus, PRIO is listed under national organizations as a Norwegian institute, but its title is "International Peace Research Institute, Oslo". On the other hand, the "ASPAC Cultural and Social Centre", in the Republic of Korea, is classified as an international

144

institute. In any case this differentiation is probably immaterial since, according to Galtung[29], "all peace research institutes are international, by definition".

The institutions listed in the Directory differ widely in many respects. Some are quite small, with only one member of staff, others are very large with a staff of several hundred. In 1978, the total size of the peace research community was approximately 5000[30].

Some institutions are of very long standing (the oldest listed began in 1889!) while others have just started. The late 1960s appear to be the period of the highest rate of increase of new institutions. Some are very active and productive (in terms of publications), others are moribund, or exist only on paper.

There are considerable differences in the type of activities carried out by the institutions. Some do actual research, while others only promote or support research by providing financial grants or facilities for publications; many institutes combine both types of activity, i.e. they carry out their own research as well as promoting research going on elsewhere. Somewhat less than a quarter of those listed in the Directory are peace research institutes "proper", in the sense of being wholly engaged in research[30].

Apart from major differences in methodology the institutions also differ widely in the actual topics of their investigations, which cover almost all social problems of modern (and past) societies. Less than one-third of all the institutions listed are connected – more or less directly – with the subject of this book, i.e. arms control and disarmament. Among these institutions only five are in the countries of the Third World, about 6 per cent of the total. This is significantly less than the proportion (13 per cent) relating to *all* peace research institutes, as listed in the Unesco Directory. This indicates that problems of arms control and disarmament have a lower priority in the developing countries. Considering that the great majority of armed conflicts since the Second World War occurred in the Third World, and that arms expenditure absorbs a very high proportion of the total budget of many of the developing countries, one may express the hope that the problems of stopping the arms race, which are in many ways different from those in the developed countries, will be studied more intensively in the future.

A few of the peace research institutions, selected mainly on criteria of relevance to the subject of this book, will be given individual attention.

United States Agency for Arms Control and Disarmament (ACDA)

With a staff of about 250 and a budget of $20 million, ACDA is probably the largest of the institutions which carry out and promote research in the fields of international relations, arms control, disarmament and military strategy.

ACDA was set up in 1961 by President Kennedy. At that time, the passing by both Houses of the American Congress of the law to establish the Agency "was considered something of a political miracle"[31], as there was strong opposition from those who considered arms control, let alone disarmament, antithetical to national defence[32], to the handing over of disarmament studies to a quasi-independent body. American scientists interested in the cause of disarmament hailed the setting up of the Agency as an important step forward; a number of distinguished natural scientists took up office in ACDA.

The primary functions of the Agency were:

1. to conduct and co-ordinate research for arms control and disarmament policy formation;
2. to prepare for and manage United States participation in international negotiations in the arms control and disarmament field;
3. to coordinate and disseminate public information about arms control and disarmament;
4. to prepare for and operate any control systems which may become part of the US arms control and disarmament activities.

All these functions were vigorously pursued from the very beginning, for example, when ACDA was actively involved in drafting a treaty for general and complete disarmament, as well as for a comprehensive nuclear test-ban treaty.

At the beginning, when the Director was the principal arms control adviser to the President, ACDA had considerable authority. Later its role diminished, and for a time ACDA was virtually excluded from policy decisions. In 1975, the American Congress took measures to enhance ACDA's effectiveness and instructed the State Department to include it in the policy process[32]. One of the Directors, Paul Warnke, was the chief American spokesman at the SALT II negotiations under President Carter.

The results of ACDA's many studies were published in reports on various aspects of arms control and disarmament, military industry and trade in arms, economic and social effects of the arms race, and on the consequences of nuclear war. The yearly publication "World Military Expenditure and Arms Transfer" presents data on the utilization of resources for military purposes and on the international trade in arms. Together with "The Military Balance", published by the International Institute for Strategic Studies in London, and the SIPRI Yearbook, they provide the best source of information on these issues.

USSR: *Scientific Research Council on Peace and Disarmament*

This is a prestigious body which co-ordinates and promotes research on peace and disarmament in the Soviet Union. It was established in 1979 under the aegis of the Academy of Sciences of the USSR, the State Committee of the Council of Ministers for Science and Industry, and the Soviet Peace Committee. Under the chairmanship of Nikolai Inozemtzev (Director of the Institute of World Economics and International Relations) it contains five sections: Problems on Disarmament – under Georgi Arbatov; Scientific and Technological Progress and the Maintenance of Peace – Jermen Gvishiani; The Developing Countries and Problems of Peace and Disarmament – Evgeni Primakov; Cooperation Among Scholars in Research on Problems of Peace – Moisei Markov; Peaceful Coexistence and Détente – Oleg Bykov. As these titles indicate, the Council has wide terms of reference, being concerned with problems of détente and the role of developing countries, in addition to disarmament. Particular attention is devoted to the pooling of the efforts to research workers in the natural and social sciences. The purpose of the studies undertaken under the aegis of the Council is "to find the best possible ways of strengthening and developing lasting peaceful relations among States and of furthering cooperation between States with different social and economic systems in solving today's world problems in accordance with contemporary international law and the generally accepted principles and standards that underlie it"[33].

The Council publishes a yearbook "Scientific Research into the Problems of Peace and Disarmament" and a series of publications under the title "Peace and Disarmament".

One of its noteworthy activities is the liaison with a Committee of the US National Academy of Sciences, to discuss specific issues of arms control negotiations between the United States and USSR. This Committee was set up in 1981, but the collaboration on these issues follows to a certain extent the East-West Study Group on Disarmament and Arms Control which started in 1964 (as an offshoot of Pugwash) and used to meet alternatively in the United States and USSR until the Vietnam war brought it to a halt.

These bilateral talks may be helped by the "Institute of the USA and Canada", another organ of the Soviet Academy of Sciences, which has been in existence since 1968. Its director is Georgi Arbatov and the staff includes distinguished scholars with specialized knowledge in the field of armaments. In the West the Institute is probably the best known of all Soviet organizations concerned with these topics. The many contacts which members of the Institute made with American and other scholars have played an important role in facilitating official negotiations between the United States and the USSR on the reduction of the arms race.

International Peace Research Institute, Oslo (PRIO)

Although of average size and budget, the Oslo Institute occupies a special place among peace research institutes by being a pacesetter and a model for many other institutions. This is largely due to the personality of its first Director Johan Galtung. One of the most prolific writers on peace research, Galtung is probably its chief theorist, who made it into a "science of peace". His thinking has influenced a large number of the present generation of peace researchers. Although at present only loosely associated with PRIO, Galtung's concepts about the contents of peace research, for example his broadening of the term violence, and the distinction between direct and structural violence, are still largely serving as guidelines for the type of research carried out by the Oslo Peace Research Institute.

PRIO was founded in 1959 as a section of the (private) Institute for Social Research in Oslo, but gradually it acquired autonomy and became a fully independent foundation in 1966. After Galtung became Professor of Conflict and Peace Research at the University of Oslo in 1969, his involvement in PRIO gradually declined and he withdrew completely on leaving Norway in 1975. Some predicted that without Galtung PRIO would expire; this did not happen, although the Institute passed through a transition period, which led to a more collective form of organization and the introduction of a salary equalization scheme.

According to the Statutes adopted in 1978, all the staff members of the Institute are collectively responsible for its operations; the administrative and other duties are shared by everybody in rotation. The internal governing body is the Staff Meeting which appoints the Executive Director – responsible for the day-to-day administration – and the Research Director – in charge of the research programme; each appointment is for one year.

The budget of the Institute (currently about 0.8 million US dollars) comes mainly from the Norwegian Government, but some support is also provided by other Norwegian sources, with small contributions from other countries. The financial aspects of the Institute are supervised by a small Board appointed by several Norwegian university and research institutions. Apart from approving the budget and the accounts, the Board also has to confirm the appointment of the Executive Director and research staff.

The staff is made up of about 40 persons, some 15 of whom are research workers in charge of individual projects; seven of them are primarily concerned with problems of arms control and disarmament. Among the staff, there are a number of conscientious objectors, mostly from Norway, who spend a period of time in the Institute instead of doing military service.

148

The programme of activities covers four disciplines: sociology, political science, law and history, but although the area under study is global, there is an emphasis on Scandinavian countries. In the field of arms control and disarmament the research projects include: proliferation of nuclear material and technology, technical aspects of nuclear proliferation, military utilization of natural resources, the doctrines and strategies of deterrence, and the dynamics of armaments.

Apart from publishing the results of its own research, PRIO produces two periodicals: the *Journal of Peace Research* and the *Bulletin of Peace Proposals*; both appear quarterly. The Journal started in 1964 with Galtung as editor and – initially – main contributor. It was originally published through the Institute of Social Research in Oslo; in 1965 it became the organ of PRIO, and since 1967 it is published under the auspices of IPRA. The Journal has been the major vehicle for the evolution of Galtung's theories of structural violence, but nowadays articles concerned with ways and means of promoting peace are favoured over purely theoretical dissertations.

The *Bulletin of Peace Proposals* was started in 1970. It was edited from the beginning by Marek Thee, currently Executive Director of PRIO. The Bulletin too is published under the auspices of IPRA but jointly with two other organizations (Institute for World Order and Berghof Foundation for Conflict Research). Armaments are the main area of interest to the Bulletin and priority goes to problems of disarmament. Apart from original articles the Bulletin prints condensed versions of articles, speeches, documents etc., from world sources grouped according to topic. This makes the Bulletin of immense value to the "amateurs" who want to keep up with developments in the field of arms control, disarmament and related subjects.

International Peace Research Association (IPRA)

IPRA was set up at a meeting held in London in December 1964. It decided from the beginning to have a rigid formal structure. At the inaugural Conference held in July 1965 at Groningen, Statutes and Bye-Laws – mainly the endeavour of the first Secretary-General Bert Röling, an authority on international law – were presented and approved. According to the Statutes, the purpose of IPRA was to advance interdisciplinary research into the conditions of peace and the causes of war; in particular:

(*a*) to promote national and international studies and teaching relating to the pursuit of international peace;

(b) to facilitate contacts between scholars throughout the world;

(c) to encourage the international dissemination of results of research in the field of and of information on significant developments of peace research.

A fourth item was added in the revised Statutes adopted in 1981, namely:

(d) to facilitate international cooperation between educators, peace researchers and activities toward more effective and wide-spread peace education.

Three classes of membership were envisaged: individual members, scientific institutes and scientific associations. (N.B. at the end of 1980 there were 303 individual members from 42 countries, and 63 corporate members in 25 countries)[34].

The general policy of IPRA is determined by the General Conference of members, which elects the governing body, i.e. a Council of 15 members. In practice the Council meets infrequently and its powers are delegated to an Executive Committee of six members. The day-to-day running of IPRA is in the hands of the Secretary-General.

Röling was succeeded in this post by Äsbjorn Eide in 1971; he in turn by Raimo Väyrynen in 1974, and by Yoshikazu Sakamoto in 1979. The headquarters of IRPA are at the residence of the Secretary-General, thus they moved from Groningen to Oslo, to Tampere and to Tokyo.

IPRA holds a consultative status with Unesco and receives a yearly grant from it; other expenditure is derived from membership fees.

Activities

The main organizational activity is the General Conference held every two years. Table 3 gives a list of the General Conferences held so far. Part of the Conference is devoted to the presentation of papers which are

Table 3. IPRA general conferences

No.	Date	Location	No. of participants	No. of countries
1.	July 1965	Groningen, Netherlands	73	23
2.	June 1967	Tallberg, Sweden	119	25
3.	September 1969	Karlovy Vary, Czechoslovakia	138	24
4.	October 1971	Bled, Yugoslavia	~150	23
5.	January 1974	New Delhi, India	~130	~20
6.	August 1975	Turku, Finland	~170	~40
7.	December 1977	Oaxtepec, Mexico	~170	
8.	August 1979	Königstein, FRG	~200	~45
9.	June 1981	Orillia, Canada	~200	~38

usually published in the "Proceedings of the IPRA Conferences". But a great deal of time is taken up in the Administrative Meeting which is concerned with organizational matters, approving the budget and electing the Council and other Committees.

The special attention to problems of the Third World was expressed by the setting up of regional organizations, the Asian Peace Research Association and the Latin American Council of Peace Research. An African regional group is being organized.

IPRA's increasing interest in peace education (cf. the addition of item d to the objectives) was manifested by the setting up in 1972 of an Education Committee, which in 1975 became the Peace Education Commission with its own Council elected at the General Conference.

The main activities of IPRA are carried out via several Study Groups, the holding of seminars, and attending various relevant conferences organized by other bodies. In the field of disarmament the activities centre round the Study Group on Disarmament which was set up in 1975, in conjunction with the United Nations First Special Session on Disarmament. Another project undertaken by the Study Group is on "Restraint and Confidence Building Measures"; this topic was discussed in several workshops. There is also a IPRA Study Group on "Militarization vs Human Rights and Development", which focusses on the world military structure and, more recently, on alternative defence strategies and the conversion of military hardware to alternative technologies.

Publications

The official organ of IPRA is the *International Peace Research Newsletter*, which was taken over by IPRA at the time of its formation from an existing publication. It is published about six times a year and contains mainly reports on IPRA activities. As already mentioned, IPRA sponsors the *Journal of Peace Research* and the *Bulletin of Peace Proposals* published by PRIO. Other periodicals sponsored by IPRA are *Current Research on Peace and Violence*, a quarterly published by the Tampere Peace Research Institute in Finland, and *Alternatives: A Journal of World Policy* published by the Institute of World Order, United States, and the Centre for the Study of Developing Societies, India.

Significance of IPRA

As an association of peace research institutes, the main task of IPRA is to promote and encourage research rather than to carry it out itself. By organizing conferences which bring together peace research workers from many countries, it provides a forum for fruitful discussion, thus stimulating further research. Its field of interest is very wide, covering the whole area of peace research, from the nuclear arms race to food policy. However, problems of arms control and disarmament have a high priority. The discussions on these topics at the General Conferences and in the Special Study Groups, as well as IPRA's publications and periodicals, have helped to increase the number of scientists interested in these problems and to induce many of them to engage in further study.

Stockholm International Peace Research Institute (SIPRI)

Among the many peace research institutes SIPRI occupies a special position, both as a source of factual information and as a centre of scientific research on problems of arms control and disarmament; it is unique in having a significant input from natural scientists who form a higher proportion among its researchers than other institutes.

Origin

The origins of SIPRI are of great interest. In the early 1960s the Swedish Parliament decided to commemorate the fact that for 150 years Sweden has not been at war with any country, by setting up an institute for research on peace and conflict. As a first step the Swedish Government set up in 1964 a "Committee on an International Peace and Conflict Research Institute", composed of several scientists and scholars, under the chairmanship of Alva Myrdal, Ambassador at large and chief Swedish Delegate to the United Nations Disarmament Committee (soon to become Minister of Disarmament). Among the groups consulted by the Committee was Pugwash, and several meetings were held with the Pugwash Continuing Committee and with members of some Pugwash National Groups. Pugwash was enthusiastic about the idea of an institute, as it saw in it a means of implementing its own projects. Many suggestions for research on problems of disarmament and arms control regularly crop up at Pugwash meetings but cannot be followed up because of the lack of a suitable organizational apparatus. The Swedish initiative was seen as an opportunity for providing a continuing effort to complement the sporadic flashes of bright thoughts. For this reason, Pugwash not only welcomed the idea but suggested a programme of work for the proposed institute, the prime recommendation being that the methodology be that employed in Pugwash, with emphasis on the approach used by the natural sciences.

These recommendations were largely accepted. In its report, issued in 1966, the Committee recommended the setting up in Stockholm of an institute to carry out research primarily directed to problems of disarmament and arms control, especially those which received comparatively little attention in existing institutes. In particular, the Committee felt that "essential scientific contributions could be made which are highly relevant to international endeavours for peace"[35], and that this could be achieved by conducting chiefly natural science research.

The Swedish Government accepted these recommendations and the Institute under the name "Stockholm International Peace Research Institute" (SIPRI) was set up in August 1966. Pugwash played a significant role in this event; the Secretary-General of Pugwash was a member of the Governing Body; Rolf Björnerstedt, the Secretary of the Swedish Pugwash Group, was appointed Acting Director of SIPRI; and the first research project, on biological weapons, was taken over from Pugwash.

International character

From the very beginning it was the intention that SIPRI should be purely international. An attempt was made later to link it with the Royal Swedish Academy but this was resisted, and SIPRI remained an independent foundation, although entirely and directly financed by the Swedish Government. (The current budget is about 2 million US dollars). The international character was ensured by the composition of the governing bodies, with representatives from many countries, and by the international recruitment of the research workers. The Statutes of SIPRI laid down that the Swedish Government appoints the members of the governing bodies, but the nominations come from other groups, and throughout the whole history of SIPRI there has been no instance of the Swedish Government interfering with the independent status of the Institute.

Governing bodies

The responsibility for SIPRI activities rests entirely with the Governing Board composed of eight members (including the Director) from several countries in the East and West, but not from the United States or the USSR. The Chairman is Swedish (currently Rolf Björnerstedt). The Board has been meeting 2–3 times a year.

To help the Board in formulating the policy of SIPRI and the selection of research projects, as well as to evaluate their results, a Scientific Council was established, with a membership of 24 drawn from many countries, including the Third World, and selected on the basis of "scientific competence or practical experience in international political affairs"[35]. Members of Council included the Earl of Mountbatten, Lord Zuckerman and Henry Kissinger. The initial intention was for the Council to meet once a year, but actually there were only two meetings in 1967 and 1971.

The actual running of SIPRI is in the hands of the Director, who is the Head of the Institute and takes care of all matters not decided by the Board. To stress the international character of SIPRI it was accepted that the Director should not be a Swede. As it happened, all Directors so far have been British: Robert Neild from 1967 to 1971; Frank Barnaby from 1971 to 1981; and Frank Blackaby since October 1981.

Initially, the research workers and staff of the Institute (at present about 45) had no formal say in its running. This has given rise to some dissatisfaction and frustration, aggravated by problems relating to tenure and to specific Swedish labour laws. The Swedish Parliament was requested to set up a Commission to inquire into the future organization and activities of SIPRI. The result of the inquiry was a report submitted in October 1979 and later approved by Parliament[35]. Among proposed changes in the structure is the setting up of a Research Staff Collegium – a formal body in addition to the Governing Board and Scientific Council – to facilitate the co-ordination of research and administration. The collegium consists of the scholars and research assistants of the Institute. One of its duties is to make nominations for the Director and members of the Governing Board; another body entitled to make these nominations is the Staff Union, composed of all members of staff (research, technical and administrative) who belong to the trade unions.

Activities

The projects approved by the Board are carried out by research workers, aided by the technical staff. There are two categories of research workers: a few are on long-term tenure and are mainly involved in the continuing projects of the Institute, such as the Yearbook; the majority are visiting scholars who are engaged for specific projects and spend a period of time at SIPRI, from a few weeks to a few years. These scholars come from many countries, including the United States, the USSR and China. Many of them are natural scientists with specific expertise in the technological aspects of the arms race. Scholars from many countries also come to SIPRI to attend specialized symposia frequently held in the Institute, just as the SIPRI scholars attend international conferences to which they are invited as experts.

As already mentioned, the initial policy was to concentrate on problems arising from armaments and disarmament, mainly the collection of relevant data and their objective analysis and presentation. The first subject to be studied in depth was chemical and biological warfare (CBW). This project was taken over from Pugwash, which had set up in 1964 a study group on the problems of biological warfare and the consequences of the possible military applications of new advances in biology. The sporadic effort of Pugwash, although very effective in its framework, was thought to be insufficient and a more sustained study was deemed necessary. The result of the SIPRI effort was a monumental publication *The Problem of Chemical and Biological Warfare* in six volumes, describing the historical, technical, military, legal, political and disarmament aspects of CBW.

Another major project was the arms trade between the developed and the developing countries; it resulted in the publication, in 1971, of *The Arms Trade with the Third World* (but the project is still going on). The statistical aspect of the study consisted of the listing of the movements of major weapons: aircraft, tanks, ships and missiles, from 11 supplying countries to 91 countries in the Third World. The other parts of the study were an analysis of the factors governing arms supply policies, and measures to limit the arms trade.

Other projects concerned a variety of aspects of warfare, particularly nuclear, and measures of arms control and disarmament. They included tactical nuclear weapons, detection of underground tests, anti-submarine warfare, outer space activities, nuclear radiation in warfare, military impact on the human environment, and problems related to the proliferation of nuclear weapons, the NPT, the link with nuclear energy, and the internationalization of the nuclear fuel cycle. All of these resulted in the publication of books or monographs.

However, the most important of the SIPRI projects is the annual publication *World Armaments and Disarmament* which became known as the SIPRI Yearbook. Started in 1968/69, it appears in June every year and is the product of the combined efforts of the permanent staff and visiting scholars. The Yearbook in an analysis of the World's arms races and of the attempts to stop them. The main features are: data on world arms production and trade, developments in military technology, and military expenditure; and an analysis of arms control measures, nuclear deterrence strategies and disarmament negotiations and treaties. The Yearbook has become a standard reference book and an invaluable source of information for all interested in the problems of the arms race and disarmament.

Publications

As a rule, SIPRI publications are issued in the name of the Governing Board and not of the actual author(s). The names of the authors are usually mentioned only in the Preface by the Director. While this procedure gives the publication greater authority, as being sponsored by the whole Institute, it is not an incentive to the author, particularly if he wants to further his own career, and may be a drawback in attracting some scholars.

Though the books are printed by a private publisher (at present Taylor and Francis, London) many copies are distributed free of charge to individuals and organizations. The expenditure on this is considered to be a legitimate and important aspect of the activities of the Institute.

The status and role of SIPRI

In the course of 15 years SIPRI has established itself as one of the world's leading centres for documentation on the problems of the arms race and disarmament. It is a meeting place for scientists and scholars from East and West,North and South, and a workshop for the staff and visitors on projects of great topicality. The Yearbook,with its impressive collection of facts and figures, has become the main source of information for individuals and governments, and is quoted in the United Nations family of organizations as the most reliable assembly of data on matters of the nuclear arms race and warfare in general. Since SIPRI does not shy away from commenting on the significance of the data it collects, and since these comments are always in the direction of emphasizing the danger of the arms race and the urgent need for disarmament measures, SIPRI has been criticized from time to time by those who do not like this kind of view. The criticism has come both from the United States, which accused SIPRI of having leftist tendencies, and from the USSR, which claimed that the information about Soviet military developments was not accurate (but without providing corrected data). The two-sided criticism is perhaps a good indication that SIPRI is being objective in its assessments. Some see a danger in SIPRI going beyond its function as collector of factual information and in acquiring an active role on the international disarmament scene. But surely it is legitimate to draw conclusions from one's own work, provided one keeps to the path of objectivity. Not only factual data, but their interpretation, are essential when there is such a dearth of authoritative evaluations on matters affecting the future of mankind.

References

1. O. Nathan and H.Norden, *Einstein on Peace*, Simon & Schuster, 1960, p. 9
2. J.D. Bernal, *The Social Function of Science*, Routledge, 1943, p.400.
3. A Report to the Secretary of War...June 1945, *Bulletin of the Atomic Scientists* vol. I. May 1, 1946, p.2.
4. Alice Kimball Smith, *A Peril and a Hope*, University of Chicago, 1965, p.236.
5. In the issues of "F.A.S. Public Interest Report".
6. Nathan and Norden. *op.cit*, p.395
7. Niels Bohr, For an Open World, *Bulletin of the Atomic Scientists*, vol. VI, July, 1950, p.213.
8. "A Report on the International Control of Atomic Energy", U.S. Department of State, March 1946.
9. "International Control of Atomic Energy: Growth of a Policy", U.S. Department of State, June 1946.
10. The Atomic Scientists Committee of Great Britain, Memo to the UN Atomic Energy Commission, *Bulletin of the Atomic Scientists* vol. I, June 1, 1946, p.6.
11. The International Control of Atomic Energy, Statement by the ASA Council, *Atomic Scientist News*, vol. II, July 1948, p.13.
12. Strontium Hazards, British Atomic Scientists Association, *Bulletin of the*

Atomic Scientists, vol. XIII, June 1957, p.202.

13. Klaus Gottstein, The Contribution of Scientists to the Arms Control and Disarmament Process, *Colloquium on "Science and Disarmament"*, Paris, January 1981.

14. Proceeding of Fourteenth Meeting of the ICSU General Committee, Dubrovnik, September 1981.

15. Roy Innes, The First Months, *Scientific World*, Anniversary Number 1966, p.11

16. A Short Guide to the WFSW, *ibid*, p.37.

17. W.A. Wooster, Some recollections of the WFSW, *ibid*, p.26.

18. *Scientific World*, vol. XIX, No. 3/4, 1975.

19. C.F. Powell, Nuclear Weapons and the Federation, *Scientific World* vol. VIII, No. 1, 1964, p.3.

20. *Scientific World*, vol. XIX, No. 3/4, 1975.

21 .*Atomic Scientists Journal*, vol. 4, No. 2, September 1954, p.33.

22. Bertrand Russell, *Autobiography* vol. III, 1969, p.77.

23. R.W. Clark, *The Life of Bertrand Russell*, Jonathan Cape, 1975, p.542.

24. J. Rotblat, *Scientists in the Quest for Peace*, MIT Press, 1972, p.33.

25. J. Rotblat, *ibid*, p.272.

26. *Pugwash Newsletter*, vol. 15, May 1978, p.106.

27. *Proceedings of the 30th Pugwash Conference*, Breukelen, August 1980, p.14.

28. "World Directory of Peace Research Institutes" (Fourth edition revised) Unesco, 1981.

29. J. Galtung, Peace Research in India, *Bulletin of Peace Proposals*, vol. 2, No. 3, 1971.

30. *Peace Research: Trend Report and World Directory* Unesco, 1979.

31. F.A. Long, *Pugwash Newsletter* Vol 1. No. 2, 1963.

32. D.L. Clarke, *Politics of Arms Control*, Free Press, New York, 1979.

33. I.P. Blishchenko and I.V. Ivanian, in *Unesco Yearbook on Peace and Conflict Studies*, 1980, Unesco, Paris, 1981.

34. Y. Sakamoto, *International Peace Research Newsletter*, vol. XIX, No. 2, 1981.

35. "Stockholm International Peace Research Institute: Organization and Activities", Report by the SIPRI Commission, 1979.

PART IV
Social responsibility of scientists

Chapter 9. Basic principles

John Ziman

Introduction

Why should scientists, of all people, have to be told to be socially responsible? By their upbringing, they ought to be highly responsible individuals, strongly oriented towards communal goals. Every scientist must go through a lengthy social process of advanced education. Every scientist must learn to take part in the intricate social activity of research. Every scientist seeks social recognition of his or her personal reputation from the scientific community. And yet, it must be admitted, these most refined representatives of our civilization seem at times to lack the most elementary sensibility of civilized people – consideration for the feelings and needs of their fellow citizens.

The conventional way out of this paradox is to say that scientists are not properly educated. It is said that they are not taught enough about the importance of value judgements in human affairs. This may well be true, but it applies equally to almost everybody in the modern world. In our democratic, pluralistic societies, we give very little formal public instruction in the basic principles of social responsibility – that is, in the basic principles of ethics, religion and politics. It is hard to believe that the average accountant, or magistrate, or factory manager, or town clerk, has had significantly more exposure to religious education, or church sermons, or party political broadcasts, or coffee house debates on contemporary issues of conscience, than the average lecturer, or medical research associate, or aeronautical engineer. The ethical codes and moral imperatives that bear upon every public issue are so convoluted, diverse and contradictory that we avoid them in academic teaching, and leave them to be acquired by personal experience. Some humanistic disciplines of higher education, such as philosophy and history, do offer specialized training in the analysis of theologies and ideologies, but at a far more advanced and abstract level than is needed for the real moral dilemmas of everyday life.

For this reason, the orthodox wisdom that scientists ought to be specially trained to be socially responsible is not so easy to put into practice. As this book amply demonstrates, scientists are often implicated in issues of great public concern, and may be called on to look deeply into their own hearts in deciding how to act upon them. It is important that they should be aware of this professional hazard, that they should be well informed of the wider social context of their work, and should have had some opportunity to rehearse in advance some of the characteristic dilemmas which they may have to face[1]. But that does not mean that we can provide them with a ready made code of all the basic principles of social responsibility – compounded, presumably, of the Ten Commandments, the Sermon on the Mount, the Koran, the Communist Manifesto, the novels of Tolstoy and Dostoevsky, the plays of George Bernard Shaw and Berthold Brecht, and the writings of selected moral philosophers, from Plato to Bertrand Russell – to meet every eventuality. It is good that scientists should be as well educated as any responsible citizens on such matters, but that is no solution to our paradox.

The real obstacle to social responsibility in science is not that scientists are peculiarly ignorant or insensitive about ethical questions, but that they acquire an armoury of precepts by means of which they defend themselves from the discomforts and dangers of social action. These precepts are not all consistent with one another, but they tangle into a web of rationalizations which scientists pick up in the course of their education, and use automatically to shield their consciences from attack. Of course we all learn to excuse ourselves as best we can when we have behaved antisocially or irresponsibly – although such excuses do not cut much ice with us when offered by other people. The peculiarity of science is that the principles which are used to excuse social irresponsibility have been elevated into a more or less coherent ideology[2]. This ideology is not well founded, but by setting science itself above all other human values it has a powerful influence within the psyche of every scientist and in society as a whole. If we are to understand the real significance of the demand for social responsibility in science, we must analyse these principles and uncover their contradictions and limitations.

Science *"for its own sake"*

The basic principle of this ideology is that the pursuit of knowledge is the most worthy of all human activities. Simply to acquire knowledge is an end in itself. A scientist has a bounden duty to explore the universe to its utmost limits, to leave no stone unturned, to follow up every curious circumstance, and so on, regardless of any other consideration.

This doctrine is usually expressed in the form: research should be undertaken 'for its own sake'. That is to say, science is disconnected from all other human activities or concerns, and has significance only in and for itself. Since there is no implication that science could somehow be bad for itself, this amounts to a total commendation of all research, without reservation. The pursuit of scientific knowledge is thus absolutely justified, as if by a universal Law of Nature or a Commandment of God.

This is clearly a metaphysical doctrine which begs innumerable questions of interpretation and validity. But it is made plausible by a germ of psychological truth. A scientist who is deeply involved in the pursuit of a particular bit of knowledge can become entirely obsessed with this inquiry, as if nothing else in the world existed. In scientific research, as in other highly skilled professions, such as master chess or legal advocacy, excellence of performance calls for total concentration of effort and will for the task in hand. The excellence thus achieved is to be encouraged and admired, if only for its aesthetic value. Considered simply as a life-long game, research is personally beguiling and satisfying for those who can do it well. No wonder many scientists want to be left alone to do their own thing, to follow their own devices, to solve the problems that they set themselves, without interference by outsiders.

There is, however, a world of difference between a professional mystique and an ethical code. Good scientists may lean heavily on a mystique of personal devotion to research to strengthen their resolve and maintain high standards of performance, just as good soldiers lean heavily on the mystique of obedience to orders and personal devotion to duty. But such a mystique is essentially a 'myth', which ignores the social significance of whatever is done in its name. Taken to its extreme, it is as individualistic as Nietsche's cult of the superman, and just as antisocial.

"All science is good science"

In practice, the circular doctrine of science 'for its own sake' is challenged whenever a method of inquiry offends against conventional ethical norms. This was obvious, in the most notorious extreme, when Nazi doctors undertook medical 'research' on the inmates of concentration camps, quite regardless of the additional sufferings their 'experiments' inflicted. At a less sinister level, this is the thread running through all controversies about experiments on human subjects, leading to considerable elaboration of the protocols for obtaining 'informed consent', whenever there might be risk to life and health. The same principle applies to experiments using living animals,[3] at least in any country where the welfare of animals is held to be of genuine moral concern. In all such cases, cruel, dangerous, or otherwise distasteful research techniques cannot be justified simply on the grounds that the acquisition of scientific knowledge is of absolute value, regardless of the circumstances. The blanket principle that 'all science is good science' is seen to be threadbare and unconvincing as soon as it is challenged on a specific issue of this kind.

The argument really hinges about the traditional ends/means axis of moral philosophy. According to this principle, one may justify the use of a relatively dangerous or obnoxious *means*, if this seems the only way to reach highly beneficial *ends*. Unless all our actions are hedged in by absolute imperatives, such as the strict Jain prohibition against killing animals, we are permitted to strike an ethical bargain, in which the potential human benefits of research outweigh the perceived human costs. But this is not a grand contract, licensing all research whatsoever, on the grounds that science has, on the whole, proved of positive value to humanity. The balance of advantage must be determined, and shown to be favourable, for each specific investigation that we propose to undertake. That is to say, we are morally obliged to give conscious attention to the objectives of our research, not simply in terms of its 'scientific merit' but also as a potential contribution to whatever is highly valued in our society, such as individual good health.

Of course any such calculation is exceedingly vague and uncertain. It is at the mercy of the unpredictability of the outcome of every experiment, and of the diversity and incommensurability of our most cherished social values. In many fields of science, the best that can be done is to establish a conventional code embodying a national ethical balance between our slightly dubious means and our somewhat distant and hypothetical ends. It is quite clear, however, from our experience with such codes that research cannot be undertaken just 'for its own sake', since it often requires to be justified on more specific grounds. This basic ideological principle is thus manifestly false.

"Scientific inquiry can know no limits"

An 'innocuous' scientific investigation is not necessarily beyond question. Even if the technique of a research is entirely harmless and inoffensive, it may still be judged morally objectionable on account of its objectives. Although we are always at the mercy of accidental discoveries which might do great harm, we are wise not to deliberately court disaster by directing research into areas where such discoveries are most likely to be made.

Many scientists dispute this opinion. It is held that scientific inquiry can know no limits, and that there is no question that a scientist may not legitimately ask and try to answer. In other words, every scientist should be free to set the goals of his or her research, without external constraint.

This doctrine arises from bitter historical experience. From its beginnnings in the 16th century, science has had to establish itself against other bodies of organized knowledge, such as revealed religion, which have claimed monopoly rights over certain areas of fact and opinion. Freedom of inquiry, which had to be established as of right against arbitrary intellectual authority, is now one of the most cherished freedoms of the open, pluralistic society. There is good, practical, social sense in the principle that nothing is altogether too sacred to be beyond factual observation and sincere criticism. As the epitome of critical rationalism, science has proved itself a peculiarly effective instrument for such investigations, and is therefore regarded as a peculiar danger by the protectors of obscurantism and privilege. Freedom of scientific inquiry is closely linked with freedom of opinion, freedom of speech, freedom in teaching and learning, and other basic human rights which must be constantly defended[4].

Nevertheless, these rights are not absolute. 'Freedom of speech' is not an open licence for slander. The scientific norm of 'organized scepticism' is not an open licence for all research, regardless of the consequences. As we have seen, there is no way of justifying the *means* of inquiry without reference to its *ends*. If those are dangerous, or malicious, or otherwise socially undesirable, then any research directed towards them can properly be called into question.

A scientific investigation is not a purely private act of thought: it is a deliberate social action[5]. An experiment, for example, must usually be elaborately planned, within a rational framework of theory and technique, to pin down a particular item of knowledge. Even though this item of knowledge is not fully known in advance, the intention behind the effort to capture it, and the foreseeable consequences of doing so, are not beyond consideration. We are quite accustomed to judging the objectives of research projects in deciding their relative merits for financial support; the whole peer review process for funding academic science works on this principle.

Of course, a research grant proposal, addressed to a public funding agency, always claims highly desirable and socially beneficial objectives. But that does not exclude the possibility that somebody might secretly conceive a research project with highly undesirable and socially malevolent objectives. The wicked scientist, doing research towards an evil end, such as the mastery of the world, is not only a familiar stereotype of science fiction; he is an imaginative warning of the consequences of the doctrine that scientific inquiry can know no limits.

In such an extreme case, we would all know that it was our heroic duty to frustrate his plans. Normally, the balance of principle between freedom of research and its potentially antisocial consequences is much more delicate and subtle. Is it not possible, for example, that research directed towards achieving a dramatic increase in the human life span would prove so disastrously unsettling, if it were successful, that it should be most definitely discouraged or even forbidden? This is not the place to enter into the immensely difficult technical, political, social and ethical consideration that surrounds such questions[6]. But by recognizing that such questions are entirely legitimate, and should perhaps be asked more searchingly and more often, we show that we cannot accept the scientistic doctrine that scientific inquiry ought *never* to be deliberately limited.

"Scientific information should be open for all"

'Communalism' is the norm commanding that scientific knowledge should be a public resource, open to all. Scientific information should therefore be published in full, at the earliest possible moment. This norm is one of the main foundations of basic science as we have known it, and has its political counterpart in the general laws that protect freedom of publication. But it is not an absolute principle licensing the disclosure of information that could be gravely damaging to innocent individuals or to society at large. It never looked remotely plausible, for example, as a justification of the actions of 'atomic spies' who deliberately betrayed military secrets to foreign countries. Normal legal and political responsibilities cannot be waived in the magic name of science, and the genuine outrage that many scientists feel about the secrecy surrounding military and commercial research can never excuse acts of bad faith and treason. Information that happens to have been gained by scientific methods, or that claims some specially 'scientific' status, is not uniquely privileged as to disclosure or dissemination.

Once more, the extreme case establishes the point in principle, whilst most practical cases are much less clear cut. The classical examples arise in medical research, where there can be a genuine ethical dilemma on a question such as whether to publish preliminary evidence suggesting that some particular treatment might prove effective against some dreadful disease such as cancer. The ultimate benefits to be derived from following the scientific norm of immediate publication may be outweighed by the distress caused by raising false hopes in a large number of very unhappy people[7].

Paradoxically, the conventions of the communication system of science are sometimes invoked *against* the publication of scientific information in a form intelligible to the layman. Scientists are often reluctant to explain briefly the essence of scientific knowledge on a vexed question, because such a statement may have to be expressed in language that lacks the formal precision of a rigorous scientific argument. This prissiness has no epistemological justification; in the final analysis, no scientific statement is logically rigorous and unassailable. When information at stake has serious social relevance – as it might be, for example, in assessing the environmental effects of a chemical agent such as tetra-ethyl lead in petrol – there is a clear responsibility on the scientific expert to bring his or her specialized knowledge into the public arena in a form that is simple enough to be matched up with the less tangible and subjective costs, benefits and values that will also enter into a policy decision.

"Science is true"

The central pillar of scientism is that science tells 'the truth, the whole truth, and nothing but the truth'. Upheld by this doctrine, the scientist feels uniquely powerful and morally unimpeachable. Conflicting assertions of fact or interpretation can be brushed aside. The servant of almighty truth need carry no burden of personal responsibility. Once it has been 'scientifically demonstrated', for example, that black people are intrinsically less intelligent than white people, who would there be to question the practices of apartheid that logically follow from this 'truth'? Indeed, in the long run, if we pursue scientific truth far enough, we may succeed in reducing the notion of moral responsibility itself to a logical paradox in a scientific theory of games and social behaviour.

This positivist doctrine is now thoroughly discredited. Although we have no reason to doubt the practical reliability of well-explored and well tested branches of the natural sciences, we are also aware of the vast extent of our scientific ignorance on most matters of real human significance. No philosopher now supports a 'scientific method' that can carry all before it in every field of knowledge. We must always ask to see the credentials of whatever is offered to us as scientific truth, look at how it is generated and validated, and make up our own minds whether it is more convincing than what we might derive from practical experience, common sense, personal insight, or social tradition.

This comparison with other sources of relevant knowledge becomes more and more apt as we move from the natural to the social sciences[8]. The would-be hard-headed scientist tends to dismiss as nonsense or prejudice every consideration that has not been formulated and superficially tested by self-styled 'scientific' techniques. But to talk about social responsibility at all, one must give adequate weight to ethical, religious, humanitarian or other precepts that cannot be derived from principles akin to the laws of physics. Just what precepts we ought to live by are matters for discussion and rational debate involving many other factors of thought, feeling and experience. It is morally irresponsible – indeed positively amoral – to refuse to enter into such debates just because they can never be decided by appeal to absolute scientific 'truth'.

Of course, a well-attested scientific fact, such as the prevention of dental caries by the fluoridation of public water supplies, is often central to a controversial social issue. The reputation of science and of scientists as the most reliable source of information within particular spheres is to be preserved at all costs. But this reputation for credibility and probity is not to be trusted in human affairs beyond the narrow limits where it has fully proved itself.

"Science is rational and objective"

Scientists present their observations and theories as precisely and logically as possible, to make them credible and convincing to other scientists. Science is a body of *public* knowledge that must continually face critical analysis and crucial tests. To give their discoveries the best chance of preliminary acceptance, scientists adopt a style of formal rationality, insisting that the conclusions they arrive at are logically compelling. This rhetorical device is assisted by an impersonal stance. Scientific papers are written 'objectively' as if the author had no hand in the matter, but were simply reporting events and arguments in which he or she had no particular personal interest.

These conventional features of scientific communication have genuine communal functional value[9]. Science is validated by active consensus. What individual scientists discover or conjecture is subjected to collective criticism until everyone is persuaded that it must indeed be so. In this process, scientific knowledge must be purged of 'subjective' elements that are not universally compelling, or which are only valid from a particular individual point of view. Scientific rationality and objectivity are the terms we apply to the consensuality and inter-subjectivity that this process achieves.

These characteristics of the creation and content of scientific knowledge are often elevated into supreme virtues. Science is held to be *perfectly* rational – i.e. logically irrefutable, from its observational premises to its theoretical conclusions, and *perfectly* objective – i.e. representing the point of view of an abstract intellect free from the defects and vices of any single human mind. Even if it does not go so far as to say that science tells the *whole* truth about life and the world, this doctrine obviously puts the scientist in a very privileged position in every practical argument. By its rationality and objectivity, his science appears to transcend foolish, fallible, corruptible, human interests and concerns. Within his own sphere therefore – say in the engineering design of an industrial production line, or the medical arrangements in support of childbirth – the scientific expert is easily persuaded that the 'scientific' solution to every problem is much the best possible.

In reality, science grows by processes that are far more fallible, far more subjective, far less disinterested, far less logically watertight than this ideology would allow. Reliable as it may be in most of its main lines of argument, and in numerous details, science nevertheless maintains many errors of fact and interpretation. Much of its rationality is superficial – little better than special pleading for an interpretation that is far from proven by the evidence. Much of its objectivity is spurious – little better than a depersonalized abstract formulation of the prejudices and interests unconsciously shared by a particular group of scientists working in a particular field. Innumerable "crackpot" theories of health and disease have been rationalized by medical science on the slenderest evidence. Deplorable 19th century theories of racial superiority, strongly influenced by the doctrines of social Darwinism and highly advantageous to the politics of imperialism, were supposed to be scientifically rational and objective. Rather than proclaiming such doctrines, it is the responsibility of the scientist to show that they grossly misuse the authority of science to rationalize particular social positions.

Although scientific knowledge on a particular point may well be the most 'rational' and 'objective' available, these qualities must be proved specifically by reference to the evidence and the arguments, not just taken for granted. In any case, these may not be virtues that ought to claim automatic deference in all human affairs. The scientist who depends solely upon 'scientific method' for his or her opinions tends to adopt an inhumane attitude which is not sufficiently responsive to historical circumstances, moral values, the diversity of human aspirations and other untidy realities that cannot be 'rationalized' and 'objectified' out of the way.

"Science is neutral"

The basic objectivity of science frees it from close attachment to the interests of particular social groups. It can scarcely be said, for example, that the law of the conservation of energy has been devised so as to specially favour the institutions of capitalism, and that socialists need an alternative theory of thermodynamics which will support their political views. Science, we insist, is 'neutral': it cannot be enlisted permanently on either side in a social conflict, although it may prove a very effective ally for any party with whose policy it is naturally consistent. The neutrality of science is a bit like that of the Angels, on whose side it is always advantageous to be.

But the strength of this doctrine obviously depends on the degree to which science is genuinely detached from particular social interests. This is a controversial issue in the sociology of knowledge, where it is pointed out, for example, that the historical development of the physics of energy was in fact closely linked to the rise of capitalism and the Industrial Revolution. Although the laws of thermodynamics would remain as valid as ever under a socialist regime, the central role of these laws in 19th century physics was a significant factor in the process of industrialization, and was not an 'objective' consequence of the purely internal development of the subject. Thus, the inventory of scientific knowledge available for social polemic in any particular epoch is not altogether 'neutral' as between the various conflicting parties.

This applies particularly when research is undertaken deliberately to settle some controversial issue. It is extremely difficult to phrase the questions to be answered, and to choose the technique of inquiry, so as not to favour one or the other party. Although many components of 'objective' science may be involved in the investigation, the circumstances in which the research is being undertaken, the sources of sponsorship, the terms of reference given, the investigators and the form in which the results are reported, all have some influence on the outcome. It must be remembered that the relative objectivity of science does not derive from its sophisticated techniques, advanced theories, and rationally ordered argumentation: it is the product of the social process of creative criticism within the scientific community, which minimizes subjectivity and the influence of particular interests. Thus, the scientist who naively believes that science is neutral in political and economic conflicts is very ill-prepared to bear the social responsibilities that these conflicts often demand.

"The scientific attitude"

Another major doctrine of scientism is that scientists, as a group, have special personal qualities. They have a 'scientific attitude' which embodies such intellectual and moral virtues as logicality, open-mindedness, curiosity, detachment, scepticism, independence of authority, etc., etc.

They should therefore be given a special place in society, with special responsibility for crucial social decisions.

This myth 'personalizes' the qualities of rationality, objectivity, etc., of scientific knowledge in the abstract. If science has these properties to a very high degree, then it is assumed that those who produce science must be correspondingly gifted. But this is nonsense. Scientific knowledge is a *social* product, and may therefore turn out far more logical, or unprejudiced, or original than any of the individuals who have co-operated to generate it. The output of a motorcar factory is a far better vehicle than could possibly be designed and constructed by any single motor mechanic!

It is true that scientists must learn certain conventions and norms in order to co-operate and compete in the scientific manner. A professional research worker soon learns from experience that it is more effective to argue coolly than to indulge in personal polemics, and that it is advisable to anticipate all possible critical objections before publishing a new idea. Within the scientific community a delicate balance is often achieved between imagination and orthodoxy, between the wisdom of age and the enthusiasm of youth, between institutional authority and individual autonomy. It is possible that the way in which the 'republic of science' conducts its own affairs might be followed to advantage by other social groups. But these are essentially professional mores, which do not necessarily fit scientists for active roles in society at large.

There are, of course, scientists, such as J. Robert Oppenheimer, who have given inspired leadership to their colleagues. Most research organizations are reasonably well managed, and science policy is as well conducted as most other government policies. But there is no foundation for the technocratic notion that scientists and other technical experts should be given special authority to determine general public policy. Scientists are often clever in peculiar ways, but otherwise they are usually quite ordinary people with quite ordinary talents. Their professional training and work experience does not fit them particularly well for high responsibility in public affairs. They have seldom had to persuade large numbers of people to support them in an uncertain enterprise; they are seldom skilled in the arts of bargaining and compromise; they have seldom had to take large decisions under severe pressures of time and ignorance; they are seldom even well informed on the larger circumstances of history, law, religion, economics, etc. within which political decisions have to be made.

The scientist who hides away in the peace and quiet of his laboratory, consoling himself with the belief that he is engaged in an honourable and beneficial profession, is not behaving quite irresponsibly. He may have judged, modestly and realistically, that effective social action calls for knowledge, insights, experience and fortitude that he does not have, and cannot afford the effort to acquire. It is not enough to be politically "enlightened", or to make an occasional gesture, like signing a manifesto or letter of protest. One must shed the arrogant notion that scientists are much wiser than politicians in the matters of peace and war, or poverty and wealth, and get down to the thankless business of understanding what is going on and trying to make it go right.

"Science has nothing to do with politics"

In its early days, science had to establish itself in a society riven with political and religious conflicts. In some countries, even now, it faces oppression from tyrannical governments. It is prudent, in such circumstances, to insist that scientific knowledge is strictly objective and neutral, and that the professional work of scientists – like the work of nurses and taxi drivers, say – is of no particular political significance. Research, we say, is just a specialized technical trade; scientists are just ordinary law-abiding citizens; learned societies and universities are just organizations for co-ordinating and advancing this innocent, useful activity.

The knowledge of what happened to science under totalitarian regimes fully justifies a general policy of 'keeping politics out of science'. The traditional norms of science cannot survive in the poisonous atmosphere of violent social conflict. A scientific institution, such as a university, that has been taken over by an anti-intellectual junta of colonels has lost its meaning and might as well be left for dead. It is obviously foolish to provoke such disasters by getting involved in politics without good cause.

But this sound practical maxim has been elevated into the doctrine that science has nothing to do with politics. This doctrine cannot, of course, apply to the response of individual scientists to the ordinary demands of citizenship. They must accept the responsibilities of life, like everybody else. It is morally offensive to suggest that they ought to have special social privileges because they are studying the eternal verities, or because they happen to belong to a professional community that transcends national frontiers. An elite of scientists who were not answerable to the laws of any nation would be just as socially irresponsible as a multinational corporation that paid no taxes and obeyed no safety regulations.

A real danger of pretending that 'science' can be separated entirely from 'politics' is that it inhibits the exercise of collective social responsibility by formal scientific organizations such as learned societies. Like the parallel doctrine that scientific knowledge is 'objective' and 'neutral', it can be used to conceal the intimate connection between research and policy, between thought and action.

This connection between science and politics is obvious in the area of 'science policy'. Modern science is not a self-contained social group like a minor religious sect; its resources come so completely from public funds, or from large private corporations, that it must be institutionally concerned about how these resources are supplied. In practice, even the most obstinately 'non-political' scientific societies find that they must express a point of view on many controversial political issues relating to science, technology, the environment, education, etc. Fearful as they may be of the dangers of getting too heavily committed to one side or another in such controversies, the leaders of the scientific community know that their formal institutions cannot afford to appear totally unconcerned about matters in which they are so very closely involved.

Indeed, science is not simply one of the institutions *of* society; it is itself a social institution. The norms and conventions of scientific life are not independent of the norms and conventions of society at large. For example, freedom of communication, which is so essential *within* science, cannot be distinguished in practice or principle from general freedom of speech, publication, assembly, travel, teaching, etc. Modern science grew up during the period when these social and political rights were being formulated and safeguarded by law, and is designed to function within an open pluralistic society where these rights are respected in practice. It is hard to believe that science as we know and value it could long survive in a society with contrary norms – where, for example, scientists were not free to communicate their discoveries and to criticize each other's research in public and private[10].

In other words, science is in politics up to its neck. For its very own existence, it must be ready to fight actively for the human rights of scientists – and hence, without distinction or privilege, for the human rights of all other citizens. The prudential acquiescence of the German scientific community to Hitler in the 1930's was a spiritual betrayal that availed it nothing; cowering behind the pretence of having 'nothing to do with politics', it did not make even a gesture against a social philosophy that was bent on destroying it[11]. One must assume that scientists take some pride in their profession – otherwise they should get out and do something more worthy, such as nursing or taxi driving. A doctrine that inhibits scientists from acting collectively, through their own professional institutions, in defence of the long term interests of that profession, is thus peculiarly irresponsible and antisocial.

"The consequences of a discovery cannot be foreseen"

The outcome of research cannot be known precisely in advance; if it could be, then there would be no need to do the research. Scientific discoveries are often hit upon by accident; but if they could be arrived at intentionally, they would not be discoveries. The irreducible element of uncertainty in science is often called upon to free scientists from responsibility for the consequences of their research.

But the same principle applies to every action that we take in life. However carefully I plan, I cannot be sure that what I do will cause no harm. My decision to set out for work five minutes earlier than usual may bring death to the child who runs out in front of my car. Through the person whom I accidentally meet at a party and subsequently marry, I may become the parent of a terrorist assassin. All moral philosophy takes account of the unintended consequences of our actions, beyond a close horizon of rational foresight. It is only what we do knowingly, with our eyes open to the outcome, for which we must bear the responsibility.

The factor of uncertainty in science provides no general excuse for social irresponsibility. As already pointed out, research itself is a deliberate activity, undertaken with conscious purpose. Even in highly academic science, most research projects must claim definite objectives to gain material support. The scientist who drafts a research grant application in terms of such objectives cannot turn round later and deny any responsibility for the obvious consequences of achieving them.

In 'knowledge-oriented' fundamental research, these objectives may be so indirectly related to human affairs that the responsibility for a scarcely imaginable outcome is minimal. Ernest Rutherford, for example, cannot justly be blamed because his discoveries in nuclear physics eventually led to Hiroshima. But the work of the great majority of scientists nowadays is 'mission-oriented'. Their research is designed to answer questions with specific ends. They are employed by organizations seeking military power or commercial profits, or public welfare, or other familiar practical goals.

Science nowadays is not just the pursuit of knowledge that might one day, just possibly, turn out to be useful. On the contrary, scientific research is largely undertaken as the most effective means of reaching *chosen* industrial, commercial, military, social or political goals which are beyond the scope of present-day understanding or technique. Science is seen as an instrument for 'solving problems' – i.e. as a means of warding off the dark dangers of misfortune, and arriving successfully at a desired future state. No scientist employed voluntarily in such an enterprise can deny some personal responsibility for what comes of it, just as no member of a gang of thieves can get away with the plea that he didn't know what they were up to and that he only went along for the ride.

"Scientists are servants of society"

Since the great majority of scientists are employed by large organizations, they are strongly tempted to unload all the blame for what comes of their research on the policies of those organizations. In other words, they plead the irresponsibility of the subordinate for what is done in obedience to orders. Often enough this plea may not be unreasonable: "Should I have really risked my whole career just because I happened to think that our new cosmetic lotion was not justifying the advertising claims for it?" Sometimes, on the other hand, it may be grossly immoral not to 'blow the whistle', regardless of personal consequences, on some socially dangerous development in a research programme[12]. That is to say, obedience to orders is not an absolute shield against personal blame, but depends very much on the circumstances. And although many of the standard examples of the need for social responsibility in science revolve around this sort of question, they really belong to the much wider issue of personal responsibility in general. This is a traditional issue of moral philosophy, and law. The responsibility of the research scientist in such cases is not different in principle from, say, the responsibility of the soldier for acts of terror carried out under orders from above, or the duty of a company accountant not to acquiesce in the presentation of fraudulent accounts.

The whole argument of this chapter would, of course, be invalid or irrelevant in a society where everybody was in duty bound always to obey the orders of higher authority. In such a society, the only principle of social responsibility would be that this duty must be performed to the utmost of one's individual powers, regardless of the consequences. Although it is not difficult to find statements along these lines from various public figures in various countries, this servile doctrine is so contrary to the elementary realities of a complex industrial society that it cannot be taken seriously, except as a deliberate attack on the spirit of licensed dissent that animates the scientific enterprise and gives scientists their personality and individuality.

"Scientists are just technical workers"

Organizations that employ scientists usually prefer them *not* to be concerned about the social consequences of their research. The job of the scientist is supposed to be simply to provide *technical* information and advice for the top policy makers who decide the commercial, military or political objectives of the enterprise. As the catch-phrase puts it:

"scientists should be *on tap*, not *on top*". Having deflated the claim that scientists are peculiarly well fitted to take such decisions, we are in no position to insist that they *ought* to have more influence of this kind than they are in fact permitted, which varies considerably from organization to organization and from country to country.

But the supposed distinction between the limited 'technical' input of the scientist and the more general policy-making inputs of other members of a large bureaucratic organization is not valid. It is simply a reflection of the myth that science itself is perfectly objective and neutral, from which it is deduced that scientists must be incapable of taking into consideration the human values and other subjective interests that enter into any policy decision in the real world. The principle that 'scientists are just technical workers' is often used to excuse them from any responsibility for the consequences of such decisions – even though these may depend very heavily on their research results or professional advice – but it is really no more than the obverse of the doctrine that science transcends the realities of the everyday world and is quite divorced from normal human concerns. It is thus a very convenient doctrine for those who want to exploit the technical capabilities of scientists without raising questions about the morality of the enterprise in which they are engaged.

"Science cannot be blamed for its misapplication"

We have now reached the heart of the matter. The fundamental question for the socially responsible scientist is whether the *search* for knowledge can be entirely separated from its later *use*. The ideology of scientism is shot through with fallacies and contradictions that can only be avoided by making a rigid distinction between the 'scientist' who makes discoveries and the 'technologist' who applies these discoveries in the form of useful devices and techniques.

A century ago, this distinction would not have been inept. In the heyday of academic science, there was little experience of deliberately organized 'research and development' to solve specific problems, or to achieve pre-conceived practical goals. A simple 'discovery' conception of science was appropriate.

But the world has been changed by science, and science itself has changed in the process. The 'instrumental' conception of science, as a positive means of getting things done, is now a practical reality manifest in numerous mature social institutions, such as industrial research laboratories and government scientific agencies. And a glance at any of these institutions shows that they are no longer based upon a sharp division of labour between 'scientists' and 'technologists', between research to gain knowledge and the application of knowledge for practical use. It no longer makes sense to suppose that these two different conceptions of science are ministered to by distinct professions, carrying out quite distinct social roles. We can only understand the science/technology complex if we accept that the discovery of knowledge and its application are merely different phases in a single social activity, different aspects of a single, coherent social institution.

Is it really necessary to give chapter and verse for a social fact which stares us in the face every time we open a popular scientific journal or switch on a television programme about 'science'? Our most self-consciously academic institutions in the most exploratory scientific disciplines, such as cosmology or molecular biology, are caught up in projects with specific military or industrial objectives. Our hardest headed practical enterprises in engineering and medicine employ basic research scientists charged with the pursuit of knowledge almost for its own sake. In apparatus, personnel, theoretical foundations, education, professional societies, managerial structure, funding arrangements, and many other features, there is such a close convergence and interpenetration of science and technology that one can no longer distinguish them by their social roles and social responsibilities.

Science is no longer an elite vocation that can shrug off its responsibilities by reference to a traditional professional ideology. Within the great complex of the R&D system, individuals undertake innumerable different, often highly specialized jobs. Some have great freedom to follow interesting lines of research wherever these seem to lead, with very little external control. Others must co-ordinate their work very closely, in large teams directed towards prescribed goals. Just as there is this wide range of personal autonomy within the research professions, so there must be a wide range of degrees of personal responsibility for what is being attempted and what has been achieved by research. The social responsibilities of scientists and technologists are as varied in character and weight as those of other citizens in other walks of life – from those of the judge or senior civil servant, say, to those of the taxi driver or barrowboy.

Basic ethical principles tell us all plainly that we have a duty to be aware of the extent of our responsibilities, as they bear upon us in our individual lives, whether as citizens, as parents, or in the exercise of our calling, and to take them up to the utmost of our strength. Whether they like it or not, this duty now rests particularly heavily upon scientists. There is great public concern about many of the effects of science upon society and upon humanity as a whole. Out of this concern there now flows the demand that scientists *must* be more careful, *must* be more responsible, in what they do, for it could bring us all to disaster. Of all conceivable disasters that might overwhelm mankind, nuclear war is far and away the most likely and terrible. Unwittingly, perhaps, the scientists made such a disaster possible; inexorably perhaps, they are driven into activities that make such a disaster ever more threatening. But whether or not they should be individually blamed for what they have collectively done for the world, not one of them can now cast off a personal responsibility to think about these matters and to act to make this disaster a little less probable.

References

1.   J.M. Ziman, *Teaching and Learning about Science & Society*, Cambridge University Press, 1980.
2.   H. Verhoog, *Science and the Social Responsibility of Natural Scientists*, Doctoral Dissertation, Leiden, 1980. This work, which goes much more deeply into the connections between various philosophies of science and varius ideologies of the social role of science, contains a very complete bibliography on the subject of this chapter.
3.   D. Morley, Dumb Animals and Vocal Minorities, *The Sensitive Scientist*, SCM Press, London 1978.
4.   Council for Science and Society, *Scholarly Freedom and Human Rights* Barry Rose, London 1977.
5.   J.M. Ziman, What are the Options: Social Determinants of Personal Research Plans, *Minerva* (to be published)
6.   G. Holton, & R.S. Morrison, (eds)., *Limits of Scientific Inquiry*, W.W. Norton, New York: 1979.
7.   D. Morley, *op.cit.*, 1978.
8.   J.M. Ziman, *Reliable Knowledge*, Cambridge University Press, 1978.
9.   J.M. Ziman, *Public Knowledge*, Cambridge University Press, 1968.
10.   J.M. Ziman, Human Rights and the Policy of Science, *The Bulletin of the Atomic Scientist*, vol. 34, No.8, 1978.
11.   J. Haberer, *Politics and the Community of Science*, van Nostrand Reinhold, New York, 1969.
12.   American Association for the Advancement of Science, *Scientific Freedom and Responsibility*, AAAS, Washington, D.C. 1975.

Chapter 10. Scientists in the contemporary world

Ivan Supek and Ignacy Malecki

Introduction

In the current fervent developments and struggles for power, science has become a fateful participant with the potential for both beneficial and harmful effects. The technological applications of science are very much evident, but the role of scientists in public affairs and their posture in relation to ruling ideologies are no less important. Only after the complex structure of mutual influences has been diagnosed, can the question of the scientists' responsibility acquire proper significance.

According to convention, the job of the scientists is to find out about "facts", how to obtain a better image of the universe, but without going into questions of social action. The celebrated "objectivism" of science carries with it a corrolary: ethical indifference. Edward Teller, the father of the H-bomb, when defending the continuation of nuclear tests, said that it is the duty of scientists to find out about all the potentials of a new discovery, but it is the duty of the politicians, the people's representatives, to decide what to apply and what to leave out. While this may be a very comfortable standpoint to take, it is bound to arouse uneasiness with most people when they consider those who are "elected representatives of the people". A model democracy would not relieve the scientists of the burden of responsibility; man is responsible for his actions, particularly if he belongs to the few who have the ability to assess, better than anybody else, the consequences of discoveries and the implications of their applications.

Gone is the vision of the lonely scientist bent on penetrating the unknown, seeking truth and reaching out for the limits of the possible. On the one hand, science and technology has grown into a mass profession dominated by team work and the mounting control of scientific activity by state and corporate interests. On the other hand, the centre of gravity of scientific pursuit has moved from basic research to the technological application of knowledge. This is especially the case in military R&D.

The idealistic image of the scientist as an independent agent, free to pursue chosen research out of intellectual curiosity, no longer fits contemporary reality. If there are still individual scientists who have retained some of their old privileges, they seem rather to be exceptions confirming the rule. And the rule is institutionalization and regimentation of science and technology. Scientists are subjected to compartmentaliza- tion which curtails mobility and deprives them of larger insight into the cummulative effort of science and technology. They are largely subordin- ated to managerial bureaucracy and discipline. This is certainly the case for the vast majority of the military R&D establishment.

Thus, an effort to infuse social responsibility into the scientific community has to address itself to the moral and ethical issues of individual scientists and even more to the structural environmental realities which tend to restrict the autonomy and the independent position of the scientists.

The basic concepts of the scientists' responsibility, considered from a variety of points of view, were discussed in chapter 9. Here we shall attempt to answer two specific questions: responsibility for what, and to whom.

Responsibility for what?

Professional responsibility

First of all the scientist is responsible for his scientific activity, for honesty in scientific research and for its objective presentation. This is the responsibility related to the job. Ethical problems arise when the scientist is subject to external influences, requiring him to abandon the truth or to leave it unsaid. This ethical conflict has occurred, in more or less obvious ways, in different historical periods, under different political systems and in different scientific disciplines. In the time of Giordano Bruno and Galileo, the conflict carried with it the threat of being burnt on the stake; in our time it is sometimes the cause of "civil death", by the removal from the place of scientific work and by preventing the presentation of points of view. At present, such conflicts arise mainly in the social sciences, and are connected with ideology and assessment of existing socio-economic relations. Nevertheless, external pressure can also be exerted in other fields of science, when the opinion of a scientist has an important bearing on practical activity, particularly if the scientist is appointed as a high ranking expert.

It is a comforting thought that even in ideological or religious conflicts, natural sciences, technology and medicine remain generally the same everywhere; not only does this contribute to better mutual understanding, but it also makes for the necessary co-operation between different countries. However, such a degree of identity has not been reached in the social sciences, particularly not in historiography and sociology. Considering the complexity of man, and the many degrees of freedom with which he operates, research in social phenomena cannot be expected to lead to impersonal deterministic laws, like those in astronomy. Not only is individual behaviour in many cases unpredictable or indeterminable, but even the judgement of a historian or sociologist about events depends very much on personal taste and habits, or on the opinions of his environment. For this reason, different approaches and syntheses will be seen in the social sciences even if the same criteria of truthfulness have been used. More complete knowledge of a historical or contemporary event can be gained only by examinations and reconstructions from different, sometimes opposing angles. The principle of tolerance, so much needed in our conflict-ridden world, is indispensable for the synthesis of various historiographic, sociological and aesthetic investigations into a world science. By respecting alien tastes and approaches developed in different civilizations, we promote a general sense of the world community. Without tolerance, science would have never attained its present standing. Such a principle most strongly confirms man's personal dignity, freedom and imaginativeness, at the same time confirming the general equality of human beings.

Responsibility for consequences

Most controversial is the question to what extent is the scientist responsible for the way the results of his work are to be used. Modern objectivism, the orientation towards a "pure" universe, does not favour the growth of socially committed people. For centuries natural scientists have been regarded as eccentrics and cranks, until various laws of gravity and thermodynamics, and the chemical, electric and nuclear forces were discovered and included into the world's assets, while at the same time education was spreading over the world in an undreamed of manner. But even during this epoch-making transformation, the researchers' ethical indifference, born in the previous centuries, persisted everywhere.

It is the responsibility for the consequences of scientific activity that gave birth to the Pugwash Movement, originating from the Russell-Einstein Manifesto (see Appendix 1).

Responsibility for dissemination

It is the moral duty of the scientist to make the results of his work part of mankind's knowledge by publishing them. Usually, no major troubles are encountered in publishing results of fundamental research. The situation is, however, different in applied research intended for use in industry or for military purposes. In such cases, the moral duty of the scientist is often presented in the reverse way, i.e. to keep his work secret. A researcher who makes the results available to anybody interested is treated as a traitor of the company or the state. It is not realistic to think that this situation can be changed substantially, nevertheless an effort should be made to minimize the number of research projects which are covered by a publication ban. This applies particularly to the results of fundamental research which are not published, in order to be on the "safe side", for the only reason that it had been sponsored by industrial or military institutions. The essential issue here is the admission for publication of a diversity of opinion, since such diversity is one of the prime movers of the advance of science. the limitation of censorship power is one of the indispensable conditions for scientists to be able to fulfil their social responsibility.

Popularization of scientific achievements is a different matter. Not every scientist is a good popularizer, but frequently the eminent scientists are the most suitable for the presentation of the issues of contemporary science to the public at large. The existing potential of scientific and cultural institutions, as well as of publications and the media, is not sufficiently utilized for this purpose. A powerful stimulus could be provided by specialized and other periodicals if they devoted part of their space to the role of the various scientific disciplines in the modern world. It would also be important to pay more attention to the situation of scholars and the role of institutions in some countries. From its very beginning science was a common human enterprise, and no scholar can be indifferent to the conditions in which other colleagues work. Several scientific periodicals, such as *Nature* and *Science*, regularly devote several pages to such issues, and it would be desirable for other science journals, to do the same. The defenders of "scientific purity" should be reminded of the fact that the virgin Science has been raped innumerable times, and that redemption from sin can be achieved only by repenting and improving. For the sake of better information, intellectuals with different opinions and from different regions shoud be invited to expose their views. Some scientific periodicals include relevant general topics, but only if they contribute to state or party propaganda; this does more harm than good.

Educational responsibility

Transferring knowledge and research methods to younger scientific workers is a noble duty of the scientist. Responsibility in this field rests formally on the scientists teaching at universities, but these scientists do not always consider teaching as a major duty. At the same time, many scientists employed outside universities appear to be exempt from this responsibility. In some countries attempts are being made to stimulate these scientists to take part in educational activities, some research institutions train their research workers using their scientific teams.

The educational function is not limited only to transferring knowledge and skill. Senior scientists are also highly responsible for shaping the moral attitudes of their disciples and co-workers. This requires a major input of time and good will, but it is essential for the proper development of science in the country.

Responsibilities to whom?

Personal responsibility

A range of responsibilities follows from absolute ethical standards; these must be observed by every honest man, but the scientist must be particularly sensitive to them in view of his social position. Primarily, this is the responsibility to his own conscience, and relates to honesty in scientific work and to its consequences.

In this connection, the notion of "academic spirit", well known by scientists employed at universities, should be mentioned. Indeed, ethics does not have to be grafted upon science from outside, for it is incorporated in the scientific enterprise. The "academic spirit" is not something exclusive or esoteric; it stresses the moral requirements of everyday life but more forcefully. When candidates for the doctor's degree take their oath, promising "always to adhere to scientific truth and to work for the benefit of all mankind" (the wording used at Zagreb University), formal emphasis is given to those principles that must guide every honest man.

Social responsibility

The scientist is not merely an observer of the reality; he is also a creator of it. Scientists are citizens with the same responsibilities as other people, but their knowledge acquired over millennia (and becoming more and more abstract and inaccessible to lay population), puts them into an exceptional position, particularly when the application of this knowledge may mean life or death.

Social responsibility is one of the consequences of research. In relation to the nation, it covers the responsibility to ensure its undisrupted existence and development. In this connection, a conflict may arise associated with research projects oriented towards the country's defence. The policies of defence and of aggression are hardly distinguishable. It should be recalled here that some scientists worked in good faith to contribute to the defeat of the Nazi war machine but later they were not brave enough (with very few exceptions) to abandon military research. But since the scientists, like those in Pugwash, consider disarmament as the key issue of the present time, they should call for a reduction of the participation of scientists in military projects to the minimum necessary to defend the existence of the nation. The sense of responsibility of every scientist should be to find out where the boundary lies.

Pasteur said once that science does not have its native country, but the scientist has. This could be interpreted in two ways: one, that a scientist must serve his country, and the other, in a more cosmopolitan way, that science is his real country. It would not be in the international spirit to deny people their patriotism. A shallow cosmopolitan approach might only accelerate the flow of intellectuals from impecunious conditions to wealthy and powerful empires.

From the social point of view, of importance is the creative role of science in culture. A particular duty falls here on the representatives of the social sciences who develop the conscience of national culture and tradition.

Scientists fostered the spirit of universality and promoted universal research procedures despite violent political and ideological differences. The community of scientists, linked by widespread publications, has over centuries and millennia been the ferment of the world community. Without the common culture to which various arts contributed considerably, it would be more difficult, even impossible, to establish a language understood by different civilizations and social systems. The works of Imhotep, Shakespeare, Darwin or Bach are accessible and intelligible to all nations. Science and art developed these universal structures most powerfully, at the same time providing the scope for freedom and imagination.

Responsibility in relation to the scientific community

The present-day scientist is linked through numerous ties with the scientific community within which he works and conducts his creative activity. He is thus responsible in relation to his social group in the same way as other professions. However, in addition there are certain aspects specific to scientists. One of these is the educational duty and the need to co-operate in the shaping of the collective moral attitude of the scientific community. This concerns relations in everyday work, and the promotion of positive scientific criticism to help in the elimination of dishonesty and humbug in the activities of the whole scientific community, and it is necessary to take into account not only individual responsibility but that of the scientific community as a whole. Depending on the organizational structure and the size of the scientific staff, this can be the responsibility of the scientific workers employed in a given unit (university, institute) or the members of a social or state organization (scientific society, academy of sciences).

The kinds of individual responsibility mentioned above concern also scientific communities. It is the duty of the community itself to take care of the scientific and moral level of its members. In this connection, it might be advisable to establish courts of honour, as it is the case at some universities and academies of sciences, with the task to admonish offenders of basic principles of academic behaviour. The establishment of an international court of honour could contribute to the strengthening of moral consciousness among scientists. Such initiative might come from the Pugwash Movement, and the international court of honour might function under the aegis of Unesco. Moreover, Unesco might issue a recommendation that all universities introduce an oath, binding newly promoted doctors to adhere to truth, foster solidarity, and work for the common good.

The degree of responsibility depends to a large extent on the authority which the given institution or organization enjoys in society and among decision-makers. Usually, the voice of an institution sounds more loudly and convincingly than that of an individual (with the exception of the most outstanding scientists) and hence assumes a larger responsibility. This responsibility concerns the relations both inside the community and vis à vis the public. Among the latter, of particular importance is the scientific expertise offered to state institutions at different levels. In what follows we shall discuss the range of responsibility of individual scientists, scientific institutions and organizations in relation to state authorities.

It is theoretically possible to speak about the collective responsibility of the scientific community of the whole country. Such responsibility appears clearly at times of particular distress to the country such as war, natural disaster, or acute economic crisis. For example, during the dramatic socio-economic changes in Poland in 1980-81, it was the subject of extensive discussion whether or not the scientists had been responsible for the heavy errors committed in the country's economic policy.

Such a global responsibility is, however, ill-defined, since the scientific community is highly non-homogeneous and represents diversified and often contending opinions. But at the time of a national ordeal, the community frequently unites to achieve common goals.

Responsibility of decision-makers

Problems related to the activity of governmental scientific experts are discussed in another chapter of the book. Here, we shall consider only the general features of the responsibility of scientists related to decision-making processes.

Scientists can play definite roles in these processes, namely:
a. they can be members of managing bodies at various levels;
b. they can perform the function of permanent advisers to the decision-makers;
c. they can prepare expert opinion for the decision-makers, either at their request or in response to initiatives from other bodies.

In each of these functions, the scientist should honestly fulfill his task, in the same way as every honest citizen given a minute portion of the country's power. However, the possession of specialized knowledge and the scientific method, and the obligations following from this, impose upon the scientists' additional responsibility and duty in performing functions related to state power. One of these is objectivity in formulating opinions, notwithstanding the pressure groups of the decision-makers. Over the past 200 years, various rulers used the authority of scientists to convince public opinion, or members of parliament, that their activities were right. In these cases, the opinion of the scientist played only a "decorative role", the conclusions had to coincide with the will of the decision-makers. However, this kind of co-operation of the scientist with decision-makers contradicts the elementary professional ethics and personal responsibility.

Another point is that the scientist employed as an adviser is capable of complex and long-term forecasts of the results of the decisions to be made. Such predictions are particularly important when they concern environmental and social relations.

In order to increase the participation of scientists in reaching important decisions, and to increase their responsibility, it would be important for them to become involved in governmental institutions, as recognized representatives of international science, sometimes as elected delegates of universities, academies, or scientific societies. It is important that research institutes should take part in determining the general trends and directions of development, and that the scientific participation should not be reduced to counselling ministers or educating specialists. The scientific advisers in government institutions must be backed by scientific criteria and the achievements of science.

If a scientist appointed by a decision-maker is replaced by a representative of a scientific institute or organization, the latter becomes partially responsible by the very fact of choosing its representative. In practice, the representative of a community is not always a better adviser than an individually appointed scientist, because of the additional limitation following from having to take into account the opinions of the given community. Expertise is usually developed by teams of scientists who bear the collective responsibility for the proposed decisions.

International responsibility

The fact that science recognizes no frontiers, and that scientists are firmly linked with the international scientific community, imposes an international responsibility. This responsibility follows also from the observation that every scientist acquires something from the world's store of knowledge, and in return makes his contribution. This is one of the reasons why international co-operation is an indispensable condition for the development of science. This responsibility is not limited only to the scientific consequences of the co-operation; it also concerns the possibility offered by contacts between scientists, in their effort to relax political tensions. Pugwash activities are perhaps the most spectacular example of this. Scientific meetings, conferences and symposia, and participation in them, should be recognized as an important part of responsible scientific work. These contacts are often limited by financial difficulties of research institutions, for this reason their importance should be adequately presented to grant-giving bodies.

An important role in international co-operation falls to non-governmental international scientific organizations; primarily to the international scientific unions which are members of the International Council of Scientific Unions (ICSU). Their plenary sessions are attended by scientists of member countries, and they are responsible for giving new impetus to international co-operation and improving their efficiency.

The organization within which science is strictly tied to political affairs is the United Nations Organization and its specialized agencies, chiefly Unesco, which is responsible for initiating and promoting scientific research and for organizing large research projects. This activity is vital for the development of science and improving the conditions of scientific communities throughout the world. For this reason, sharing in the common responsibility of scientists for what is happening in United Nations organizations is theoretically beyond any doubt. In practice, however, scientists have to fight for their representation not only in the Secretariats of these organizations but also on the governing General Assemblies. It is the usual practice that during these Assemblies the issues of science are discussed and decided by ministerial officials of Member Countries who must bear the responsibility for erroneous decisions. The aim of national and international scientific communities, and of bodies responsible for science policy, should be to change this state of affairs. The responsibility of scientists on the international forum can be implemented only if they themselves participate in the decision-making.

Responsibility of scientists in developing countries

This is a very extensive issue, discussed in numerous reports and at the UNCSTD Conference held in Vienna in 1979. Here, only some problems related to the responsibility of scientists will be mentioned, taking into account the specific features of the work of scientists in developing countries.

The key problem involves the influence of the scientist on the whole society, including the scientific community within which he works. The behaviour of the scientist has, as a normal and habitual standard, a much wider significance here than it does in highly developed countries. At the same time, due to the lamentable shortage of scientific staff, the scientist must educate co-workers, often starting from the very beginning. In many cases, the scientist is the only representative of his discipline in the scientific community. He has no opportunity to discuss scientific problems and to face constructive criticism. Thus, he depends much more on self-control in his scientific work and on limited international contacts.

The culture-creative and popularizing role of scientists is more vital in developing countries than anywhere else. The scientists whose task is to investigate and record disappearing traditions and customs bear a special responsibility. No less is the responsibility of the national or foreign scientists charged with the function of governmental advisers. In general, these scientists enjoy higher authority in the community and can exert more influence on governmental decisions than is the case in highly developed countries. Very difficult situations may arise, however, because the scientist enjoying governmental confidence has to decide whether to consider the country's interests as a whole, instead of forcibly promoting research in fields in which he is particularly interested but which may have only a prestige value. The very expensive but hardly used nuclear laboratories installed in several African countries, demonstrate the lack of responsibility of many advisers.

* * *

This survey of the forms of responsibility of the scientists is, of course, incomplete. A simplified approach to very complex problems has been unavoidable. Many of the questions are treated more extensively and thoroughly in other chapters of this book. However, the synthetical and classifying approach to the diversified aspects of the responsibility of scientists may be useful in the assessment of their activity both by themselves and by public opinion.

Chapter 11. Comment on the social responsibilities of scientists

Mark Oliphant

Introduction

The present escalating arms race is a clear indication that organizations like Pugwash, and individuals of goodwill, have failed to persuade either people, or the governments they elect, that nuclear weapons, and all other weapons of mass destruction, should be eliminated from the armouries of the world. Despite their dedication and great endeavours, the possibility that large scale war will break out is greater now than when their efforts began. Attempts to examine this question yield no satisfactory explanation of this failure, nor do they offer any very promising possibilities for future success. Yet, the disease of war remains the greatest problem faced by all who care for the future of the human race, as it was when Bertrand Russell and Albert Einstein issued the Manifesto calling upon the scientists of the world to meet and discuss the dilemma.

Influencing governments

Reading statements on the question of scientific and technical advice to governments, by those who have had experience in that duty, and listening to their speeches, one cannot but recognize apologia, in which they reveal not success, but failure, in the promotion of disarmament and peace. They experience that frustration which comes to those who, in other areas, spend much time and effort on committees appointed to report on an important issue, only to see their document pigeon-holed, and their recommendations ignored. Also, governments can change overnight, and the new government is generally reluctant to follow a policy of the old.

National leaders are unlikely, in any case, to appoint advisers whose views are incompatible with their policies. Because of the nature of scientific knowledge, and the ethos of the search for information about nature, compromise does not come easily to men of science. Thus, Freeman Dyson[1] was able to remark that Robert Oppenheimer and Edward Teller, by becoming embroiled in political policy, each in his own way destroyed himself. Other areas of knowledge also demand adherence to truth, however uncomfortable. In his writings as diplomat and teacher, George F. Kennan makes it clear that he was unable to persuade the government which he served as Ambassador to the USSR that "Both sides must learn that there is no security in the quest for military superiority... There is a very special tragedy in this military competition. It is tragic because it creates the illusion of a total conflict of interest between the two societies; and it does this at a time when their problems are in large measure common ones".[2]

Self-interest is an overriding objective of most human beings. Politicians, scientists, and other intellectuals, are rarely exceptions. There have been unsavoury examples of this in many nations during the last few decades, mostly associated with greed for wealth or power. Advice which conflicts with self-interest is likely to be witheld by the adviser, or ignored by the recipient. In any field of human endeavour, good or bad, there are those whose services and support can be bought. The price is not necessarily money. It can be the opportunity to work in an area of particular interest, to exercise power, or to seek fame. Thus, there are medical men, ostensibly devoted to human welfare, who will co-operate in work on chemical or biological warfare; physicists who will develop new forms of nuclear weapons; or psychologists who will lend their expertise to the promulgation of pernicious doctrines or habits. Many will support the concept of a winnable nuclear war, the sale of tobacco or drugs, or the export for profit of baby foods to developing countries where they will be misused.

It is noteworthy that almost every advance in methods of mass destruction has been made, not in response to demands from the armed services, but from proposals put forward by men of science. All nuclear weapons originated in this way, as did the inertial and other guidance systems for the vehicles which deliver them. Some, like Robert Oppenheimer or Andrei Sakharov, have made weapons because of intense loyalty to their countries, but in the end have experienced feelings of guilt, and of anxiety for the future of mankind. But most scientists get on with an interesting and challenging task, without much concern for the social, political, or economic consequences of success.

Indeed, in relation to the nuclear arms race, which feeds on the continuous input of scientific innovation and technological skill, these factors have acquired a momentum of their own, they have become the masters instead of being the tools. There is much truth in the statement that nowadays technology dictates policy, that new weapons systems emerge not because of any military or security requirements but because of the sheer impetus of the technological process. This is forcefully expressed by Lord Zuckerman, for many years chief scientific adviser to the British Government:[3]

> "Here the armaments experts rule, and when it comes to nuclear weapons the military chiefs of both sides – who by convention are the official advisers on national security – usually serve only as a channel through which the men in the laboratories transmit their views for it is the man in the laboratory – not the soldier or sailor or airman – who at the start proposes that for this or that arcane reason it would be useful to improve an old or to devise a new nuclear warhead. And if a new warhead, then a new missile; and given a new missile, a new system within which it has to fit.
>
> It is he, the technician, not the commander in the field, who is at the heart of the arms race, who starts the process of formulating a so-called military nuclear need. It is he who has succeeded over the years in equating, and so confusing, nuclear destructive power with military strength, as though the former were the single and a sufficient condition of military success. The men in the nuclear weapons laboratories of both sides have succeeded in creating a world with an irrational foundation, on which a new set of political realities has in turn had to be built. They have become the alchemists of our times, working in secret ways which cannot be divulged, casting spells which embrace us all."

Thus, those who seek the abolition of war from earth, beginning by outlawing nuclear weapons, have to overcome the opposition, not only of those whose business is war, but of almost half of all scientists whose jobs depend upon a continuance of the arms race. President Eisenhower, probably on the advice of George Kistiakowsky, warned of the pressures from the military-industrial complex, whose desire for power and profit threatened all people. Years ago, at a time when rational thinking about war seemed to be gaining ground, Niels Bohr and the writer were shown over a large factory by the chairman of the board of the company. Noting the preponderance of arms manufacture, we asked what the factory would do if peace broke out. Our guide replied that the possibility of such an event gave him many sleepless nights!

In the fields of science and technology the problem of influencing government, other than with advice it wants to hear, is exacerbated by the existence of an entrenched bureaucracy, whose background is in other areas of knowledge, but whose senior members regard themselves as the founts of all wisdom. As shown so well in the remarkable BBC production "Yes Minister", bureaucrats, who in their careers serve many ministers, tend to insulate their masters from the real world, and from much outside expert advice.

Influencing public opinion

After a lifetime in international affairs and politics, always fighting for disarmament, Philip Noel-Baker has concluded, as earlier did Bertrand Russell and Albert Einstein, that only sustained public pressure from an overwhelming proportion of the peoples of the world, can ensure that disarmament negotiations are meaningful. The problem is how to generate the pressure and make it effective. In co-operation with Lord Fenner-Brockway, he has launched a World Disarmament Campaign, asking the citizens of all countries to sign a Petition addressed to all governments, and to the United Nations General Assembly at its Second Special Session Devoted to Disarmament in 1982. The Petition is worded:

"We, the Peoples of the World, demand:-
1. The abolition of nuclear weapons and all weapons of mass destruction.
2. The abolition, by agreed stages, of conventional arms, leading to:
3. General and complete disarmament.
4. Transference of military expenditure to end world poverty."

There is a growing enthusiasm for such an approach. People are beginning to realize that once they have elected a government to power it does what it wants to do, rather than what the people desire. In the end, however, except under a dictatorship, the voters have the power to dismiss a government, and to demand that those they then elect shall work towards disarmament. The apathy which characterized the public's reaction to government policies in the past is beginning to give place to realization that it is in their own interest, and that of their children, to banish war from earth.

This crack in the armour of the military–industrial complex must be widened by people of goodwill, especially scientists, who are prepared to give time and effort to spreading knowledge of the inevitable consequences of modern warfare, and the futility of defence against modern weapons. The possibility of winning a war fought with nuclear weapons must be countered whenever it is suggested.

The importance of movements like Pugwash, or of publications like the *Bulletin of the Atomic Scientists*, does not lie in their ability to influence directly either public opinion or governments. They are important because they encourage and help all associated with them to spread the knowledge that peace *is* possible, that the arms race is unable to preserve peace or freedom, but is immoral and an amplifier of the fear and distrust which created it. They provide facts about the enormous waste of human effort and world resources required to make weapons and deploy them – effort and materials sufficient to remove poverty and hunger from the planet. And Pugwash is especially important because it alone brings together scientists and others, from both sides of the conflict, to discuss the issues free from the restraints placed on representatives of governments. Having discussed the problems, however, participants must report, repeatedly and in person, to the people of their nations, and not only to officials or governments. Moreover, when necessary, they must be prepared to speak and write against the policies of their own country. The discreet and surreptitious approach has achieved little in the past, and is unlikely to succeed in the future.

The world media are little interested in peace. Their favoured headline is catastrophe or death. The ordinary man does not read the *Bulletin of the Atomic Scientists* but the popular press; he watches Star Wars, not a portrayal of the bestiality of war; he goes to a football match, not to a rally for peace. Indifference, combined with a feeling of helplessness when faced with forces over which he has no control – this is the outlook which must be changed if the pressure of public opinion is to force governments to work for disarmament and peace. Fortunately, the very excesses of the warmongers are creating suspicion and opposition against them, a situation which can be used by advocates of disarmament.

Based on experience, it appears that the most effective way to influence public opinion is through talks and discussion with 'captive' audiences. A subject, such as "Science, Technology, and the Future", creates the opportunity, for it is constantly called for by organizations like Rotary, Lions, and other service clubs; by professional societies and associations; by trade unions, student clubs, science teachers in schools; by farmers, beekeepers, local authorities and churches. It enables discussion of both the use and the misuse of knowledge. Such talks are non-political, even when addressed to groups of the extreme right or left. Discussion following a lecture of this kind can be both heated and fruitful, providing headlines for the media, angry comment from veterans' clubs, subjects for sermons, and often much correspondence. In this field, as in politics, demagoguery can sometimes be useful.

It is perhaps unfortunate that so great an emphasis has arisen on the dangers of nuclear reactors and uranium mining. These issues are important and real hazards are involved, but the number of people at risk from them is minuscule compared with the large fraction of the human race which would die or suffer in a nuclear war. People are far more concerned with the here and now – in Australia, for example, with uranium mining and export – than with the growing threat of nuclear war. Victor Weisskopf [4] emphasized this surprising concentration upon worry about, and discussion of, nuclear reactors rather than on nuclear bombs. A lecturer must continually emphasize the absolute priority of the weapons issue.

Scientists, and others who have served a government in any capacity, and who thereby have greater knowledge of weapons of war and of strategic and tactical policies, are often prevented, by the need to obey security laws and official secrets acts, from active participation in the influencing of public opinion, other than in support of government policy.

So, the task falls on those on the periphery, able to use their background knowledge to deduce much of what is going on in the armaments field.

While spreading the fullest possible information about the arms race, and its inevitable consequences if the process is not halted or reversed, it is essential to avoid producing a sense of impotence, of inability to influence events because of the great chasm between those who are governed and the governors. Except through a close personal relationship, like that between Lindemann and Churchill, or Kistiakowsky and Eisenhower, the individual, however well informed, cannot do a great deal to influence politicians and governments. However, the creation of a mass movement for peace, great enough for the political future of individuals in government to be threatened, could bring about reforms.

The Vietnam war came to an end because people antagonistic to involvement demonstrated against it. Opposition was not party political, but included people with all party affiliations. Large numbers marched in processions and attended gigantic rallies. Noting what was happening, governments recognized the political dangers of continuing to send troops to fight an unpopular war.

The current growing public opposition to the presence of nuclear weapons in Europe – as exemplified by the massive demonstrations in many European countries, including the Socialist bloc – has already won partial success: it has forced the governments of both sides to sit down at the negotiating table. The continuation of such an expression of public opinion, with scientists supporting it by providing factual information about the consequences of a nuclear war, is needed to influence political events and to exert pressure on the negotiators to bring about real measures of arms limitation and disarmament.

References

1. F. Dyson *Disturbing the Universe*, Sloan Foundation, New York, 1979.
2. G.F. Kennan, *Bulletin of the Atomic Scientists*, vol.37, May 1981, p.4.
3. Lord Zuckerman, *Science Advisers, Scientific Advisers and Nuclear Weapons* The Menard Press, London 1980
4. V.F. Weisskopf, *Bulletin of the Atomic Scientists*, vol. 36, Feb. 1980. p.1.

PART V
Measures to encourage scientists to be actively concerned with disarmament

Chapter 12. Use of science and technology for arms control and peace keeping

Bernard Feld

Introduction

"If you want peace, prepare for war". This stupid dictum – largely responsible for the fall of the Roman Empire – has, through the ages, led to more misery and bloodshed than all the plagues put together. And still, even now, this calumnious cliché continues to be echoed, blindly, unthinkingly, by political and military leaders throughout the world.

It has been argued in the past that some wars were just wars, and that some even resolved important issues. The Second World War is generally cited as the prime example – the Allied nations had no choice but to respond by force to Hitler's aggression. But accurate as this statement is, it represents only a part of the story, in so far as it discounts the historical truth that the Second World War would have been entirely unnecessary if the so-called democratic nations had – instead of permitting the League of Nations to die – acted in concert early enough, when it would still have been possible to stifle fascist expansion by collective economic actions. Nor has the final verdict of history yet been rendered as to the justification for replacing the Hitlerian policy of genocide by the indiscriminate, so-called strategic bombing of undefended population centres, culminating in the total elimination of two Japanese cities – Hiroshima and Nagasaki – by single nuclear weapons in the concluding days of the war.

Indeed, the Second World War – the bloodiest war in mankind's history, in which more people perished than in all previous wars put together – was practically predestined by the unsatisfactory resolution of the European bloodbath of 1914–18. And it is equally clear that the seeds of the Second World War were planted in the last war's concluding and immediate postwar years.

Today's situation is, however, radically different from that which has prevailed until now in the entire checkered and bloody history of mankind's slow social evolution from the cave to the skyscraper. In the words of Albert Einstein, one of the spiritual fathers of Pugwash, "The unleashed power of the atom has changed everything save our modes of thinking, and thus we drift toward unparalleled catastrophe."[1] This is in large part the consequence of indiscriminate technological progress.

Indeed, the problem we now face is stark and inescapable. Again in the words of Einstein (this time, jointly with the British sage Bertrand Russell): "We have to learn to think in a new way... Shall we put an end to the human race, or shall mankind renounce war:"[2].

Another world war could well be mankind's last. The United States and the Soviet Union have between them (in roughly equal numbers) some fifty thousand nuclear weapons, most of them vastly more powerful than the "primitive" bombs that annihilated Hiroshima and Nagasaki. A nuclear war between these two superpowers, in which a substantial fraction of this nuclear stockpile were exploded (and nobody knows whether or how such a nuclear war could be kept limited) would, within hours, eliminate the major part of the populations of the protagonists; the resulting radioactive fall-out (which could cover with lethal radioactivity an area of approximately ten million square kilometres) would within days spread comparable devastation very widely over the rest of the Northern hemisphere; and the worldwide atmospheric contamination would raise the level of exposure to radiation from natural sources by an order of magnitude and could, over a period of months or years, very seriously raise the burden of damage and defect in the pool of genetic material, carried by us all, designed by a benign evolutionary process to ensure the survival and slow improvement of all species.

But this is only the tale of two giants. Already four other nations have demonstrated nuclear weapons capabilities; by the end of this century as many as twenty others will have acquired both the technical ability and the necessary materials to produce their own "modest" arsenals of nuclear devastation.

Can any sober individual doubt that war, as a means of settling anything, is a hopelessly – no, insanely – obsolete concept?

Some history

It is generally accepted that it is the military application of science and technology that has placed civilization, not to speak of the human race itself, in such serious jeopardy. As new technologies have been exploited in a race to seek military advantage in an ongoing technological arms competition between the two superpowers, the security of the technological giants, rather than being enhanced, has steadily been diminishing. The dilemma is that each new military advance, heralded by its proponents as

200

the answer to their needs for achieving decisive military superiority, has – within the relatively short time required for the other side to emulate the originator (the technological "catch-up time" in the past has averaged around 5 years) – only served as a ratchet for screwing up the spiral of mutual destructability to an even higher and more dangerous level.

Thus, for example, what apparently started out as an attempt by both sides to develop assured retaliatory forces – to serve as a deterrent against any temptation by the potential antagonist to introduce nuclear forces into one of the periodic confrontations that have been occurring since the end of the Second World War – has turned into a nightmare of assured escalation of even a conventional confrontation into a large-scale exchange of nuclear annihilation. It has become abundantly clear that the only hope of salvation lies in the superpowers finding some formula for agreement, first to halt this deadly upward spiral of lethal armaments, and then, to reverse it.

The history of the past forty years is characterized by a dreary succession of lost opportunities. In the early 1940s, when the atomic bomb was being conceived, it was widely hoped, by the scientists involved, that the "secret" – at least, of the existence of a vigorous effort to investigate the feasibility of a fission weapon – would be exchanged with our Russian allies. But the political leaders in the West, after the untimely death of Roosevelt, were not able to muster the breadth of vision to recognize the vastly greater long-term benefits that would have followed from an open sharing with the Russians of information on the possibility of a nuclear bomb. Instead, they chose the route of secrecy and deception, thus laying the groundwork for the Cold War that poisoned the postwar international atmosphere, and whose echoes still inhibit the achievement of the East-West co-operation necessary for curtailing the ongoing futile and self-destructive race for the accumulation of nuclear overkill.

We now know that all efforts in the West to monopolize the so-called secret of the atomic bomb were completely futile, destined from the start to failure and frustration. First of all, the Soviet scientific community, under the inspired leadership of Igor Kurchatov (see p.86) and his able team of associates, including Lev Artsimovich and Andrei Sakharov, was thoroughly equal to the task of producing a nuclear weapon from scratch – especially once they knew that it was possible and they had been released from the immediate exigencies of preventing the German armies from overrunning their homeland. Furthermore, it was not at all necessary for them to go through all the trials and errors of the Manhattan Project – even without the inside information provided by an effective espionage network, including Klaus Fuchs and Allan Nunn May – thanks to the clear and accurate map of the route to the production of an atomic bomb that had been laid out in the official Smyth Report[3].

In retrospect, it is now obvious that once the secret of the successful achievement of an atomic bomb was out – and that occurred with its use for the destruction of Hiroshima – it was merely a matter of a few years before the Soviet scientific community would be able – even without any additional knowledge from the outside – to repeat the feat of scientists in the West. Knowledgeable scientists, who had participated in the American, British, and Canadian efforts to produce the first atomic bomb, predicted that the time for a technologically competent nation such as the USSR to repeat their feat would not be more than about five years. While this was disputed by the military bureaucracy that had managed the Western effort – in particular, by General Groves, the head of the wartime Manhattan Project that had organized the American bomb production – the scientists' estimate turned out to be quite accurate. The Russians achieved their first test explosion of a fission bomb in 1949[4].

Furthermore, the failure of the United Nations to place nuclear energy under effective international control – as was envisaged in the Acheson-Lilienthal-Baruch proposals and might well have been possible in the late 1940s – represents a tragically missed opportunity.

The Problem of nuclear weapons proliferation

The historical point is worth emphasizing in view of current discussions on the problems and prospects of nuclear weapons proliferation. There is a great deal of confusion in current discussions between the role of technical secrecy and the role of political constraints in preventing the future spread of nuclear weapons into the Third World. There is no question that, as far as the scientific and technical know-how is concerned. "the cat is out of the bag". There no longer exist any basic "secrets" – neither scientific nor technical – concerning the workings of the atomic bomb and the requirements for its production, that are not available in the open literature to any with the minimal technical competence required to understand them. Even a relatively unsophisticated group of technicians in almost any country, *given* the availability of the requisite quantity of weapons materials (some 20 kg of highly enriched uranium-235 or 10 kg of a relatively pure plutonium), would be capable of fabricating a crude atomic bomb by using this material, and the designs are already widely disseminated in the open literature in the West.

There is, however, still a considerable technical effort involved in the application of available knowledge to the actual *production* of the fissionable materials needed for nuclear bombs.

Unfortunately, for almost any "practical" purpose, it does not much matter whether the weapon produced by some aspiring power elite or terrorist group is highly efficient or relatively inefficient. For almost any purpose important to an aspiring non-superpower nuclear weapons producer, there is no practical difference between a ninety per cent efficient "device" (approximately 200 thousand tons of TNT equivalent) and a one per cent efficient (2 thousand tons) "dud". Two thousand tons of high explosive is more than enough to obliterate the heart of any modern city.

Under the circumstances, the problem with which the world is faced is no longer one of maintaining the "secret" in the hands of a few "reliable" nations, but rather one of preventing the uninhibited availability of the 10 kg plutonium which would permit the fabrication of a nuclear "device" by almost any government, or even any relatively well-organized extra-governmental group with access to a moderate number of competent technicians and engineers and the moderate resources needed to support their efforts.

The Safeguards problem

Concern for this problem is part of the rationale for the establishment of the International Atomic Energy Agency (IAEA) in Vienna. It was originally intended that all future atomic energy programmes of all but the nuclear-weapon states would be conducted under its auspices and control. The hope was that the Agency should be able to maintain sufficient control over all weapons-capable fissile materials, to prevent their diversion to military uses. At the same time, by permitting the Agency access to the most advanced peaceful technology available, the smaller nations of the world should find it overridingly in their interests to accept the IAEA sponsorship, with its concomitant safeguards, over their atomic energy programmes. Such acceptance would be more palatable if the same safeguards were also applied to the peaceful nuclear programmes of the superpowers.

However, it has been recognized from the start that the Agency concept – even recognizing the effectiveness of its current safeguards programmes – also presents a serious problem. For once such smaller nations have used the Agency to help build up their peaceful nuclear power programme, they will also have acquired the indigenous capability for going it alone, without having to live with the inhibitions associated with IAEA "safeguards" over their nuclear programme.

With respect to this problem of the future effectiveness of IAEA safeguards, the most promising suggestion for the prevention of nuclear weapons spread appears to lie in the direction of a "Fort Knox solution" – that is, a solution which, by putting these materials under physically effective lock-and-key, prevents any military significant amounts of plutonium or highly enriched uranium from falling into the hands of *any* unauthorized individuals, groups or governments. Such a solution, it almost goes without saying, requires the existence of an international agency that can be universally trusted with the guardianship of these materials. Presumably, the IAEA – appropriately strengthened with the requisite authorities – would be the international agency that could eventually assume such a role.

The key to the effectiveness of international safeguards lies in their emphasis on *physical* protective measures. It would be difficult to make a case for the long-term efficacy of purely accounting measures, or of occasional inspections by International Atomic Energy Agency employees, especially given the political nature of the Agency's charter. None of these approaches is capable of providing the close to 100 per cent assurances against diversion that are required if small nations are to be guaranteed their security against possible surprise nuclear attack by an aggressive neighbour. In the view of most students of the problem there is really no acceptable solution to the nuclear weapons proliferation dilemma short of such complete physical control, by a trusted international agency, over the materials required for nuclear weapons production.

Such controls, and in particular the maintenance of effective and believable inspection procedures, required to guard against unexpected violations of the prohibition against diversion of fissile materials from civil applications to nuclear weapons production, will require a very high order of technological competence on the part of the international inspectorate. The inspectors will need to know at least as much about the workings of uranium separation plants, of nuclear reactors and fuel reprocessing facilities as their designers and operators. They will, of course, also need to have continuous and *completely* uninhibited access to the relevant plants and their records.

Furthermore, in order to know what kind of "violations" are most sensitive the inspectorate will also need to have considerable knowledge of the technology of nuclear weapons design and their use. This is a rather "tricky" aspect of the nuclear materials verification problem that may require considerably more study and discussion at the international level.

In any case, whatever the limits on its mission, the IAEA system must be as "fool-proof" as any such system – even given its built-in restraints on physical access – can possibly be. This will require the IAEA to call on the most sophisticated technologies available for remote-control monitoring, and for computer-based accounting. For example, the American Arms Control and Disarmament Agency (ACDA) has been developing a regime for the internal monitoring of United States nuclear programmes – the IAEA problem in microcosm. Many aspects of this programme referred to as RECOVER (Remote Control Verification) are being adapted to IAEA use, with improvements being continuously introduced[5].

The problem of remote-control monitoring or inspection is, of course, not a new one. In the early discussions leading to the nuclear weapons Test Ban Treaty of 1963, the problem of verification of small underground tests was the main obstacle (and remained so) to the conclusion of a comprehensive treaty. The problem of achieving effective "on-site inspection", without providing a licence for uninhibited intelligence activity, was and remains the major stumbling block. At the time, the concept of "black-box inspection" was introduced at one of the Pugwash Conferences at which ideas were exchanged on these issues (see p.139).

The "black-box" concept is simple: in lieu of the physical presence of actual inspectors, instruments would be placed at strategic locations in the nation being inspected (i.e. small seismographs for the detection of underground disturbances that could be associated with underground nuclear weapons tests). These instruments would be continuously monitored at stations located outside the borders of the nation under inspection, by an international inspectorate with presumably accepted neutral credentials. Ambiguous signals, if they could not be satisfactorily explained by the nation concerned, would serve as grounds for requests for permission for "on-site inspections" by teams from the international agency. Such requests could not be refused on trivial grounds, but they would also – by the same token – require serious reasons before they could be advanced.

Such black-box control came very close to being accepted by both the United States and the USSR in the 1963 negotiations on the test ban, which were initiated in reaction to the Cuban missile crisis. Its acceptance foundered on the inability of the two sides to compromise between the Western insistence on 7 annual mandatory on-site inspections and the Eastern willingness to accept three.

However, the black-box concept should be applicable to many other problems of inspection of arms control agreements without unacceptable intrusion. Technology of detection and communication, in many areas including seismology, has advanced a great deal since 1963. The use of black-box verification may well be a technology whose time has finally come.

In the long run, however, in the absence of significant changes in the international regime of sovereign and independent states, it is difficult to conceive of any international inspection system that would be completely foolproof against determined evasion by a sovereign state. Completely effective inspection requires absolute access to the material and facilities under inspection. Limited measures, requiring national acquiescence – a situation which has, until now, been the case for practically all the nations involved in international energy programmes – will work only so long as such national co-operation continues, even assuming complete acceptance of the international control regime. But as the recent Israeli aggression against the Iraqi reactor has demonstrated, not all states are prepared to accept as adequate the present IAEA safeguards.

Nuclear-weapon-free zones

In spite of verification problems, however, the concept of nuclear-weapon-free zones is becoming increasingly attractive, especially as the superpower rivalry in the accumulation of ever-more sophisticated weapons grows and the concomitant doctrines proliferate for justifying their early introduction into "conventional" conflicts. The classic examples of such areas are Antarctica – which has been completely demilitarized by formal agreement of all interested parties since 1961 – and Latin America, by virtue of the Treaty of Tlatelolco of 1967. (Although Brazil has signed the Treaty, it still does not accept it as being in force, since not all Latin American countries (e.g. Cuba) have yet joined.) The Tlatelolco Treaty, although it is a regional agreement, is accompanied by a protocol in which the nuclear weapon states agree to respect the nuclear-weapon-free status of the area.

Serious discussions are taking or have taken place with respect to the possible establishment of such areas in Africa, the Balkans, Europe, the Middle East, the Nordic Area and South-east Asia. However, such discussions have, at least up to now, usually been thwarted by the unwillingness of one or more of the key nations in the region to join in the negotiations. However, as the Latin American case has shown, a treaty can be effective in respect to a given area even if not all the major actors are immediate adherents.

In this regard, it is important to emphasize that the nuclear-weapon-free concept is *not* wed to the existence of contiguous areas of application. All that is required is the acquiescence to the concept of a sufficient number of nuclearly-capable states in an area. This possibility has sometimes been referred to as the "Swiss cheese" zone concept.

Basically, states will agree to remain non-nuclear – that is free of nuclear weapons and of the facilities for producing them – so long as it remains in their basic security interests to do so. In this regard, one of the major instruments, available to the nuclear weapons states for promoting this concept of enhanced security deriving from non-nuclear status, is the guarantee of no-first-use of nuclear weapons against such nations.

Until now, the no-first-use pledges of the superpowers have been rather more limited: both have proclaimed the non-use of nuclear weapons against non-nuclear-weapon states which are not aligned or allied with any nuclear weapon state. There would be, however, considerable advantage to the superpowers to extend this concept to *all* states refusing to acquire or store nuclear weapons, since this would greatly encourage already existing tendencies within both NATO and WTO to reduce, and eventually eliminate, their dependence on so-called tactical or theatre nuclear weapons for their defence.

But beyond such limited application, it can be persuasively argued that the universal acceptance of the no-first-use concept with respect to nuclear weapons would represent a tremendously important step towards the avoidance of nuclear war. Despite the argument that this would be purely an expository step, without any enforceable or even verifiable aspects – nor would there be any requirement for associated reduction in nuclear weapon stockpiles and their further development and deployment – there is an important historical precedent which speaks for the effectiveness of such an agreement.

The Geneva Protocol of 1925 (banning the use of chemical, bacteriological and analogous weapons) was very widely interpreted as simply a no-first-use agreement. Nevertheless, it provided very effective inhibitions, especially during the Second World War, against the use, and even development of such weapons. And it laid the groundwork for an eventual Convention Prohibiting the Development, Production and Stockpiling of Bacteriological (Biological) and Toxin Weapons, and providing for the destruction of existing stockpiles (1972). A similar treaty with respect to Chemical Weapons has been under serious negotiation.

With the help of a no-first-use arrangement for nuclear weapons, one might be permitted to hope that international developments (assuming the avoidance of nuclear war) would encourage a universal agreement to ban such weapons and eventually to eliminate them from the arsenals of all nations.

Verification of arms control agreements

With respect to the proliferation problem, in today's world it is necessary to operate on the assumption that programmes for nuclear power production are destined to be with us for some time, and we must learn to cope with the problems of weapons proliferation associated with such programmes. Just as the most sophisticated technology is today the backbone of the nuclear weapons development and deployment programme of all the major powers, so must a comparable technological sophistication serve as the backbone of any system for the verifiable control, limitation, reduction and eventual elimination of nuclear armaments from the world's military arsenals. For it must stand as given that neither of the superpowers, not to speak of the other nuclear weapon states, will acquiesce to a very substantial reduction, let alone elimination, of its nuclear weapon capability if it is not unequivocally sure that no virtual antagonist could possibly maintain a nuclear attack potential at the end of the disarmament process. Verification is *the key* to any significant nuclear arms limitation, and especially reduction, now and in the foreseeable future.

Unfortunately, our experience until now with the international verification of arms control arrangements is not too encouraging. Even though problems associated with such verification have received serious consideration, both on the national and the international levels, since the late '40s, the history of international acceptance of verification procedures has been uniformly disappointing. It has never been possible for the United States and the USSR to agree on any formal arrangement involving any form of international agency with intrusive inspection capabilities with respect to the two superpowers. Both superpowers have been willing to envisage intrusive IAEA inspection of nations outside their own immediate strategic orbits; but if ever any question of restricting their own national sovereignty has arisen, both of the nuclear giants, as well as the other nations that have come to regard themselves as nuclear powers, have always insisted on "drawing the line". In reality, the world is still a very long way from the acceptance of any of the forms of supranational control over activities of military significance that might signal the initiation of a serious regime of international order.

Satellite inspection

Nevertheless, in spite of the determined insistence of all nations on the inviolability of their sovereign territories, a great deal of international inspection has been going on for quite some time. To a large extent, both the Soviet Union and the United States are now capable of continuously monitoring the military potential (and even more) of the other side, by means that lie entirely within their own (national) control. Such monitoring of the capabilities of the other side no longer depends on the effectiveness of clandestine intelligence activities – efficient as these have become as a result of the use of the most modern surveillance and communications techniques. Beyond the conventional intelligence gathering techniques, the availability to both sides of reconnaissance satellites – capable of the essentially continuous monitoring of practically the entire area of the other nation by photographic means, coupled with the use of a variety of sensors using other regions of the electromagnetic spectrum – has resulted in a situation of more-or-less complete openness, as far as the significant physical activities of any nation are concerned. Any major military programme, and especially one that might significantly alter the *status quo*, would almost certainly be detected through the continuous monitoring of both ground and air-based activities, that is now being carried out by the surveillance satellites of both the Soviet Union and the

United States.

The extent of this revolution in observational capabilities that has taken place in the last 20 years or so, since the Soviet launching of the Sputnik in 1957, is still not sufficiently understood in Western defence analysts' circles; the extent to which these revolutionary changes are taken into account in equivalent Eastern "think-tanks" is not known to this author.

The simple fact is that the entire area of both nations is now being continuously scrutinized by the other side, with observational instruments that are capable of reading the numbers on car licence plates, or the headlines of newspapers. Having made this statement of technological capability – and it is essential that the high level of this capability, now being exercised by *both* sides, be recognized and accepted – it is of course necessary, however, to put forth some obvious caveats. Observation by sensors of this degree of resolution cannot be continuous, due to the vicissitudes of weather and the limitation on the number of satellite photographs that can be seriously analysed in a finite time by a finite number of photo-analysts. Nevertheless, it must be accepted as a fact of contemporary international life that any reasonably large-scale enterprise, that would be capable of appreciably altering the military capability of either side, is exceedingly unlikely to escape the almost-continuous scrutiny to which both the United States and the Soviet Union are now subjecting each others' activities.

The capability of reconnaissance systems to detect change is of particular importance. One of the most significant technological developments of recent years has been in this area. If it were necessary for the military establishments of both sides to analyse all the photographic data on the activities of the other, this would represent an impossible task for any system with finite resources. However, there now exist systems that can provide automatic comparisons between two photographs of the same area, taken at different times, and call attention to any significant differences between these two photographs. Thus, the system need not be capable of analysing the activities in any given area, but only of detecting any "significant" change (which can be appropriately defined in advance) that has taken place in the time interval between the two photographs.

The problems are not simple, of course. Too loose a definition of "change" will result in a swamping of the system by spurious data or could subject the system to easy misdirection by a sophisticated opponent; too tight a definition could permit important evidence to leak through the sieve. However, given the high degree of input into these systems, and the great amount of "redundancy" that has traditionally been built into military systems, it is a good guess that any significant alteration of military capabilities by either side would not escape detection by the sophisticated reconnaissance, surveillance and espionage capabilities of the other for long.

In respect to such reconnaissance satellite systems, it is important that both the United States and the Soviet Union have recognized the value to their own security of maintaining this "open skies" situation. Thus, a number of agreements exist, (e.g. the Outer Space Treaty of 1967, the Direct Communications Link Modernization Agreement of 1971, the Accidents Measures Agreement of 1971, the SALT I and the ABM Agreements of 1972, as well as the International Telecommunications Conventions), some being informal but nonetheless essential, that bind each superpower to respect the satellite verification systems of the other. Other industrialized nations – in particular France – also have serious and active satellite reconaissance programmes under way, so that the super-power monopoly in this field cannot continue indefinitely.

Clearly, in respect to such satellite observation, we are in the midst of a continuing technological race between the "hiders" and the "seekers". Even if techniques can be developed which – at least for some short time – may succeed in camouflaging some significant military activity, thus preventing its detection by the other side, any advantages thereby achieved must perforce be short-lived. Meanwhile, however, new techniques are being developed on both sides, mainly of mobile missile deployments (the MX on the part of the United States and the mobile SS-20 and its offshoots, on the part of the USSR), which are deemed by many to threaten the stability of the mutual deterrent posture that, for some time now, has seemed to ensure an accepted balance between the two superpowers.

Of particular concern, with respect to their possible impact on arms control prospects, are three areas of new technical developments: cruise missiles, anti-submarine warfare techniques, and directed energy (particularly laser) sources. The first is, in fact, a rather old idea – arising from the German V-bombs, of the Second World War – which has recently been revived in a much improved manner, mainly through the development of strong, light-weight metallic alloys and highly efficient jet engines. Cruise missiles are pilotless, drone aircraft, travelling at subsonic speeds, capable of delivering conventional and nuclear weapons on specific targets. Owing to modern guidance technology, they can be given pinpoint accuracy, and owing to their ability to fly at rooftop levels, and even to manoeuvre on their course, they are almost invulnerable against conventional anti-aircraft defences. Because of their light weight, they can be launched from aircraft, and dispatched at considerable distance from their intended targets. (They can also be carried by freight trains, ships, submarines, trucks, etc.). They are obviously easy to conceal and almost impossible to verify as to their number. Hence, the deployment of cruise missiles on a large scale will hugely complicate the achievement of a verifiable limitation on numbers of deliverable weapons.

The danger of cruise missile deployments represents a good illustration of a recurring problem of American-Soviet arms control. This is the problem of the "illusive advantage", sometimes referred to as the "fallacy of the last step". The idea – always an attractive one to military leaders whose horizons rarely extend beyond the last conflict – is that it is possible to maintain a constant military advantage over the other side by being one step ahead in the race for new weapons technologies. Fortunately, the world has never come to the point of an actual conflict between the United States and the Soviet Union, where some elusive but immediate advantage might count. The actual facts of life have dictated that every new deployment on either side has been followed, within a very short time, by either the deployment of the same system by the other, or the introduction of a new system that has served to counteract the "advantage" of the first. Until now, the Soviet-American military competition has represented a "no-win game".

Another example is the competition, still not definitely resolved, in the realm of anti-submarine warfare (ASW). In the immediate post Second World War period, it was generally believed in the West that the Soviet Union would be content with its pre-eminent status as a major continental power; the control of the seas would remain within the prerogative of the triumphant Western allies of the Second World War.

However, any serious analysis of Soviet military concerns must conclude that the control over the sea lanes in and out of the Soviet Union is a matter of life-or-death concern to Soviet leaders. Hence, the very concept of a submarine threat to surface shipping, and possible means of its denial, would be of immediate concern to the Russians. It is thus rather difficult to understand in retrospect, why almost all studies in the West, to date, on ASW prospects, have completely ignored Soviet concerns. Nevertheless, this has been the case.

Assuming that this deficiency will be remedied in such studies in the future, it is necessary to be concerned with the mutual East-West developments in anti-submarine warfare techniques, not because these represent any possible breakthroughs in new technologies, but because the inability of either side to comprehend the realities of the current technological standoff could introduce dangerous instabilities into the current East-West competition.

The third technological threat, that of directed energy weapons – particularly laser beams – is of a different nature and involves a much longer time horizon. Although the weapons prospects of intense beams of particles or electromagnetic energy has been a subject for science fiction for decades, technology has only recently attained the level necessary to permit serious consideration of such possibilities.

Compelling arguments have been advanced as to the practical short-term infeasibility of long-range particle beam weapons[6]. Neverthe-less, it appears to be rather more difficult to discourage laser-beam weapon enthusiasts, especially in respect to the possibility of using space-based lasers as the primary components of an anti-ballistic missile or ballistic missile defence (ABM or BMD) system. This is not the place to analyse thoroughly the technical arguments as to why such an ABM system is not likely to prove effective against an antagonist with the technical capabilities of the Soviet Union[7]. However, suffice it to note that any attempt by either side to develop a space-based ABM system would not only demand the abrogation of the heretofore effective ABM-Ban Treaty of 1972, but it would also start a dangerous and futile race in the deployment of offensive weapons in space – a medium that until now has blessedly been reserved for peaceful scientific exploration.

In essence, then, the major powers would be extremely well advised to avoid any attempts to obtain transient military advantage through the secret exploitation of some imagined technical possibility in the space realm. On the contrary, in the current competitive atmosphere, any element of technological surprise is more likely to to be dangerously destabilizing rather than being conducive to the avoidance of conflict; either way, it is certain to be transient.

The Future of space exploration

In any case, the level and capabilities of current reconnaissance deployments on both sides are such that it is exceedingly unlikely that any significant, let alone permanent, advantage could be achieved by either side through a clandestine programme. Furthermore, the grave danger that the ultimate discovery by the other side – which is highly likely over any significant time period – of such secret deployment would lead to a breakdown of the system of international arms control, and to the initiation of an expensive and extremely dangerous open-ended arms race, should act as an effective deterrent against any such unilateral effort at evading the presently accepted Russian–American arrangements, minimal as they are, to restrain nuclear weapons growth.

Nevertheless, there is a growing concern among defence specialists over the escalating superpower competition in space. Both sides have mounted large programmes of space exploration, involving both manned earth-orbiting vehicles and unmanned planetary explorers. In spite of the fact that there is no obvious, immediate military application for any of the space programmes mounted to date, there is growing evidence that both superpowers now look on their space programme as being highly competitive in the military sense. If this situation should continue, not only would the above-mentioned dangers be intensified, but this would also represent the loss of a unique opportunity for a breakthrough in peaceful East-West co-operation for our mutual benefit.

At this stage, Soviet and American interests in space exploration are not only completely uncompetitive, but they have a large overlap in interests and effort. Both nations have invested considerable sums in space research, most of which have been channeled through programmes of a non-military character. Thus, even though the military establishments have maintained great interest in their national space programmes, the fundamental interests on which support for these programmes has been sought and achieved, have been – and continue to be – primarily related to the public interest in the romance of the exploration of the cosmos. This is a distinct international asset, which arms control advocates should be at great pains to maintain and foster.

Thus, the involvement of peaceful space exploration in the military competition would not only be unfortunate from the arms control point of view; it would also represent the loss of an unprecedented opportunity for co-operation at a level that could provide very positive benefits to both parties. The operative question, therefore, is how is it possible to channel the current competitive modes of non-military space research by the superpowers into a mode of mutual co-operation.

Off hand, this sounds like a Utopian ideal, given the present atmosphere of East-West antagonism at almost every level. Nevertheless, it is important to emphasize the traditions of East–West co-operation in the scientific realm. We have been through other periods of severe "confrontation", but the scientific community has somehow always been able to continue its dialogue, and even to maintain programmes of international scientific co-operation, despite the political vicissitudes.

Assuming that a co-operative space programme makes good scientific and economic sense, it is very useful to consider what might be the dimensions of such co-operation. At a minimum, such a co-operative programme must involve an extensive exchange of information on the characteristics of specific space-probes (either in earth orbit or beyond) launched by both parties. But a mere exchange of information (which is, in any event, already the norm to a considerable degree), is only a bare and rather insubstantial minimum.

In actual fact, it makes little, if any, sense for the USSR and the United States to conduct two separate scientific space exploration programmes in complete independence of each other. More to the point: considering the great scientific and economic resources involved in such programmes, and considering the very great overlap – not only in interests but also in the actual physical activities involved – between the two programmes, it does not make any sense whatsoever for the United States and the USSR to continue to follow completely independent pursuits of the same goals via substantially similar programmes.

It would, in fact, be distinctly to the advantage of both the Soviet Union and the United States to establish a programme of co-operative space research. Both countries are deeply committed to the concept and practice of space exploration. Both have already invested vast resources – monetary and technical – in space programmes. Both have succeeded – quite independently of each other – in launching exciting programmes of manned and unmanned exploratory vehicles into the solar system and beyond. And yet, in defiance of all logic, these programmes are being carried on completely independently, each as though the other were non-existent. Viewed by a man from Mars, this makes absolutely no sense whatsoever.

On the other hand, there is a vast scope for co-operative programmes. Both the United States and the Soviet Union are currently being forced to curtail the space exploration (and especially space science) programmes for want of available resources. And yet, if such programmes were assumed as a co-operative venture, the relative costs to each country would, in the end, be far less than what would be needed to mount independent and competitive ventures. Furthermore, in the longer (and not too long-term) view, the savings that would be mutually afforded by the avoidance of a military confrontation in space are almost incalculable. Co-operation in space would accelerate scientific and technological progress, save large amounts of expenditures that would otherwise go into competitive and redundant programmes, and avoid a dangerous area of military confrontation that could otherwise lead to unnecessary tension and dangers of war.

In short, a joint Soviet–American space programme is an obvious channel through which mutual co-operation could eventually supplant antagonistic competition, to great mutual benefit. Even if we cannot yet agree on the just division of the resources of this planet Earth, recognition of our mutual interest in the rational exploration of the rest of the solar system should not be a point of contention. Perhaps the vision of a common future in space might even eventually help to bring us to admit to our common humanity.

* * *

In the end, if you want peace, you must prepare and work for peace. At this tail end of the 20th century, science and technology have become indispensible tools in any such programme for permanent peace.

References

1. O. Nathan & H. Nordon, *Einstein on Peace*, Simon and Schuster, 1980, p.376.
2. The Russell-Einstein Manifesto, see Appendix 1.
3. H.D. Smyth, *Atomic Energy for Military Purposes*, Princeton University Press, 1945.
4. H. York, *The Advisors: Oppenheimer, Teller and the Superbomb*. Freeman, 1976.

5. F. Prokoski, *IEEE Spectrum*, July 1981.
6. J. Parmentola and K. Tsipis, Particle beam weapons, *Scientific American*, April 1979.
7. A. Chayes and J.B. Wiesner (editors), *ABM*, Harper & Row, New York, 1969.

Chapter 13. Peace research

Bert Röling

Introduction

Peace research is a scholarly pursuit concerned with the causes of war and the conditions of peace. Peace science, or polemology, or "Friedenswissenschaft", is a problem-oriented branch of scholarship. The regular occurrence of war is a social problem. Peace researchers presume that more knowledge about the causes of war and about the conditions under which peace can be maintained will contribute to more rational behaviour in international relations, and thus contribute to solving this social problem.

Peace research emerged from anxiety rather than curiosity. It is a branch of the social sciences born in the atomic era. The introduction of nuclear weapons brought danger to the world surpassing anything mankind had encountered previously. Awareness of the extreme danger has generated the peace research movement throughout the world. When nuclear weapons made war unbearable, means had to be discovered to eliminate such a confrontation. The spreading interest in peace research sprang from an urge to contribute to more rational foreign policies and more peaceful international relations, through better insight into the causes of war and the conditions of peace.

The theory of international relations is a well established branch of scholarship. It originated after the First World War, which showed the need for a clearer perception of international relations. This fairly new field of research emphasized state sovereignty and state power. Government-sponsored "societies for international relations" appeared in almost all European countries. Like the League of Nations, their point of departure was the maintenance of the *status quo*, which included the dominance of European states and the United States, over large parts of the non-white world in colonial and imperial relations; the dominance of the victors in the First World War over the vanquished.

It is easy to understand why in the course of time the war–peace problem acquired an evermore prominent place in the theory of international relations. Especially after the Second World War, the awareness grew that maintenance of peace was in the primary national interest. But the approach to the problem of war and peace remained to be based on the traditional standpoint, with emphasis on the significance of the armed power of the national soveriegn state. "Peace research" was born out of discontent with the *status quo*, which was considered to be a dangerous conflict-ridden situation. It was critical in its attitude regarding traditional state policy and questioned the value of the existing concept of national sovereignty. It suspected that the emphasis on national military power would irrevocably lead to arms races, over-kill and weapon-postures, and to increased danger of war. It differed in its paradigmatical approach by taking not the national but the global view-point.

A similar ambiguous relation exists between peace research and "strategic studies", that is research concerning the optimal use of armed power. In principle, both kinds of research should come to the same rational conclusions. The difference in outcome is due to the military origin of "strategic studies" which may explain the trust in power to achieve political ends.

Theories of peace research

Peace research is a recent phenomenon. The science of peace and war is young and as such it has features which are common to most young social sciences. In all social research the tendency exists to give expression to the prevailing value-judgements. A social group which opposes a particular social institution will be tempted to impute a great many social evils to that institution. The kings were seen as the cause of war during the epoch of absolute monarchy. Nowadays, those who have misgivings about the capitalist or the communist system will be inclined to impute the occurrence of war to capitalism or communism. Technology, which at one time was seen as the cure to all social evils, was then regarded as the hoped for road to peace. Today, the inclination exists to ascribe much of the evil to technology, including the arms race and the occurrence of war. For the very reason that social sciences are concerned with evaluations, the prevailing moods may, and will, influence the social scientist.

Another pitfall is the tendency to generalize research findings and to yield to emotion that goes with discovery. Most social scientists start their task by fighting superstitious beliefs and traditional thinking. If they discover a real cause of a social evil they will be inclined to regard it as *the* cause. Lombroso's theory of "born criminal" reigned for a long period in criminology. In socialist doctrine each society engenders the crime it deserves. Society is of course to blame, but not for all crimes.

These primitive scientific "truths" were in fact vital errors but they fulfilled the important function of breaking through traditional mistaken opinions. When social science comes to maturity it corrects the generalizations. It becomes more sophisticated, more complicated, more realistic, more aware of the fact that many factors are involved in every social event and that it is often very difficult to determine their relative strength. At this stage the findings of the social sciences are more in conformity with reality but more difficult to adapt by decision makers. The "vital error" is perhaps more effective than the "sterile truth". The history of every social science shows the road it travelled, a road paved with the names of famous scholars who erred in their one-sidedness, but who focussed attention on previously neglected aspects of social phenomena.

It is difficult to establish in which phase peace research finds iself at present. Some radical theories, such as those which label the capitalist system as the cause of war and claim that there can be no peace without the elimination of capitalism, or those which blame structural violence and social injustice as the cause of all evil, would suggest that peace research is still in the early phase. A just world does not necessarily mean a peaceful world! A peaceful world needs a stable structure along with a generally acceptable just order, a structure that is able to withstand a crisis.

In theories which stress specific aspects of a problem, too much may be hidden in the metaphors used in social theory. In his article "Twelve friendly quarrels with Johan Galtung", Kenneth Boulding[1] suggests that many terms used by Galtung, such as negative and positive peace, personal and structural violence, top-dog and under-dog, centre and periphery, are introduced as metaphors and gradually applied as models. A metaphor is the emotionally loaded image of one aspect; a model is the cool simplification of the whole. Boulding states: "perhaps one of the great dilemmas of the human race is that metaphors are persuasive and models are not"[2].

In this connection it is worthwhile to stress the point that the peace researcher tries, as objectively as possible, to describe and analyse the social reality confronting him. Distinction should be made between the "hard facts" and the real world, e.g. the existing weapon potential, and what one might call the "soft facts", the existing perceptions, opinions and evaluations. If one analyses the hard facts it may be possible to discover what would be needed to cope with them. The hard facts determine what society needs if it is to continue and prosper, and the changes necessitated by the "natural law of the atomic age", such as general disarmament and some form of federal world structure. But the soft facts, the attitudes, opinions and short term interests, often prevent the realization of those changes, even if they were considered necessary for survival. These soft facts determine what is possible in human society. William Fulbright[3] stressed the gap between "our needs" and "our capacities".

The hard facts determine the final goal that should be reached. The soft facts determine the small steps that are feasible. It is typical for those who are primarily confronted with the hard facts, e.g. the nuclear physicists, to demand the radical implementation of the steps needed to prevent disaster. But soft facts also belong to reality, they often prevent radical solutions. Peace researchers take them into account. And if the capabilities of mankind are insufficient to cope with dangers for survival, they stress the need to find out by what ways and means these capabilities can be influenced and changed. This problem may be one of the most important tasks of peace research.

It remains to be seen to what extent decision-makers and the masses are capable of adopting a long-term interest in peace as their guiding principle. It is the aim of peace research, peace action and peace education to promote this long-term view of world interest. There is a growing awareness in the world that the environment is of primary interest for every living being. But the environment of a state is the world. It is of vital national interest for every state that this world is at peace.

In conclusion: prevailing opinions determine what is politically feasible. The difference of opinion with respect to the maintenance of peace does not mean a clash between noble doves and evil hawks. It is not a question of moral pacifism against amoral political action. Peace action, which aims at creating opinions and attitudes favourable to peace maintenance, pleads for rationality. It is based on rational, prudential pacifism; it adds good sense to good-will. The question is, what is and can be made politically feasible? As Henry Kissinger said: "progress towards peace can be thwarted by asking too much as surely as by asking too little."[4]

Hard and soft research

Great differences exist within peace research with respect to the contents of this problem-oriented branch of scholarship, although opinions are united about the multi-disciplinary character of peace research. Whatever the issue, human beings as well as states are involved, and the international structure must have a great impact. Hence the need for the collaboration of psychologists, sociologists, political scientists, historians, lawyers, economists, cultural anthropologists and experts in international relations and organizations.

Great differences also exist with respect to the methodology. A problem-oriented social science, such as criminology, or polemology, does not recognize a single method of research. It makes use of the different methods applied in the different disciplines. Every director of a peace research institute knows of the extreme difficulty of inter-disciplinary co-operation.

A major difference among social scientists concerns the controversy regarding "hard" and "soft" research. Soft research is regarded as the traditional method of historians, sociologists, psychologists and lawyers, who rely as much as is possible on hard statistical facts but also draw conclusions from specific events and observations by way of analogy and generalization. The danger of this approach is subjectivity. Hard facts, statistics, experiments, which time and again confirm the tested hypothesis, assure greater objectivity. Hence the tendency among social scientists to follow the example of the natural sciences and to exclude the so-called non-scientific method, and replace conjecture with respect to war, by explanation. Scholars, who have confidence only in quantitative analyses based on measurable facts, reject the traditional, qualitative approach, as not trust worthy. The most impressive example of this kind of research is that of David Singer[5], based on the study of 93 international wars during the past 150 years. He admits that "From a humanitarian point of view, that may have been 93 wars too many, but from a scientific point of view it was too few." This may explain Singer's admission of the discouraging fact of "our failure to achieve any significant theoretical breakthrough."

There are many reasons for "hard research", based on numbers, statistics, curves and models. The desire to prevent the criticism that peace research is but "politics in disguise" may be one of the motives for restricting research to empirical facts and verifiable quantitative data.

Most peace researchers, however, concede that restricting peace research to "hard research" amounts to restricting the roads to "reality". Statistics are almost exclusively concerned with the "surface facts". Hard research excludes research on qualitative issues, which may be of the greatest significance, as for example the intensity of a collective memory, or the deep-lying bases of public conscience. Such issues, not being measurable, cannot be researched by counting data. Moreover, they cannot be communicated sufficiently by statistics. Suffering is not expressed by the exact number of mega-deaths. Some truths cannot be imparted by numbers. The statement that each truth needs its special form of expression may be too strong, but it is undeniable that numbers and figures often fall short of the truth they try to express.

The central problem of peace research is often the question whether or not alternatives are feasible for present day thinking and acting. Peace research concerns structures and attitudes which do not yet exist and which therefore cannot be weighed or measured. Futurological research has to be part of scholarship in all the social sciences, if these are not to deteriorate into an advocacy of the *status quo*, and if they are to contribute favourably to changes in society, changes made inevitable by factual developments, such as technology.

Either method of research has its *raison d'être* and should be pursued, but so far hard research has not made many significant discoveries. Dedring[6], while concluding that so far the findings of specific hard research were insignificant, nevertheless recommends that this research should go on. Either method is indispensable. Empirical research should be undertaken wherever feasible, but it should be complemented by soft research, which often leads to convincing conclusions about the probability of future events and feasibilities.

Futurological peace research

A distinction has to be made between two different areas of peace research; *futurological peace research* and what might be called *existential peace research*. The former deals with scholarly speculations about the future, the latter with the world as it is today.

Peace plans and suggestions for global organizations capable of maintaining the peace are centuries older than peace research. They were mainly introduced and propagated as the possible realization of global justice. Further analysis of the plans, however, leads inevitably to the conclusion that they served the special interests of a certain state or a group of states[7]. The rhetorics used to support these early peace efforts were in essence an *"oratio pro domo"*, an argumentation in the service of particular interests. The proposed organizations might be called *"organisationes pro domo"*, ostensibly set up to be in the service of global justice and universal peace, but in reality being organizations favouring the special interest of one state or a group of states. The League of Nations may be considered as an *"organisatio pro domo"*, as it was an organization for the maintenance of the status quo, i.e. the dominance of the white part of mankind over large parts of the non-white world, and, within the white world, the dominance of the victors in the First World War over the vanquished. Even the United Nations Charter envisages a world organization favouring the special interests of a group of states: it regulates the colonial relationship; it does not mention world poverty; it almost neglects the topic of disarmament. However, the United Nations practice changed all that.

The Baruch proposals (see p.120) are a clear example of an *"organisatio pro domo"*. These proposals suggested that all states should refrain from producing nuclear weapons and that a global mechanism for verification should be established. In the meantime, the United States would be permitted to keep her nuclear armed power without any restriction, until the American Senate would decide that the global machinery for inspection was watertight. Acceptance of the Baruch proposals would have legitimized American preponderance in armed power for an indeterminate period.

When evaluating schemes proposed for arms control and disarmament, the concept of the *"organisatio pro domo"*, should be taken into account. Many proposals in the past were unfair and served the special interests of one of the parties. Arms control proposals and the verification machinery that goes with it should serve the common interest of all parties and should not give special advantages to one of them, neither in the final result nor in the different stages of the disarmament process. An application of this principle can be found in the United Nations resolution on disarmament which states: "The whole programme to be such that no State would have cause to fear that its security was endangered".[8] This provision refers to the practice of the Cold War parties who used to suggest comprehensive disarmament plans, but to begin disarmament with those types of weapons in which the opponent had preponderant strength, i.e. conventional weapons (United States) or nuclear weapons (USSR).

An important part of futurological peace research concerns relevant Utopia's, preferred worlds, and world order models as feasible alternatives for the present system. The theory of international relations deals with the factual situation, the permanent existence of sovereign states in an anarchical international setting[9]. But "world order" plans consider alternatives to this statist standpoint. Richard Falk[10] makes a fascinating distinction between the different modern world order plans. Type I approach is Western, non-marxist and associated with the ideology of liberal internationalism. The emphasis on world order in the Type I approach is principally an attempt to adopt statist orientation to economic interdependencies. Its essence can be nicely summarized by the notion "the management of interdependence", in which the managerial approach to the various issue-areas of world politics has to be contrasted with both the traditionalist preoccupation with power and the alleged utopian insistence on transcending the state system[11].

Type II posits images of preferred worlds not as mere manifestations of a lively imagination, but as projects to be realized in the world. The blueprints of this model for the future are often built around advocacy of some form of world government. They rest their claims upon appeals to reason and self-interest, an approach that derives from a kind of rational, universal humanism. In economics such an approach is for example Tinbergen's Report to the Club of Rome[12]. In the political field Clark and Sohn's *World Peace Through World Law*[13] calls for a world structure to cope with the existence of atomic weapons. Hence the need for general disarmament, a world military force, a court with compulsory jurisdiction and an equity court. However, cultural differences in the world are neglected, and the way such a plan could be realized is not dealt with. The poverty problem receives only superficial attention, and the proposal concentrates only on the transfer of capital, disregarding the need of a New International Economic Order. The proposal leads to a world organization for the maintenance of a system of free enterprise. As such it falls under the projects of "covert imperialism"[14]. The proposed world organization has all the features of an *"organisatio pro domo"*.

A different Type II proposal takes into account the cultural differences in our world and explores the ways and means to arrive at a peaceful and generally acceptable new world order. The most concerted effort is that of the World Order Models Project (WOMP), which started as a transnational exercise in 1968. It seeks to combine the notion of a preferred world with the promotion of specific world order values (peace, equity, social and political justice, ecological quality, humane governance). WOMP's initiative induced a number of scholars from different parts of the world to work out their version of a preferred world[15]. A serious effort is made to exclude all features of cultural imperialism and to harmonize some basic values within the diversity of cultures, presupposing different transition periods for different world regions. Whether cultural imperialism, hidden in the concepts of socio-political justice and humane governance, can be excluded, in the main question. This benign form of imperialism may, however, be inevitable, especially since every region in the world wants the benefits of technology. The introduction of technology is not restricted to the transfer of machinery. It inevitably includes the transfer of many of the accepted values existing in the developed parts of the world.

Arms control and disarmament

However important futurological peace research may be, we still live in a world that is rightly called an "endangered planet"[16]. Its dangers are pressing. Research is badly needed, particularly to diminish the danger of nuclear war. Mankind cannot wait until a new world structure has been established, or until a more just order has been realized. We must ask what can be done, here and now, within the framework of our conflict-ridden system. What should be the conduct of states to prevent violent conflicts? In what manner would it be possible to influence the many causes of tension: armaments and the arms race, poverty and development, racial discrimination, violation of human rights, nationalism, political ideologies, overpopulation? What kind of peace education and peace action could lead to more rational governmental decisions?

This is not the place for a survey of the results of peace research concerning all these different topics. This book deals with arms control and disarmament, and therefore the discussion will be restricted to these items of peace research.

Peace research arose out of the anxiety caused by the emergence of nuclear weapons. A considerable part of peace research is devoted to the dangers to humanity stemming from the technological weapon development. For the first time in history the question of survival has become a serious topic. Much research and many publications are devoted to the analysis of the dangers of modern weaponry and the prevailing strategic theories. The deeper one penetrates into the present weapon situation and the prevailing military theories, the more worried one becomes. Peace research has the important task to follow the arms developments closely and continuously, evaluate these developments and give the world the much needed information. Governments would presumably act differently if they were aware of the existing macro-risks. "Blindness in involvement" plays an important role. The dictum that between the weapon-reality and its perception lies a gap that opens the road to Armageddon contains much truth.

Another aspect of research into these matters is concerned with the factors which play a role in the arming process. What causes governments to spend so much of their resources on arms? National armed power is a logical consequence of an international system consisting of sovereign states which must ensure their own security. But what can be the reason for the excessive armed power existing today? What can explain the existing mindless arms races?

Two extreme theories attempted to supply an explanation. According to one theory the excessive arming stems from an arms race fed by technology and is dominated by an action-reaction process. Fear of new technological developments compel the adversaries to concenrate on technological arms research. Any new development is immediately applied and gives one side a temporary advantage until the other side restores the balance. In a situation like the present Cold War, each side strives for superiority. Hence the current arms race.

The assumption that the strategic arms race follows from the action-reaction syndrome is refuted in the theory of Dieter Senghaas[17] which states that to a large extent governments base their armaments and deterrence policies on autonomous, inner-directed motives. Apart from the "military–industrial complex", this theory involves the psychological aspect of social "autism" which leads to a very distorted view of the outside world.

A major proportion of peace research is devoted to the analysis of armaments-dynamics in which internal and external factors intermingle. The lack of sufficient empirical evidence precludes a clear picture of the different forces determining the "deadly logics" of the threat system.

A similar controversy exists in relation to the general theory of the present function of military power.

NATO and WPO account for approximately 70 per cent of the world's arms expenditure, of more than 500 billion US dollars per year. The introduction of weapons of mass destruction, such as nuclear arms and sophisticated rocketry, have made it quite clear that an all-out nuclear war between the two alliances would end in mutual destruction. Such a suicidal war is unacceptable and totally different from von Clausewitz's concept of war, and his description of war as "a continuation of politics". However, such a total war might still occur accidentally or inadvertently, as a war indicating the breakdown of policy. At present the concept of "limited war" keeps creeping up. This is a von Clausewitz type of war which would be fought out in Europe and on the high seas, without the involvement of the devastating central systems strategic nuclear weapons. Opinions are divided about the feasibility of keeping such a war restricted, but experts agree that the risks of escalation are too high.

Modern weapons are so destructive and there is no possibility of real defence, that the reasonable conclusion must be that military power is non-usable. However, it would be wrong to draw the conclusion that national armed power should be abolished. If one of the two major military alliances were to disarm unilaterally, the weapons of the other alliance would then become usable thereby giving the Soviet Union or the United States absolute power. Such a situation is not attractive. History teaches us that a state usually misbehaves according to its might. Hence the need of countervailing armed power. Modern weapons are unusable but indispensable. This is the problem of present weapons, and it will remain a problem until it is solved by arms control and general disarmament.

What is the function of military power in such a situation[18]? Here, too, there are many different opinions. If any employment of military power carries with it macro-risks, the rational conclusion would be that the function of military power should be restricted to preventing its use in battle, i.e. deterrence. Deterrence aims not only at preventing the factual use of the sword in battle, but as well the rattling of the sword.

Many objections have been raised to such a radical conclusion about the function of armed power. It has been pointed out that military intervention against economic measures exercised by a Third World state, or opposition to ideological developments, may appear attractive. The American "rapid deployment forces" are destined in part to protect economic interests against non-military violations. This is an example of the concept of the political use of military power, the indirect or oblique use of force[19].

Experts may agree that the only function of armed force is to provide for peace and security, but opinions differ about the very concept of security. Security usually means military security with respect to the military power of a possible opponent; this might rather be called "enemy security." But with the present technological weapon developments

226

another danger arises, a danger hidden in the weapon-postures themselves. There are forms of destabilizing weapon-postures, such as the capacity to launch a successful surprise attack. War would be likely if one side acquired a first strike capability; it would be almost inevitable if both acquired it or thought they had acquired it. The premium on haste would have an almost absolute character.

Another aspect of a dangerous premium on haste concerns the situation when war has broken out. If one party has vulnerable weapons of mass destruction, e.g. eurostrategic weapons, the other may be inclined to destroy them immediately. The possessor, on the other hand, may be inclined to put them into action before that destruction. The premium on haste thus leads to a quick escalation, even when both sides have a vital interest in keeping the fighting under strict control, to give diplomatic action a chance.

Another "weapon-danger" is caused by the existing overkill. Use of the nuclear weapons available at present would lead to the total destruction of both sides. Such a threat is not needed for effective deterrence. But if a war started, – probably an inadvertent war, in a situation in which a local conflict could not be kept under control because of miscalculations or misperceptions – this overkill might lead to unimaginable disaster.

Thus, military security comprises not only "enemy-security" but also "weapon-security". The distinction is relevant. Steps to enhance enemy-security often diminish weapon-security, not only in bilateral relations. Vertical proliferation of nuclear weapons may easily enhance horizontal proliferation, and the spread of nuclear weapons all over the world would increase the weapon-insecurity.

There is a tendency at present to broaden the concept of security. State interests can be perceived to be violated by means other than military, e.g. by ideological developments or economic measures. Great powers are inclined to protect their interests against such violations by military means, and the military preparations in connection with scarce materials, such as oil, are prominent illustrations. Growing economic interdependence contributes to the fears of the developed nations of the collapse of their economy, through the loss of scarce materials. This has resulted in the ominous revival of the idea of protection of economic interest by military means.

The broadening of the security concept to "economic security" and "ideological security", with its corollary, the extension of the function of military force, may have disastrous effects. Threatened by one of the superpowers, Third World countries may seek protection by turning to the other superpower. This will strengthen the drive for superior military strength and preclude any chance of arms control and disarmament. By the same token, the Third World states may see strong incentives to arm themselves, even to "go nuclear", in an endeavour to prevent great power intervention.

Willingness to use armed force when national interests are threatened or violated by ideological or economic means, indicates a preparedness to disregard the prohibition of the use of force, enshrined in the United Nations Charter, according to which armed force is only to be employed as a reaction against an armed attack. This strict prohibition is reaffirmed in the definition of aggression adopted in 1974 by the General Assembly. The implied elimination of the legal prohibition of the use of force – the ground-rule of the United Nations structure – contributes to the misgivings of peace researchers about the broadened concept of security.

If the only legitimate function of national armed power is restricted to providing miliary security, a progressive development of international law, forbidding military capabilities beyond that function, would be feasible. Offensive, destabilizing and excessive postures would be prohibited. In accordance with the present legal situation of the law of arms control and disarmament that "the right of a state to possess arms is not unlimited", the United Nations General Assembly might be assigned the task of elaborating guiding principles for arms control negotiations, based on the restricted function of armed power. These guiding principles might later harden into binding rules of law: the much needed new chapter of international law restricting the sovereign national freedom of possession of armed force.

A more radical view concerning the present function of military power stresses the need to replace this power by non-violent means of defence, non-violent resistance and non-cooperation. In the domestic field the potential of non-violent resistance is impressive, because the power of a government is based on the obedience of its citizens. If this obedience is collectively renounced, a government becomes powerless. But such a relation of obedience does not apply to international relations, and therefore the prospect of non-violent resistance has less impact on the behaviour of a would-be aggressor. In a situation of occupation it again becomes a powerful tool to influence the behaviour of the occupying power[20]. How far civilian-based defence – a term used to indicate a defence policy against foreign invasions and internal take-overs relying on prepared non-cooperation and defiance by the trained civilian population and their institutions to deny the attacker's objections and make lasting control impossible – can be effective, is questionable. The conclusion of most peace researchers is that more research is needed on this topic[21].

Substantial research is in progress in the area of arms control and disarmament; on the forces which prevent effective arms control and disarmament; on reasonable measures to curb arms proliferation; and on the different methods to achieve results in this field. The usual method is that of negotiation ending in a treaty. The outlook for this method is not promising if one considers the outcome of 35 years of negotiations. Of other methods proposed, the most spectacular alternative is the daring process of "Graduated and Reciprocated Initiatives in Tension Reduction" (GRIT) proposed by Osgood[22]. This method involves a series of relatively small but not negligible unilateral steps taken publicly as a sign of readiness to go further if the opponent follows suit and as an invitation to reciprocate in like form.

The main research pertaining to arms control and disarmament deals with the opposing arguments and with the forces preventing effective agreements and arms control. These are the same forces in society which contribute to arms spending and the arms race, namely the military–industrial complex, the arms technologists, the bureaucracies, the hawks who only believe in power and the martial spirit of the population.

The concept of disarmament is clear. Alva Myrdal, in her book *The Game of Disarmament*[23], uses disarmament as a generic term, with a larger connotation than elimination of armaments. It covers all degrees of reduction of armaments, and it includes the preemption of options for further arms development (non-armament), as well as measures for regulating the production or use of arms quantity or "quality." This extension of the concept of disarmament is perhaps related to her strong rejection of the concept of arms control. Her book gives a fair description of the disarmament failure. She blames the superpowers in particular, who aim to maintain their status of superpower and thus seek to keep the distance between themselves and the rest of the world. She argues conclusively that the small powers have sinned by their silence. Now that the superpowers have failed to achieve substantial disarmament the small powers should take the lead. It is their historic mission to compel the world powers to behave more rationally.

Arms control comprises all measures to assure that armed power can fulfill optimally its reasonable function, which is, to provide for peace and security, by ensuring that the opponent's armed power will not be used for war or for the threat of war. This means the prevention of provocative, offensive features of armed postures, as well as of destabilizing characteristics, arms and arms systems which put a premium on haste to start a war, as in the case of a disarming first strike capability, or a capability of an effective surprise attack. Thus, as part of the SALT II agreements, the United States and the USSR agreed "to seek measures to strengthen stability by, among other things, limitations on strategic offensive arms most destabilizing to the strategic balance and by measures to reduce and to avert the risk of surprise attack"[24]. Arms control would aim at the right measure of armaments: sufficient to deter, but not leading, in case of failure of deterrence, to mutual annihilation.

To put it another way: arms control implies all measures to ensure that the weapons do not become disfunctional. Technological developments have brought about weapon-postures that can add to the existing tensions and dangers. The first function of arms control is the elimination of the dangers that stem from the weapon-postures themselves, from their offensive character which feeds the arms race, and from their destabilizing character which incites to early action.

The distinction between "arms control" and "disarmament" should be maintained, even though arms control may imply abolishing existing armed power. Arms control has no connection with the existence of détente, or the intensity of existing friendly relations. No "linkage" should be attempted between the willingness to negotiate arms control agreements and the political good behaviour of the other party. Indeed, arms control measures are even more needed in a period of tension or crisis. On the other hand, disarmament, the reduction of armed power to lower levels, aiming at general and complete disarmament, strongly depends on a peaceful climate. Here a "linkage" does exist.

Some balance of power will be needed as long as the anarchical international system is maintained. Disarmament theories are therefore closely related to theories concerning deterrence strategies. The radical analysis leading to the thesis "peace can only be maintained after elimination of deterrence" is less helpful for a rational approach than the search for optimal forms of deterrence. Maximum deterrence is rejected by most researchers, because it leads to endless arms races. A deterrence posture should not scare the opponent into rearmament. Minimal deterrence is preferable. This might take the form of inoffensive deterrence, or defensive deterrence, i.e. enough military power to make war an unacceptable prospect, but not enough military power to be able to start a successful offensive action. If both parties, eager to prevent nuclear war, would accept the strategy of defensive deterrence as a starting point, agreements which would make both parties more secure seem feasible with considerably fewer weapons at considerably less costs. The overkill would be eliminated and with it a risk that the disastrous weapons created to deter a von Clausewitz type war, would be used in an unforeseen and unexpected military confrontation, which might occur like a traffic accident in the existing hazardous international traffic.

References

1. *Journal of Peace Research*, Oslo, 1977, pp. 75-86. See further elaboration in Boulding's contribution "Metaphors and Models in the International System" in Akkerman, van Krieken and Pannenborg (eds), *Declarations on Principles. A Quest for Universal Peace*, Leyden 1977, p.311-321.
2. *Ibid.* p.83.
3. J.W. Fulbright, *Prospects for the West*, Cambridge 1963, p.43.
4. H. Kissinger at UN General Assembly, 23 September 1974.
5. J.D. Singer *et al: Explaining War*. Selected Papers from the Correlates of War Project, Sage Publications, London 1979, also J.D. Singer and M.D. Wallace: *To Augur Well, Early Warning Indicators in World Politics*. Sage Publications, London, 1979.
6. J. Dedring, *Recent Advances in Peace and Conflict Research, A Critical*

Survey. Sage Publications, Beverly Hills, London 1976.

7. J. van Kan in his L'idée de l'organisation internationale dans ses grandes phases, *Recueil des Cours de l'Academie de Droit International*, 1938, Vol. IV, p. 259-611.
8. UN General Assembly Resolution of 4 November 1954.
9. H. Bull, *The Anarchical Society. A Study of Order in World Politics*, London 1977.
10. R. Falk, On Writing a History of the Future, in H-H. Holm and E. Rudeng (eds): *Social Science. For What? Festschrift for J. Galtung*, Oslo, Bergen, Tromso, 1980, p. 87-91.
11. S. Hoffman, *Primacy or World Order*, New York, 1978.
12. J. Tinbergen, *Reshaping the International Order*, New York, 1976.
13. G. Clark & L.B. Sohn, *World Peace through World Law*, (3rd Ed) 1966.
14. R.A. Falk, The International Dimension of a New International Order, in A.J. Dolman, *Global Planning and Resource Management*, Pergamon Press, 1980, p. 87-102.
15. R. Kothari, *Footsteps into the Future*, New York, 1974; A. Mazrui, *A World Federation of Cultures: an African Perspective*, New York, 1976; R.A. Falk, *A Study of Future Worlds*, New York, 1975; G. Lagos & H. Godoy, *Revolution of Being: A Latin American View of the Future*, New York, 1977; J. Galtung, *The True World; A Transnational Perspective*, New York, 1980.
16. R.A. Falk: *This Endangered Planet: Prospects and Proposals for Human Survival*, New York 1971.
17. D. Senghaas, Abschreckhung und Frieden. *Studien zur Kritik organisierter Friedlosingkeit*, Frankfurt, 1972.
18. IISS Adelphi Paper 102: Force in Modern Societies. Its Place in International Politics, London 1973, and B.V.A. Röling, The Function of Military Power, in *Arms Control and Technological Innovation*, London, 1977, p. 288-302.
19. See S. Hoffman, *The Acceptability of Military Force*, in Adelphi Paper 102, p. 2-13.
20. G. Sharp. *Social Power and Political Freedom*, Boston, 1980.
21. For further elaboration of aspects of "civilian defence" and "social defence", see A. Roberts: *The Strategy of Civilian Defence. Non-violent Resistance to Aggression*, London 1967; G. Geeraerts (ed), *Possibilities of Civilian Defence*, Amsterdam and Lisse, 1976.
22. C.E. Osgood: *An Alternative to War or Surrender*, University of Illinois Press, 1962.
23. Alva Myrdal, *The Game of Disarmament*, New York 1976.
24. US v USSR Joint statement on SALT II. Vienna, June 18, 1979.

Chapter 14. Disarmament education and research

Swadesh Rana

Introduction

This chapter describes the purpose of education for disarmament, and the need to encourage people to be actively concerned with disarmament. In doing so, an attempt is also made to: (*a*) identify some of the existing obstacles to promote education for disarmament; and (*b*) suggest some major themes for research which should be incorporated in a curriculum for disarmament education both at the formal and informal levels.

One of the basic purposes of all education, in essence, is to equip human beings with an ability to understand their environment and to overcome its inherent constraints. The human environment, in its entirety, encompasses not only its specific physical and material features but also the politico-economic and socio-cultural order of human life[1]. Today, human beings, as a race, command a historically unprecedented understanding of their environment. Never in human history has the human race had so many resources, so many technical skills and so much potential for overcoming the constraints inherent in its environment as it has today. Nor ever before has it been better equipped to destroy completely, what it has created, in a matter of less than an hour.

Armament vs. disarmament

The world-wide weapons arsenals, involving a purely financial cost of over a million dollars per minute, constitute an almost incalculable loss of opportunities for the entire human race, and particularly for the poorer sections of society[2]. To the extent that the human and material resources consumed by the global military sector represent an economic waste, an

233

ecological hazard, a political risk, a societal penalty or a moral affront, those employing their education for promoting the armament phenomenon are negating the basic purpose of education. Nearly 50 per cent of the world's adult population, out of a total population of 4500 million people, cannot afford literacy[3]. But over 50 million people who have received some degree of technical training or formal education are directly or indirectly engaged in the designing, production, procurement or deployment of armaments. This figure includes: (*a*) some 25 million persons in the world's regular armed forces; (*b*) roughly 10 million world-wide in para-military forces; (*c*) approximately 4 million civilians currently employed in defence departments; (*d*) an estimated 500 000 scientists and engineers engaged in research and development for military purposes; and (*e*) at least 5 million workers directly engaged in the production of weapons and other specialized military equipment[4].

The world-wide weapons arsenals contain some 3–5 tonnes of explosives for every man, woman and child on earth. But the process of actually negotiating a reduction and eventual elimination of these arsenals remains highly concentrated in a few thousand people, who constitute a barely calculable fraction of 0.01 per cent of those involved in making and deploying them.

Simply stated, the statistics mentioned above demonstrate a serious lacuna in the existing institutionalized attempts to bring about disarmament through a process of negotiation alone. Too many of the world's educated people are involved in the phenomenon of armament; and too few of the world's educated people have been entrusted with the responsibility to negotiate disarmament. Two very obvious results of this regrettable situation can be easily identified.

In the first place, the arguments in favour of armament have generally appeared to be better informed than those against it. The need for disarmament has been mostly projected in terms of the virtues of peace and the horrors of war. It has essentially assumed the characteristics of an appeal to the conscience of mankind, almost always stirring a nagging sense of unease but seldom acquiring the force of a rational imperative. The arguments in favour of armaments, on the other hand, are usually forwarded with an apparently strong appeal to human rationality and supported by meticulous concern for conceptual clarity and empirical quantification. Armament spending is demonstrated as having a positive effect on economic growth; armament technology is projected as producing valuable spin-offs for the civilian economy; the armament sector is portrayed as creating job opportunities; export of armaments is sometimes described as a way of improving the balance of payments. And if none of these arguments proves convincing in a total tally of the short and long term consequences of the armament phenomenon, the entire debate is subordinated to the near universal appeal in favour of purchasing national security, regardless of cost. Notions of national security vary from a direct and tangible threat to geographical frontiers, to the real and perceived challenges to national ideologies, not to mention the personal ambitions of national elites. The proliferation of armaments tends to expand in proportion to the multiplicity of meanings attached to the notion of national security so that those responsible for defining national security have an almost inexhaustible range of choices available to strengthen the case for more and more armaments.*

Secondly, the process of negotiating disarmament has been complicated by the role of some of the most highly educated among the world's total literate population i.e. the scientists and engineers, and the strategic analysts. The scientists and engineers in the military sector, particularly those in the R&D field, have imparted an element of near automaticity to military technology which tends to race ahead of disarmament negotiations and destabilizes the base-line of negotiating positions. The strategic analysts, particularly those committed to perfecting confrontation tactics with existing or future adversaries, tend to broaden the area of agreed negotiations by linking disarmament measures to a broad range of issues relevant to the politics of negotiating but not always directly covered by the range of negotiable problems. One of the tenacious problems currently bedevilling the SALT II process, for example, is the attitude of the major negotiating parties about the 'grey areas' in their strategic calculations or, in other words, the conflict situations in the Third World. Apart from the obvious fact that these so-called 'grey areas' are not themselves participating in the negotiating process and, hence, may or may not endorse the agreements reached therein, their implicit or explicit inclusion among the negotiable problems will inevitably complicate and delay the SALT II process.

The anomalies in the present situation have given rise to a growing public concern about the military orientation in the existing system of education, as well as the limitations of treating disarmament as a subject of negotiation alone. Touched by an anxiety over the future and a sense of powerlessness over the present, people are coming forward in new combinations, often by-passing existing social and political structures, to seek ways and means to influence the outcome of decisions affecting their lives. Consumer advocates, trade unions, environmentalists, religious groups, health and care specialists, economic planners, energy conservationists, and several other specialized interest groups, are trying to mobilize public opinion with a view to articulate it at a point where it becomes a factor in the decision-making processes relating to disarmament. Their motivations vary from broadly altruistic to strictly personal:

---

*The 25 references to national security in the Final Document of the First United Nations Special Session on Disarmament use the term as threats of a military aggression across national frontiers.

some of them are seeking disarmament as a prerequisite for a more equitable distribution of the world's finite resources; but for many of them it also means an attempt to establish public accountability of a process which is surrounded by a complexity that debars a thorough assessment of its socio-economic costs and benefits.

No other aspect of the contemporary armament phenomenon has generated a more co-ordinated reaction than that accompanying the growing application of science and technology to the military sector. Traditional channels of communicating public concern have been supplemented by new forms of political agitations such as demonstrations, plebiscites and social rejection of technological decisions made within a framework of closed politics. Several factors have contributed towards making the scientific and technologically-related issues pertaining to the military sector different from other issues commonly associated with public controversies and participatory movements[5].

In general, the rapid pace of change in military technology creates an unsettling effect in the public mind about its potentially dangerous side-effects. Even those who vote for nuclear-generated energy pause before endorsing a decision to have a nuclear reactor in their neighbourhood without having some understanding of the risks of ecological pollution, hazards of waste disposal, and dangers of contamination at the work place. Some irreversible effects may not be immediately visible but have a long-term social relevance. For example, the cumulative impact of nuclear testing on the ozone layer, or the inevitable implications for personal privacy of the security precautions surrounding military installations, go far beyond the present predictive capacity of a public understanding of the armament phenomenon.

The horizons of optimum feasibility of military technology, and the limits of public understanding about its concrete and intangible implications, simply do not coincide. Government secrecy about information pertaining to the military sector is mostly upheld on the grounds that only those parties having a special interest and competence should be allowed access to the relevant information. The gap between those educated sections of society which directly or indirectly contribute to the knowledge that constitutes the information withheld from the public at large, and those whose lives are affected by the application of this knowledge, continues unabated. Public anxiety about the decision-making processes in the disarmament negotiations is aggravated by an awareness, that the full range of political choices, available to serve the purposes expected to be pursued by the armament phenomenon, is not likely to be explored since there is a demonstrable tendency by the decision-makers to subordinate broad political problems to narrow technological solutions. The existing institutionalized attempts to control the armament phenomenon through the process of "closed" negotiations have, thus, come perilously close to tilting at windmills.

Education for disarmament can capitalize upon the growing public anxiety about the armament phenomenon and strengthen its claims for participating in the process of disarmament negotiations by filling in the information gaps perpetuated through a denial of access to the armament-related body of knowledge. As a separate field of study, education for disarmament may still appear to be a discipline in search of a definition. But the objectives of such an education can be clearly spelt out precisely in the terms applicable to the need for education in general: to understand the human environment and to overcome the hazards it has accumulated on account of the armament phenomenon. A demilitarization of existing educational priorities and a democratization of the process of disarmament negotiations constitute the twin objectives of education for disarmament. The need to demilitarize education and democratize negotiations was tacitly accepted by the 1974 Unesco Recommendation on Education for International Understanding Co-operation and Peace and Education Relating to Human Rights and Fundamental Freedoms, which called for: (i) a global perspective, an understanding and respect for various cultures and an awareness of global interdependence; and (ii) decision-making based on rational analysis of relevant facts and factors. Moreover, the principles of disarmament education, as defined by the World Congress on Disarmament Education include preparing students "to resist incitement to war, military propaganda and militarism in general." (see p.263)

The Role of Unesco

The levels at which education for disarmament should be imparted, and the form it takes, have been the subjects of continuous concern for Unesco which has placed repeated emphasis on making education an instrument of transition from an armed to a disarmed world. The scale of transition required is matched only by the urgency to do so before a seemingly endless arms race irreparably narrows down the socio-cultural and politico-economic choices available to a world increasingly vulnerable to the immediate and cumulative effects of the armament phenomenon. The transition to a disarmed world will inevitably involve parallel attempts at arresting the damage to the total human environment – as defined earlier – and also a reversal of the trends perpetuating the armament phenomenon.

The major challenges facing those interested in promoting education for disarmament are also recognized by Unesco: the abundance of different political and strategic doctrines concerning the foreign and domestic security of states; the politics and economics of the international traffic in arms; the conditioning of public opinion and of children from an early age to accept a glorified vision of military personalities, feats of arms, wars and conquests; the spread of certain fashionable theories in the sphere of mass-psychology; and the impact of mass media. In meeting these challenges, education for disarmament confronts several obstacles which can be generally grouped under three categories: political, perceptual, and pedagogical[6].

A major political obstacle is in the international system itself which, on the one hand, renounces the use of force and, on the other, accepts the right of all nations to arm in self-defence. Conventional and juridical renunciations of the use of force for aggressive and repressive purposes run against the historical experience of the recent and not too recent past. Visions of a disarmed world continue to belong to the realm of aspirations, whereas memories of being witnesses to, or participants in, conflicts involving the use or threat of use of force are imbedded in reality.

Among the perceptual obstacles to disarmament are fear and ignorance. Fear of the economic consequences of disarmament, including dislocation and unemployment; fear of the real or perceived adversary in a world where not every nation will be equally disarmed; and fear of the unknown, dominate perceptions fed by formal and informal education. Information and knowledge likely to change these perceptions do not figure prominently in teaching curricula and priority research areas in the current educational systems. Ignorance about the complexities of the problems involved in disarmament is perpetuated by a lack of understanding of all the facts and factors, and is reinforced by the secrecy surrounding matters pertaining to the armament phenomenon.

The pedagogical obstacles, stemming both from the political and perceptual, involve the affective and the cognitive domain. National educational systems are still inadequately equipped with the tools and resources required to transmit the fullest implications of contemporary global interdependence. When pupils of yesterday become decision-makers of today, their reactions to issues confronting them tend to be dominated by a tendency to fight off the ghosts of the past rather than to meet the challenges of the future, unless their socio-cultural milieu governs the primacy of their responses. Observations, in this context, are made by some peace educators who were heartened by the fact that in the language of some of the tribes living in primitive conditions, the word "war" did not exist. Betty Reardon[6], for example, has observed that among some cultures which put a higher premium on tradition and human relations rather than on competition and efficiency, group co-operation is a strong socializing force. She also notes that the highest degree of competitive socialization, with an emphasis on winning, predominates in societies which are also most active in the armament phenomenon.

While admitting the role of the cultural milieu in determining human responses, it needs to be emphasized that no national culture, howsoever primitive or modern it may be, lacks the basic values which put a premium on mutual recognition of, and respect for, the right of survival of each human being. Education for disarmament, therefore, does not need a new glossary of elementary values to be learnt in teaching respect for human survival. Nor does a demilitarization of education require an alienation of individuals from their immediate cultural ethos. What is urgently needed, however, is a fuller understanding of the common destiny of mankind: political, social, economic and ecological. Conceptually sound and empirically quantifiable analyses of the negative impacts of the armament phenomenon, and the mutually advantageous consequences of disarmament measures, should become a part of the curriculum designed for disarmament education.

A growing literature on the subjects which could be included in the curriculum is already available in the pronouncements and publications of the various interest groups concerned with disarmament-related issues. Its incorporation into tools of formal or informal education within the national educational systems requires a scale of co-ordination and planning which may exceed the human and material resources available to a single nation. Also, the evolving national perspectives dominating educational planning in each country need constant juxtaposition to the world educational milieu to overcome some of the political and perceptual obstacles described earlier. It is here that Unesco can play a vital role as a catalyst and a co-ordinating body.

Through a series of symposia, seminars and conferences (see p.260) Unesco has been promoting an awareness of the need for, and the purposes of, disarmament education. More recently, it has provided a forum for pooling the global intellectual resources required to overcome the challenges emerging from traditional approaches towards strategic interests, threat perceptions and military doctrines. In pursuing its goals further, Unesco can derive strong sustenance from the priority consideration being given by the United Nations to disarmament issues, including the factors affecting the process of disarmament negotiations. A relatively recent development in this respect has been a number of expert studies undertaken by the United Nations Centre for Disarmament pertaining to the socio-economic opportunity costs of the arms race, the nature and magnitude of the nuclear threat, the reduction of military budgets and the relationship between disarmament and development.

Along with the conceptualization embodied in the relevant resolutions on the subject, particularly the Final Document of the First United Nations Special Session on Disarmament, these United Nations studies can provide Unesco with some major themes which could be purposefully incorporated into Unesco's programme for making education an instrument of transition from an armed to a disarmed world. To specify some of these:

1. All the problems and difficulties of transition connected with

disarmament could be met by appropriate national and international measures. There should thus be no doubt that the diversion to peaceful purposes of the resources now in military use could be accomplished to the benefit of all countries and lead to the improvement of world economic and social conditions. The achievement of general and complete disarmament would be an unqualified blessing to all mankind[7].

2. The arms race must be stopped not only because of the immediate perils it holds for us all, but because the longer it continues, the more intractable the problems of economic growth, social justice and environment will become. A halt in the arms race and a significant reduction in military expenditures would help the social and economic development of all countries and would increase the possibilities of providing additional aid to developing countries[8].

3. National and international efforts to promote development should be neither postponed nor allowed to lag merely because progress in disarmament is slow. However, disarmament and development can be linked to each other because the enormous amount of resources wasted in the arms race might be utilized to facilitate development and progress. Furthermore, the blatant contrast between this waste of resources and the unfilled needs of development can be used to help rouse public opinion in favour of effective disarmament, and in favour of the achievement of further progress in development, particularly of the developing countries[9].

4. The social, political, technological and industrial options of countries are affected by their participation in the arms race. International policies, not only in the military field, but also in the fields of international trade and of co-operation and exchanges generally, are influenced by the climate of confrontation and apprehension engendered by the arms race. Many of the major problems faced by the world community, problems of development, economic imbalance and inflation, pollution, energy and raw materials, trade relations and technology, and so forth, are enhanced and exacerbated by the arms race. Progress in other areas, such as health, education, housing and many more, is delayed owing to lack of resources[10].

5. The arms race between the superpowers is by far the most precarious. It involves the greatest diversion of resources and the greatest inherent dangers, and it constitutes the principal driving force of the world-wide arms race. This competition is even more intense than is suggested by the immense size and the rapid expansion of their arsenals, because it takes place primarily in a qualitative rather than quantitative dimension, each new generation of weapons being more complex and more destructive than the ones replaced[11].

6. Despite all arguments, some countries have chosen to base their

security on nuclear weapons. In trying to maintain a balance of deterrence each superpower is concerned that the other might achieve nuclear superiority, and thus the nuclear arms race continues. In the light of their awesome capabilities, nuclear weapons have now acquired a unique role in international relations and the future of mankind is a captive to the perceived security of a few nuclear weapon states, most notably that of the two superpowers[12].

7.   Progress in disarmament, both nuclear and conventional, and avoidance of policies and actions leading to a deterioration of the political and security conditions at the global level, would greatly facilitate agreement on effective measures in each region. Equally, progress in regional disarmament, the equitable solution of problems, and the just settlement of disputes at the regional level, could create conditions that would promote disarmament and the relaxation of tension at the global level[13].

8.   The adoption of the disarmament measures should take place in such an equitable and balanced manner as to ensure the right of each state to security and to ensure that no individual state or group of states may obtain advantages over others at any stage. At each stage the objective should be undiminished security at the lowest possible level of armaments and military forces[14].

9.   The economic and social consequences of the arms race are so detrimental that its continuation is obviously incompatible with the implementation of the new international economic order based on justice, equity and co-operation[15].

Study of disarmament and development

Primarily because of the nature of its findings and partly also to describe the process whereby a world-wide research on the subject was conducted, the recently concluded United Nations expert study on Disarmament and Development provides an illustrative example of encouraging a body of knowledge, whereby the arguments in favour of disarmament acquire the same kind of well-informed appeal to rationality that is generally associated with the arguments in favour of global military activities. The *ad hoc* group of 27 governmental experts appointed by the Secretary-General to conduct the study were provided with specific terms of reference determined by the General Assembly itself at its first Special Session on Disarmament held in 1978. In accordance with the general guidelines given in Document A/S-10/9, which served as its mandate, the Expert Group addressed itself to the following main areas of investigation:

(*a*) present day utilization of resources for military purposes;
(*b*) economic and social consequences of a continuing arms race and of the implementation of disarmament measures;
(*c*) conversion and redeployment of resources released from military purposes through disarmament measures to economic and social development.

The Group's mandate recognized that, in view of the broad and complex field to be studied and in the interests of securing the broadest possible participation in the project, it would be desirable to draw on expert assistance from all over the world. To achieve this, the Group drew up a list of researchers and institutes around the world considered to be knowledgeable in the various fields of study relevant to the Group's terms of reference. All those on the list were invited to submit research proposals for evaluation by the Group.

In total, the Group received some 75 research proposals. In the selection process, the Group endeavoured to meet a number of criteria. The primary considerations were that the commissioned proposals should collectively cover the areas of research in the Group's mandate as completely as possible, that the proposals be original and well-constructed, and that the responsible researchers be manifestly competent for the task. In addition, the Group endeavoured to ensure that the research would focus on as many countries and geographic regions as possible, and that those responsible for the research would come from countries at different stages of development and be representative of different economic and social systems. Furthermore, the Group considered that the problem of the conversion of resources from armaments to economic and social development, particularly for the benefit of developing countries, was of special importance; this also influenced the selection of proposals.

A total of 45 research projects were eventually commissioned by the Group; forty of these were actually submitted. Apart from the commissioned material, the Group also utilized the results of the on-going research in many institutions around the world, including the United Nations Industrial Research Development Organization (UNIDO), the United Nations Institute for Training and Research (UNITAR), the United Nations Conference on Trade and Development (UNCTAD), the International Labour Organization (ILO) and the Stockholm International Peace Research Institute (SIPRI). Similarly, the results of several international conferences and symposia, on subject-matter directly or closely related to the Group's term of reference, provided relevant inputs. Finally, the Group solicited the views of non-governmental organizations – including trade unions and other professional organizations – both as inputs to its work and with a view to facilitating the wide dissemination of the findings of the final report. The Group also attempted to solicit the views of employers' organizations.

In examining the findings of the inputs available to it, the Group was guided by the directives of the General Assembly which specifically required that this study "should be forward-looking and policy-oriented and place special emphasis on both the desirability of a re-allocation, following disarmament measures, of resources now being used for military purposes to economic and social development, particularly for the benefit of the developing countries, and *the substantive feasibility of such a re-allocation*" (emphasis added). The terms of reference for the research undertaken for this study placed special emphasis on strengthening the socio-economic case for an empirically quantifiable and rationally imperative relationship between disarmament and development, based upon the emerging mutuality of interests in a world increasingly pushed towards growing economic interdependence. This perspective also remained at the forefront of the Group's concern in conceptualizing the relationship between disarmament and development; in calculating the magnitude of real resources claimed by the world-wide military outlays; in assessing the opportunity costs of the arms race for societies at different levels of development and with different economic and social systems; in examining the technical feasibility of converting armament-related efforts into developmental channels; in projecting the direct and indirect benefits of disarmament; and finally, in examining the possibilities for some institutional arrangements to facilitate the transfer of disarmament-related financial resources for the benefit of the developing countries.

Among the major conclusions of the Disarmament–Development Study, the following can provide some useful guidelines for the present and future analyses of the armament phenomenon:

1. Military outlays, by definition, fall into the category of consumption and not investment.
2. A co-existence of high rates of military spending and high rates of economic growth does not reflect a causal linkage between armaments and development.
3. Economic growth promotes development but is not coterminous with it.
4. The dynamics of the arms race involves more than the mere number of its participants and the sum total of the expenditures nationally consumed for military purposes.
5. Up to 6 per cent of the world resources – few infinite, some non-renewable and many scarce – are annually consumed by the arms race. This fact accentuates the inefficient allocation of the remaining 94 per cent of resources – both human and material – within and among nations.
6. The arms race and development are in a competitive relationship not only in terms of resources but also in the vital dimension of attitudes and perceptions.

7. The world can either continue to indulge in a mindless arms race or make deliberate attempts to establish a more sustainable international economic and political order. It cannot do both.

By an analysis of military spending as an impediment to economic growth, and of the arms race as an obstacle to the establishment of a new international economic order, the study has strengthened the economic case for a disarmament-development relationship. By projecting the arms race as a threat to international security, and by outlining the dimensions of non-military threats to national security, it underlines the strategic considerations pertinent to a realistic assessment of the potentials for reversing the arms race and reducing the national military outlays. In suggesting that policies aimed at implementing the disarmament-development relationships are likely to broaden the base of East-West détente and put the North-South dialogue in a mutually advantageous frame of reference, the study projects the direct inputs for development as indirect investments into détente.

References

1. Luis Echevara, "Survival Demands the Creation of New Models of Development", *United Nations Environmental Programme: Annual Review 1979*, Nairobi, 1980.
2. Ruth Leger Sivard, *World Military and Social Expenditures*, Leesburg, Virginia, 1981.
3. *World Development Report 1981*, OECD, Paris, 1981.
4. *Study on the Relationship between Disarmament and Development*, United Nations A/36/356, 1981.
5. *Technology on Trial: Public Participation in Decision-Making Related to Science and Technology*, OECD, Paris, 1979.
6. Betty Reardon. "Obstacles to Disarmament Education", *Obstacles to Disarmament and Ways of Overcoming Them*, Unesco, 1981, p. 113-134.
7. Report of the Secretary-General on the Economic and Social Consequences of Disarmament, UN Publication 62. IX. 1, p. 52.
8. *Economic and Social Consequences of the Arms Race and of Military Expenditures*, UN Publication E.73. IX. 16, p. 38.
9. *ibid*, p. 22.
10. *Economic and Social Consequences of the Arms Race and of Military Expenditures*, UN Publication E. 78. IX. 1, p. 72.
11. *Official Records of the Preparatory Committee for the Second Special Session on Disarmament*, A/AC. 206/9 p. 4.
12. *ibid*, p. 24.
13. *ibid*, p. 30.
14. Final Document of First UNSSOD, p. 8.
15. *ibid*, p. 6.

Chapter 15. Social consciousness and education for disarmament (How to learn to think in a new way)

Sergei Kapitza

Introduction

Disarmament is undoubtedly one of the most complex issues of our time. Its scale is determined by the reverse process, that of the arms race, which is considered by many as an intersocial global problem[1]. World expenditure on arms is now more than one billion dollars a day. It is estimated that about half of all scientists in the developed countries are, in one way or another, involved in the arms race. Armaments are an even heavier burden for the developing countries, where the relative costs, in terms of the GNP are often greater than in the developed countries.

After having gone through two World Wars in this century, Europe has now experienced peace for 36 years. But on this Continent, we have at present the greatest concentration of the most diverse and powerful instruments of destruction. For the whole planet the explosive power in the nuclear arsenals is equivalent to 3-5 tons of TNT per capita, but for Europe, with its high population density, the tonnage is ten times greater; one railway truck of high explosives for each of the 700 million Europeans, or one kilogramme per square metre.

If these numbers are not impressive enough, imagine what could happen if nuclear power stations, of which more than a hundred are now operating in Europe, were attacked with nuclear weapons. The destruction of a reactor in a power station by a nuclear explosive injects into the atmosphere radioactivity which decays more slowly than that of the bomb itself, contaminating vast areas for much longer periods. Thus, nuclear reactors, and nuclear fuel processing plants, could become components of a most lethal radiological weapon[2].

Consider also the consequences of the collapse of the complex infrastructure, the highly developed and interconnected mechanism of our life, in the wake of nuclear war.

Social consciousness

However sophisticated and powerful nuclear weapons may be, the main factor that determines their use is human consciousness, or to be more specific, its surrender to unreason. Of all the aspects of the problem of disarmament – historic, economic and social – let us consider the part played by technical and scientific progress in relation to the consciousness of the human being.

It would be appropriate to quote here the moving words of I.P. Pavlov, from his preface to *Lectures on Conditioned Reflexes*[3]:

> "Let the mind rise from victory to victory over surrounding nature, let it conquer for human life and activity not only the surface of the earth but all that lies between the depth of the seas and the outer limits of the atmosphere, let it command for its service prodigious energy to flow from one part of the universe to the other, let it annihilate space for the transferrence of its thoughts – yet the same human creature, led by dark powers to wars and revolutions and their horrors, produces for itself incalculable material losses and inexpressible pain and reverts to bestial conditions. Only science, exact science about human nature itself, and the most sincere approach to it by the aid of the omnipotent scientific method, will deliver man from his present gloom, and will purge him from his contemporary shame in the sphere of interhuman relations."

It is now generally recognized that subjective factors must be taken into consideration when dealing with problems of arms and conflict. Human behaviour, human consciousness, built up into a system of ideas expressed in different forms of social consciousness through ideology, has contributed to the arms race. But human reasons can and should prevent a nuclear holocaust; it should guide us away from the present state of affairs and help us in developing the means to resolve the broad, truly global problems that face the world.

Scientists have for many years expressed concern over these matters. In recent years consideration has been given to the subjective factors in disarmament issues. For example, in Pugwash steps were taken to investigate psychological approaches in resolving critical situations. While the main Pugwash activities are directed towards scientific, technical and military aspects of the arms race, in 1980 and 1981 special workshops were convened on the role of the mass media in averting nuclear war. An important development is the involvement of psychiatrists and doctors in discussions on these matters. The new international movement of physicians has proved to be very successful in drawing attention to more than just medical problems. Doctors have managed to deliver their message better than scientists, by using a more direct and personal approach.

In discussing Pugwash activities it has often been suggested that the scientists, meeting in private, and directing their efforts mainly to other scientists and decision makers, should also attempt a wider dissemination of the results of their deliberations. It should be specially noted that the founding fathers of Pugwash – Russell and Einstein – in their Manifesto signed by a group of eminent scientists, have explicitly shown how to act. They did everything they could to spread the message on the danger of nuclear war to the widest possible audience. The Manifesto (see Appendix 1) also invited us to "learn to think in a new way"; in other words, to change our thinking and our mentality on matters of armaments. This point has been extensively discussed by M. Markov.[4]

Education for disarmament

The principles and moral issues to which a child is exposed in its home and family, the education that it later receives at school, college or university, determine attitudes and *Weltanschauung*. In studying physics and biology, chemistry and astronomy, one acquires an understanding of the working of nature, one is exposed to the power of the scientific method. Unfortunately, the traditional way science is taught, usually dividing everything into separate subjects, does not lead to a systematic approach. This lack of interdisciplinary thinking looms even larger when we consider the connections between the humanities and sciences, the dichotomy usually designated as "the two cultures".

To what extent do we use quantitative thinking when studying literature, history or the arts? To what extent are we shown its limitations? In a broader sense, to what extent does the study of history prepare us for the pressing issues of our time, marked by a complex interplay of science and society? To what extent could the symptoms of fear and apathy – demonstrated by escapism and lack of interest shown by the younger generation in some countries – be related to this lack of an integrated approach in our educational system? To what extent can the whole issue of the emergence of irrationality be traced to defects in modern education, to a lack of a more general scientific and social outlook, without which it is very difficult to start thinking in a new way not only on matters of disarmament, but on the social impact of science and technology?

A more integrated, interdisciplinary approach is crucial not only in the case of disarmament but also for all the problems that are complex and global in their nature. For example, one should certainly introduce the concepts of ecology in teaching biology. In teaching physics one should provide the elements for a better understanding of the problems of energy in its broader implications. There is quite a long list of problems that should be reconsidered and brought into the school curriculum if we are to prepare the next generation for a better comprehension of the set of global problems.

One of the most necessary conditions for disarmament is the development of an understanding of other nations, other cultures, the variety of customs and traditions that make up the world. At present, on the suggestion of Unesco, a comparative study has been done on history books. It would be interesting to find out to what extent this had led to a revision of the way history is taught, to a more considerate treatment of the "other man's point of view". The recent curtailment of cultural and scientific exchanges has been a most unfortunate development, occurring at a time when mutual understanding is so important.

On the tertiary level, the development of the necessary educational prerequisites to disarmament faces many of the same difficulties as at school. Perhaps the most important one is the necessity to develop a systematic and integrated approach; paradoxically, it is absent at this higher level. The modern trend of specialization, both in training and in acquiring academic recognition, does not help to encourage education in the field of interdisciplinary studies of global problems. Most universities, which by definition should and do have the facilities for a really universal training, are hardly in a position to encourage these studies under present conditions.

The main criticism that has been directed at the first, manifestly path-finding study *"The Limits to Growth*[5], was that it was limited in expertise and methodology. But it is the positive result, the new dimensions that have been added to social, scientific and technological issues, that is really significant. This set of problems has gained recognition and has been brought to the foreground of research with the development of new methods; and it is this, rather than the detailed recommendations that could seemingly follow from the models, that is the important message. It is training through research that has been the main educational method, and has led to the spread of these studies and to the development of the whole field. That is why it is difficult in this field to teach a formal course, as the whole subject is rapidly evolving.

Much of what has been said had direct relevance to disarmament. The problem is recognized; parts of the subject can and are examined by existing special fields of study; but what is wanted is an integrated approach to the whole subject. It is certainly most necessary to provide special training in this field at the first degree or doctoral levels. We can only hope that the number of people trained in this field will be larger than the immediate requirements of governmental organizations, the military establishment and international organizations. How small the effort is can be illustrated by pointing out that in the United States the total expenditure on research on disarmament is much less than on military bands!

A concentrated effort in the field of disarmament is related to the creation of a system for re-educating people, for guiding their energy and ideas which for ages have been conditioned on the principle that "might is right". This is why a widespread long term effort is necessary. We may ask what the international scientific community has done to enhance these efforts, to give more support to Unesco, to international research institutes such as SIPRI, or the International Institute for Applied Systems Analysis (IIASA), or to other bodies that can contribute to education and study on disarmament. Finally, a greater effort should be directed to the follow-up of the policies of those countries which have managed to develop a concept of security not based on massive armaments, and to the educational effort and public opinion background that support such policies.

Public opinion, the media and disarmament

As an educational tool and informational channel the mass media are the most powerful means to influence public thinking and guide public opinion about the realities of ideology. This is not the place to consider the full impact which the mass media have on the individual, and on the way people and society act, but, of all the media, some consideration will be given to television. Television came into being at approximately the same time as nuclear weapons. Both are the direct result of scientific and technological developments with a major social impact. Compared with the press and radio, television has a much greater emotional impact, it appeals to feelings and can be used an an instrument of persuasion. The atom bomb too can be used in such a way, but rather more as an instrument of fear and horror, as the ultimate psychological weapon of terror. It would be interesting to reflect on the comments of a future historian in comparing the social impact that these diverse developments of science and technology had on human thinking and behaviour in our time.

On the other hand, television can certainly be used to propagate the message of science. At present, we can see that by informing the public on scientific matters, by popularizing the broader facts of science, television can help to advance more general socio-scientific concepts, and the incorporation of science into our modern culture. In the Soviet Union, the author has had wide experience with a regular fortnightly programme under the title "Things obvious yet incredible" in which scientists from many countries have participated. In the past 8 years the programme has received recognition by being transmitted nationwide to the largest audience that exists in a country spanning ten time-zones of the globe. These programmes are aimed at developing attitudes to scientific matters, and helping to incorporate science into our cultural and public thinking. On a number of occasions science, armaments and peace were discussed. Well known are the series "The Ascent of Man" by J. Bronowski and the recent serial "Cosmos" by C. Sagan, in which an effort has also been made to explain the menace of nuclear arms. On this subject special mention should be made of "Nuclear Nightmares" by Nigel Calder. Programmes of this type, disseminating the message of world science, also help in developing an understanding among people on an international scale. In introducing scientific thinking, such programmes help to develop attitudes to global problems and a new awareness on these subjects.

An interesting analysis of the place and role of the mass media is contained in the Unesco report "Many Voices, One World"[6] prepared by the MacBride Commission. A whole section of Chapter IV, "Images of the World" is devoted to issues of war and armaments.

This document contains outspoken criticism of many of the aspects of the mass media in the Western countries. On matters of disarmament and public opinion the following statement made by Mr. MacBride in an address delivered at the University of Peace, Brussels in 1979, is of interest:

> "The absence of an adequate public opinion in support of world disarmament is in part due to the failure of the media – electronic and written – to give priority to disarmament issues. Apart from the direct influence which they can, and do, exercise on governments, the military establishments wield a considerable amount of indirect influence by feeding material to the mass media so as to create fears in the minds of the people. This is done by exaggerating the dangers posed by a likely enemy. It is also done by exaggerating the military and armament potential of the other side. The only way of overcoming the pressures that are exerted on governments to increase military expenditure and armament is through public opinion. Public opinion has now become much more powerful than ever before and it is in a position to force governments to comply with its wishes".[7]

The Commission of Unesco experts particularly felt that the press and media should in no way encourage the distribution of false or alarming information on strategic armament and on other military matters. The report further noted from a paper submitted to the Commission that:

> "Even such an illustrious event as the United Nations Special Session on Disarmament received scant treatment. Before the Session it was difficult to get it mentioned at all: I am reliably informed that the Government itself was "desperate" to obtain publicity for its own proposals. The huge Assembly for Disarmament and Peace obtained scarcely a mention, although 730 people attended it, and it was the biggest peace conference for years. At the same time a propaganda campaign developed in the press generally designed to pose a most serious threat to the West, emphasizing how our "defence" preparations were falling behind those of the Soviet Union, and how essential it was for us to spend more on 'defence'. What a good preparation for the Special Session! It could not have been more effective if deliberate!"[8]

Finally, in the recommendation we read:

> "Due attention should be paid to the problems of peace and disarmament, human rights, development and the creation of a new communication order. Mass media both printed and audiovisual, should be encouraged to publicise

significant documents of the United Nations, of Unesco, of the world peace movements, and of various other international and national organizations devoted to peace and disarmament. The curricula of schools of journalism should include study of these international problems and the views expressed on them within the United Nations.

All forms of co-operation among the media, the professionals, and their associations, which contribute to the better knowledge of other nations and cultures, should be encouraged and promoted.

Reporting on international events or developments in individual countries in situations of crisis and tension requires extreme care and responsibility. In such situations the media often constitute one of the few, if not the sole, link between combatants or hostile groups. This clearly casts on them a special role which they should seek to discharge with objectivity and sensitivity."9

The events of autumn 1981, with the massive anti-nuclear demonstrations in Europe, have shown to what extent public opinion has become aware of the immediate issues of the arms race in Europe.

In developing attitudes towards global problems and disarmament much could be done by using the existing consensus of opinion worked out by international organizations, such as IIASA, SIPRI, Club of Rome, etc.

These materials could help in the preparation of special TV programmes, such as a whole series produced nationally or in collaboration with different national networks. One can envisage public lectures, "round-table" discussions on these matters with participants from different countries. In the preparation of nationally distributed programmes much could be done by the pre-distribution of appropriate illustrative material which could then be commented upon by a moderator. When preparing internationally produced programmes one must bear in mind the necessity not only of dubbing them into another language but of matching them to another cultural environment. Much needs to be done to realize fully the potential of such messages and of properly delivering their meaning.

This is especially important in dealing with such sensitive subjects as nuclear war and disarmament which can easily generate an adverse reaction, and lead to greater fear and insecurity. However complex the question may be, one must recognize that apocalyptic doomsday philosophy, having a great shock value, cannot in all cases be considered to be constructive. One has probably to persuade by more reasonable means, even though these may take a longer time to develop in the public mind.

On the other hand, the militaristic propaganda has been aiming at persuading the people to accept the idea of a limited nuclear war, to come to terms with the possibility of nuclear arms being used. An example of this is Hackett's book *The Third World War*10. The influence of such publications is not very significant in their immediate effect, but they have to be considered as symptoms, as signals of a less conspicuous, deep-lying tendency to develop complacency to the issues of a nuclear war.

In this respect in the 1960s the films "On the Beach", "Dr. Strangelove" and "Fail Safe" were produced. Somehow such films have ceased to appear, and it seems that the whole issue of the danger of nuclear war is not finding its way into modern art and writing as it did in the recent past. In the last decades there has emerged a well defined trend in Soviet literature on the Second World War. The epic writings of K. Simonov, novels by V. Bykov and V. Astafiev, to name only a few, films made following these books, have vividly shown all the horror and devastation of the war to a generation that happily missed this terrible experience. Special mention should be made of 20 films of a Soviet-American co-production TV serial "The Great Fatherland War" directed by R. Karmen and circulated in the West as "The Unknown War".

Attention should be drawn to a recent film in the Soviet Union by A. Tarkovski, "Stalker", in which a post-nuclear world is presented in a most striking (and depressing) way. In 1980 a remarkable book by perhaps the most prominent living Soviet writer Ch. Aitmatov, *A Day Longer than an Age*[11], was published which also portrays a rather fearful metaphoric image of a major global issue and the impotence of the superpowers in facing it.

How much the image of a nuclear war is fading is perhaps best illustrated by the suggestion made by Sigvard Eklund, the former Director-General of IAEA, to stage a nuclear explosion for the purpose of educating some statesmen!

This shows how much needs to be done and how extensive the problem of educating for disarmament is. The whole issue is not only linked with global problems, but also with the ideals and values that govern society.

Soviet attitude to disarmament

The idea that "disarmament is the ideal of socialism" was stated by V.I. Lenin[12]. The pursuit of disarmament has become one of the most important components of Soviet diplomacy and foreign policy. This has been expressly stated in the "Programme for Peace" proclaimed at the 24th Congress of the Communist Party of the Soviet Union and further developed at the 25th and 26th Congresses. In the Soviet Union war propaganda is forbidden by law, and the practice over the years of the Soviet mass media is a powerful demonstration of these trends. The Soviet people understand that "to try to win in the arms race, to think that one can win a nuclear war is a dangerous delusion"[13]. At present there is certainly "no other issue more important than to sustain peace on an international scale for our party, for our people, for all people of our planet".

We should go back to the example set by the Russell–Einstein Manifesto by initiating an authoritative international committee of scientists, and find ways and means to deliver their message to all people of the world. This specific suggestion of President Brezhnev should help in defining the system of measures necessary to develop the attitude of the public, and the consciousness of every person on these most urgent matters.

Conclusion

It is important to have more understanding and trust between peoples of the world. This must be done at all levels of education and teaching; it should become a natural and inherent element of modern culture.

Basing our thinking on historical optimism, and guided by political realism, we should seek ways and means to prohibit any use of weapons of mass destruction. Scientists, engineers, and the military have a professional understanding of the consequences of a modern war. But only when a commonly developed attitude towards these matters finds its way into the minds of everyone, becomes part of our thinking and is deeply embedded into the human mind, into the consciousness of people, into the mentality of the rulers, into the plans and actions of Governments, shall we finally reach a state which excludes nuclear war, or any war, from the destiny of mankind. A prerequisite to this is the formation of a new mentality, a new consciousness on these matters.

We have to adjust and reorient our educational system in a broad sense to take into account the social consequences of the enormous advances of science and technology; of all global problems the arms race is one of the most conspicuous, costly and inherently dangerous.

The history of mankind and the development of man have demonstrated that, on a number of occasions in the past, technical and scientific advances have overtaken social development. Today this gap is so great that the very existence of our future depends on it being closed.

References

1. V.V. Zagladin and I.T. Frolov, *Modern Global Problems: Scientific and Social Aspects*, Moscow, 1981 (in Russian).
2. S.A. Fetter and K. Tsipis, Catastrophic releases of radioactivity, *Scientific American*, April 1981.
3. I.P. Pavlov, *Lectures on Conditioned Reflexes*, Petrograd, 1923 (in Russian). New York, 1928 (in English).
4. M.A. Markov, Have we learnt to think in a new way? *Bulletin of the Atomic Scientists*, November 1977.

5.   D. Meadows, *et al. Limits to Growth*, New York, 1974.
6.   *Many Voices, One World*, UNESCO, Paris, New York, 1980.
7.   *Ibid*, p.178, footnote 1.
8.   *Ibid*, p.177, footnote 2.
9.   *Ibid*, pp.271-272.
10. J. Hackett *et al. The Third World War: August 1985*, Macmillan, London, 1978.
11. Ch. Aitmatov, *A Day Longer than an Age,* Novi Mir, No. 11, Moscow, 1980.
12. V.I. Lenin, *Collected Works,* fifth ed., 30, p.153.
13. Proceedings of XXVI Congress CPSU, Moscow, 1981.

PART VI
Role of the United Nations

Chapter 16. The role of Unesco in disarmament and the status of scientists

Stephen Marks

Introduction

Ten years before Bertrand Russell and Albert Einstein issued the Manifesto which led to the founding of Pugwash, the Founding Conference of the United Nations Educational, Scientific and Cultural Organization met at Church House, Westminster, in London. The meeting drew on the work of the International Institute for Intellectual Cooperation, which had functioned in Paris between the two World Wars in association with the League of Nations. The Institute has been described as a society "whose members included such personalities as Salvador de Madariaga, Paul Valery, Albert Einstein, Sigmund Freud and many others. They held impressive dialogues with one another, a very elevated correspondence, but neither activity had much hold on the reality of affairs".[1]

The founding of Unesco is relevant to the subject of disarmament and the responsibility of scientists for two reasons: (i) the founders were essentially the victors of a world war which had just ended and (ii) the organization was set up as a means of utilizing "the moral and intellectual solidarity of mankind"[2] as a defence of peace. Regarding the first point, the preamble to the constitution of 16 November 1945 contained the declaration "that the great and terrible war which has now ended was a war made possible by the denial of the democratic principles of dignity, equality and mutual respect of men, and by the propagation, in their place, through ignorance and prejudice, of the doctrine of the inequality of men and races".[3] On the second point, the preamble not only contained the declaration, so often quoted, "that since wars begin in the minds of men, it is in the minds of men that the defence of peace must be constructed" but also stipulated "that peace based exclusively upon the political and economic arrangements of governments would not be a peace which could secure the unanimous, lasting and sincere support of the peoples of the world, and that the peace must therefore be founded, if it is not to fail,

257

upon the intellectual and moral solidarity of mankind".[4]

The purpose of the Organization, as defined at the London Conference, "is to contribute to peace and security by promoting collaboration among the nations through education, science and culture in order to further universal respect for justice, for the rule of law and for the human rights and fundamental freedoms which are affirmed for the peoples of the world, without distinction of race, sex, language or religion, by the Charter of the United Nations".[5]

Among the functions by which the Organization is to accomplish this purpose is "encouraging co-operation among the nations in all branches of intellectual activity, including the international exchange of persons active in the fields of education, science and culture..."[6]

In order to dispel an often heard misconception of the role of intellectual and moral co-operation, it should be stressed (as many scientists[7] have said and as peace and conflicts studies show) that understanding other peoples does not of itself constitute an effective break on war-making. Nor is it because scientists or other professional groups agree upon certain principles concerning the role of scientists in the arms race and disarmament, or because governments adopt solemn resolutions on general and complete disarmament and on the creation of a climate of public opinion favourable to disarmament, that the arms race will grind to a halt or that military force will not be used by some of the very sponsors of these resolutions. That the causes of conflict are much more complex is in fact the reason for the existence of the peace research institutes described elsewhere in this book (see pages 144-156).

Nevertheless, the exchanges among scientists that Unesco has organized since its creation have done much to develop and disseminate knowledge on science and technology and to apply this knowledge to development. The first Director-General of the Organization, Julian Huxley, was himself an eminent scientist.

The inter-relations of science and peace were frequently brought out in the early programmes of the organization. Further to a decision of the second session of the Unesco General Conference in 1947, a long range project on tensions was launched covering six fields of inquiry for social scientists[8]. A number of publications were issued under the title "Tensions and Technology", later called "Tensions and Society", including a project on the social and moral implications of the peaceful use of nuclear energy[9].

However, it is not the purpose of this chapter to review the history of Unesco's role in promoting international scientific co-operation[10], but, more modestly, to stress the link between that role and the Organization's activities concerning the social responsibilities of scientists and its contribution to understanding the obstacles to disarmament and the ways of overcoming them. Thus, a few comments will be made on the recommendation on the status of scientific researchers and on recent disarmament-related activities and publications of Unesco.

The Recommendation on the Status of Scientific Researchers

The role and responsibility of scientists has been a matter of special concern for Unesco, by virtue of the Constitution itself, as already stressed. Organizations such as Pugwash, and most of the others described in the chapter on movements of scientists against the arms race (see pages 115-144) take positions under the sole responsibility of their members, acting in their individual capacity. On the other hand, a pronouncement by the General Conference of Unesco reflects the official positions of the major actors in international relations, namely the Member States themselves. It is in this light that the Recommendation on the Status of Scientific Researchers takes on particular significance.

The premise of much of what is said in this book about the responsibility of scientists is that scientists have a special mission to contribute to human progress. In the preamble to the Recommendation, the General Conference recognized that:

> "scientific discoveries and related technological developments and applications open up vast prospects for progress made possible in particular by the optimum utilization of science and scientific methods for the benefit of mankind and for the preservation of peace and the reduction of international tensions but may, at the same time, entail certain dangers which constitute a threat especially in cases where the results of scientific research are used against mankind's vital interests in order to prepare wars involving destruction on a massive scale or for purposes of the exploitation of one nation by another, and in any event give rise to complex ethical and legal problems."

As representatives of governments rather than individual scientists, the delegations at the General Conference immediately related the above principle to the responsibilities of States:

> "To face this challenge, Member States should develop or devise machinery for the formulation and execution of adequate science and technology policies, that is to say, policies designed to avoid the possible dangers and fully realize and exploit the positive prospects inherent in such discoveries, technological developments and applications."

The operative part of the Recommendation (reproduced in Appendix 2) then sets out the provisions which Member States should apply by taking whatever legislative or other steps may be required.

These provisions detail the role of scientific researchers in national policy-making, their education and vocation, their working conditions and career development, and the role of their associations. The text stresses the need for the utmost respect for the autonomy and freedom of research necessary to scientific progress.

It provides further that Member States should seek to encourage the conditions in which scientific researchers have certain responsibilities and rights, including the right to work in a spirit of intellectual freedom; to pursue, expound and defend scientific truth as they see it; to contribute to the determination of the methods to be adopted which should be humanely, socially and ecologically responsible; and to express themselves freely on the human, social or ecological value of certain projects. For an analysis of the role of scientists in the arms race, it is particularly noteworthy that the Recommendation also recognizes the right of researchers, in the last resort, to withdraw from projects if their conscience so dictates.

As regards freedom to publish, the Recommendation considers that it should be standard practice for employers of scientific researchers, including states, to regard it as the norm that scientific researchers be at liberty and encouraged to publish the results of their work; to minimize the restrictions placed upon scientific researchers' right to publish their findings, consistent with public interest and the rights of their employers and fellow workers. Among the other provisions, of particular relevance to the role of scientists in the arms race and disarmament are those relating to the possibility of scientific researchers to travel abroad and to communicate with colleagues throughout the world without hindrance. Member States are urged to co-operate with organizations representing science and technology educators and learned societies and indeed to

> "enlist the vigilant and active co-operation of all organizations representing scientific researchers, in ensuring that the latter may, in a spirit of community service, effectively assume the responsibilities, enjoy the rights and obtain the recognition of the status described in this Recommendation."

There is clearly a direct relevance of this Recommendation to the measures which can be taken to encourage scientists to be actively concerned with disarmament. Action by scientists and their organizations consistent with their social responsibilities is not only a concern of the individuals and organizations directly involved; it is also in conformity with the status of scientific researchers as recognized by the Member States of Unesco.

Some recent disarmament-related activities

The disarmament-related activities of Unesco for the period 1977–82 have been carried out pursuant to the first Medium-Term Plan, adopted by the General Conference at its 1976 session. The Plan sets out some fifty "objectives" for that six-year period, including:

> "Promotion of peace research, in particular on manifestations of violations of peace, causes preventing its realization, ways and means to eliminate them and

proper measures to be taken in order to maintain and reinforce a just, lasting and constructive peace at the level of groups, societies and the world."[11]

One of the "principles of action" of that objective reads as follows:

"Increased emphasis should also be placed on studies which can be used to explain the origin of the tensions on the world and the factors determining the arms race which can be used to promote disarmament and eliminate obstacles to it."[12]

In accordance with that plan and in preparation for the Tenth Special Session of the General Assembly Devoted to Disarmament, Unesco organized on 3–7 April 1978 an expert meeting on "The Obstacles to Disarmament and the Ways of Overcoming Them". After discussing the prevailing international climate, the typologies relating to the obstacles to disarmament, the economic factors, the negotiation process, security doctrines and cultural and psychological factors, the meeting examined the role of educators and scientists. Regarding the latter, the meeting considered that the role of scientists was a major factor in the search for disarmament since they occupy the key position in the race in technology which, in fact, is what the arms race is all about. Military research and development was considered to affect many aspects of life and create a technological momentum and a technological imperative which, in the view of some of the experts, were stronger than governments, although others saw the will of governments as paramount.

In its recommendations, the meeting devoted particular attention to science. It considered proposals relating both to natural sciences and social sciences. International co-operation relating to research in both these fields was considered as an essential task for Unesco in overcoming the obstacles to disarmament in its spheres of competence. Unesco was urged to expand its efforts to involve scientists in the study of disarmament problems. In this regard, it was suggested that Unesco convene a conference of scientific and other workers engaged partly or entirely in military industries to consider the problems of conversion and of ways of bringing pressure on their governments to begin such conversion.

The meeting recommended that research programmes co-ordinated by Unesco should be implemented in close co-operation with relevant international scientific organizations, universities and research institutions.

The responsibility of scientists was considered one of the key factors in overcoming the obstacles to disarmament. It was suggested that an oath for scientists could be drafted according to which they would commit themselves to working towards disarmament.

Among the numerous themes of research projects and/or symposia which Unesco could carry out or encourage, the meeting suggested the following:

(*a*) military research and development and its impact on the arms race;

(*b*) role of various scientific disciplines in developing new military technology;

(*c*) impact of contemporary strategic doctrines on the international climate;

(*d*) costs and consequences of war in general and of nuclear war in particular;

(*e*) non-military alternatives and strategies for assuring security of states, including non-violent ones;

(*f*) the semantics of disarmament and its impact on the various negotiations;

(*g*) human rights aspects of the arms question including the relationship between militarization and repression;

(*h*) new developments in the problem of reconversion of military industries to civilian uses;

(*i*) the decision-making process as applied to disarmament negotiations.

The meeting also felt that Unesco could do more to bring the role of scientific research in fueling the arms race to the attention of scientists and science teachers through scientific organizations, conferences and journals. Semi-popular publications on the impact of science, technology and medicine on war, both in historical and in modern times, could be a useful way of stimulating the interest of scientists and science teachers and in promoting public opinion in favour of disarmament.

One of the background papers for that meeting dealt specifically with the role of scientists, particularly in military research and development[13].

Further to its recommendations, the proceedings were published[14] and a vast programme of disarmament education, defined for the first time at the meeting, was proposed by the Director-General of Unesco to the General Assembly in his address to the Special Session on 26 May 1978[15].

In its Final Document, the Special Session gave Unesco a mandate in four areas: dissemination of information about the arms race[16]; research and publications, especially in developing countries[17], relations with non-governmental organizations[18], and, most important, disarmament education[19].

Unesco carries out this mandate in close collaboration and co-operation with the United Nations Centre for Disarmament, which exercises a leading role as regards disarmament-related activities throughout the United Nations system. Indeed, the General Conference of Unesco invited the Director-General

"to maintain co-operation with the institutions of the United Nations system, and, in particular, with the United Nations Centre for Disarmament and the United Nations Institute for Disarmament Research, attached to the United Nations Institute for Training and Research"[20].

This collaboration and co-operation is realized through regular contacts between the units concerned, through *ad hoc* inter-agency meetings and through mutual representation at meetings. It has led to a satisfactory division of labour according to which Unesco's activities, directed essentially towards the scientific and educational communities (as well as to the general public), avoid duplication of or overlapping with the work of the Centre.

The general approach of Unesco has been to respect high standards of scientific rigour and plurality of views on controversial matters, always with the aim of meeting the needs of educators and performing a responsible role in the field of public information. The Director-General declared before the Special Session of 1978 that "action to influence 'the minds of men' should naturally not take the form of propaganda, but of information."

Unesco's disarmament-related activities (described in greater detail in the various volumes of the *United Nations Disarmament Yearbook*) cover all its fields of competence:

Education

The specific tasks assigned to Unesco by the Special Session in the field of disarmament education have been carried out essentially in relation to the World Congress on Disarmament Education. Following a preparatory meeting held in Prague in June 1979, the World Congress met in Paris in June 1980 and adopted a number of principles, major recommendations and detailed proposals to be considered for an action plan[21]. A draft of an action plan, worked out by an international consultation held in Paris in August 1981, covers the entire Second Disarmament Decade, that is, activities to be carried out up to 1989[22].

The work of the World Congress on Disarmament Education is relevant to the matter of the role of scientists in the arms race and disarmament in several ways. Not only is science education concerned with the whole concept of disarmament education but two of the ten guiding principles of disarmament education adopted by the Congress have a special meaning for scientists. One concerns the relation of scientific research to decision-making:

"In addition to reaching the general public, disarmament education has a more specific and equally crucial task of providing rational arguments for disarmament based on independent scientific research which can guide decision-makers and, to the extent possible, rectify perceptions of a potential adversary based on incomplete or inaccurate information."

The other is related to the reliability of information, which has often been a difficult problem for scientists concerned with disarmament questions:

"Disarmament education requires the collection and dissemination of reliable information from sources offering the highest degree of objectivity in accordance with a free and more balanced international flow of information. It should prepare learners, in the strictest respect for freedom of opinion, expression and information, to resist incitement to war, military propaganda and militarism in general."

While the principles adopted by the Congress do not commit Unesco itself or the Member States, the General Conference has adopted regularly a resolution on the "creation of a climate of public opinion conducive to the halting of the arms race and the transition to disarmament." At its twenty-first session (1980) the resolution bearing that title[23] addressed the issue of information. The General Conference invited Member States:

"to take the necessary steps to make adequate information available on matters concerning disarmament, in order to make meaningful and informed disarmament education possible"

Of direct relevance to the concerns of Pugwash and to the mobilization of scientists in the field of disarmament is another paragraph of the same resolution in which the General Conference invited Member States:

"to encourage public and private scientific research institutions which could usefully contribute to a better understanding of the problems relating to disarmament"

Similarly, the Director-General was invited, in addition to carrying out various specific activities in line with the aims of the resolution:

"to continue to stimulate and support activities of the international non-governmental organizations which are directed to achieving disarmament objectives within Unesco's fields of competence"

As regards concrete activities in disarmament education, publications have been issued and a series of regional training seminars has been planned for university teachers of the subject, the first one of which took place for the region of Latin America and the Caribbean in October 1981 in Caracas, Venezuela.

In short, disarmament education, as promoted by Unesco, constitutes an effort to respond through international co-operation, to the appeal of the Russell-Einstein Manifesto "to learn to think in a new way"[24].

Science

The periodical of the Science Sector of Unesco *Impact of Science on Society* has devoted several issues to disarmament-related subjects. The April-June 1971 issue, for example, contained an article by Milton Leitenberg on 'Social Responsibility: the classical scientific ethic and strategic weapons development". In the July-September 1972 issue, articles by U Thant, Alva Myrdal, William C. Foster, K. Subrahmanyam, Fyodor Burlatsky and Sigvard Eklund were published under the issue title "A forum on nuclear armament".

The January–June double issue of 1976 was devoted to "Science and War". The editor of that issue felt that the title could have been "Science and Madness", for, he explained,

"with the refinement of our scientific knowledge and its immediate transformation into usable technology, a disproportionate part of our endeavour in scientific technology seems inevitably to become converted into the wherewithall of war."

In the January–March issue of 1981, the subject was again dealt with in the pages of *Impact*, this time under the title of "Weapons from Science: civilization's pitfall." The issue focussed on military R & D, and contained the report of the Pugwash Symposium on the use of military and civilian satellites for peace-keeping.

Social sciences

One of the major recommendations of the World Congress on Disarmament Education was that Unesco

"strengthen social science research activities on disarmament, peace and international relations with a view, *inter alia*, to improving education and information programmes in these fields, in collaboration with the United Nations, in particular with the Centre for Disarmament and the Institute for Disarmament Research, with national and international research bodies, and with appropriate non-governmental organizations."

Among the relevant recent publications are a issue of the *International Social Science Journal* on "The Infernal Cycle of Armament" (vol. XXVIII, No. 2, 1976), *Armaments Arms Control and Disarmament; a Unesco Reader for Disarmament Education* (1982); *Obstacles to Disarmament and Ways of Overcoming Them* (1981); *Unesco Yearbook on Peace and Conflict Studies* (published since 1980); *World Directory of Peace Research Institutes* (1981).

A recently completed project of particular interest to this book is an international research project entitled "Military Research and Development: its Relation to the Arms Race and Development."[25] Professor Raimo Väyrynen (of the University of Helsinki) co-ordinated a team of scholars from different parts of the world who prepared studies on various dimensions of military R&D in industrialized countries and in the Third World. Chapters of the study deal with the involvement of the scientific community in military R&D, the interests behind it and its effects on science policy, the quest for self-reliance, and on the transfer of military technology to the Third World. As Alfred Kastler reiterates in the Preface:

"it is no longer, as in the past, the strategic needs of the military that govern the development of weapons; it is technological innovations that are imposing strategies on the military and compelling the political decision-makers to step up arms expenditure year after year."

Other chapters deal with the prospects for co-operation among scientists in promoting disarmament and in resolving problems relating to the reconversion from military to civilian production. A concluding chapter discusses the potential role of science in realizing a demilitarized world order.

Other on-going projects in the social sciences include:
– strategic doctrines and their alternatives;
– militarization of society and its economic, social and cultural effects;
– perceptions of security and their effects on the arms race.

Culture

The culture dimensions of the obstacles to disarmament are often overlooked, while in reality the acceptance of armed – or overarmed – defence as the only foundation of security for practically every country has profound cultural implications. The glorification of war and military exploits, the ideologization of violence and the propensity towards militarism are first and foremost cultural phenomena. It was the role of culture that the Director-General was referring to when he told the General Assembly at its first Special Session devoted to Disarmament that "the reduction of armaments and their progressive elimination would be the most striking proof that mankind has at last become reconciled with itself and can one day look forward to experiencing that peace in justice and fraternity which has been its aspiration from time immemorial"[26].

In 1966, the General Conference of Unesco proclaimed the Declaration of the Principles of International Cultural Co-operation, among which is that "in cultural co-operation, stress shall be laid on ideas and values conducive to the creation of a climate of friendship and peace." More recently, in a resolution on "international cultural and scientific co-operation", the General Conference invited Member States to broaden cultural and scientific co-operation "as an important factor in strengthening peace, friendship and reciprocal understanding among peoples"[27].

On the subject of culture, it may be interesting to recall that Einstein published in the December 1951 *Unesco Courier* an article entitled "Culture must be one of the foundations for world understanding."

In order to begin an in-depth examination of the relation between disarmament and culture, a research project has been undertaken by Unesco on the axiological content – such as acceptance or glorification of war – of the images or war and peace conveyed by various forms of cultural expression[28].

Communication and information

As proposed by the 1978 meeting, the recommendations concerning information were brought to the attention of the International Commission for the Study of Communication Problems, which took them into account in its final report, *Many Voices, One World. Communication and Society, Today and Tomorrow* (1980). Extracts from that report appear in another chapter of this book (see p.250). New activities, based on the recommendations of the 1978 meeting, are planned to examine the role of the media in disarmament matters. Moreover, several principles of the 1978 Declaration on the mass media concern strengthening peace and international understanding, and countering incitement to war[29]. This declaration which seeks to encourage the contribution of the media to peace without infringing on the freedon of information, essential to the media's task, has been translated into over fifteen languages and is being widely disseminated.

In addition there are, of course, the extensive activities in the area of public information, including publishing special issues of the *Unesco Courier* and contributing to Disarmament Week. Several issues of the *Unesco Courier* have in fact been devoted to popularizing the results of Untied Nations studies on disarmament[30].

Conclusion

As the specialized agency within the United Nations system with the constitutional mandate for promoting co-operation among scientists for peace and security, Unesco has a special role relating to the responsibility of scientists in general, and to the encouragement of positive action by scientists in favour of disarmament in particular. However much may have been accomplished so far, which this chapter has briefly outlined, the major task lies ahead. Russell and Einstein considered in 1955 that "the men who know most are the most gloomy". Scientific research provides no less reason for gloom nearly thirty years later. In 1930, Einstein warned that:

> "Science ennobles anyone who is engaged in it, whether a scholar or merely a student... Yet science cannot liberate us from the scourge of war. Science is a powerful instrument that can enhance or destroy life. Nothing can save us from the horrors of war but man's resolve to abolish it, and his unconditional refusal to allow his energies to be misused for an evil cause."[31]

In the imagination of a contemporary writer[32], we are living in a "century of destruction". The author invents a history of the earth (called Shikasta) from the perspective of several centuries' hindsight and the distance of another planet. The role of science is dealt with in the following very harsh terms:

> "Science was the most recent ideology. War had immeasurably streng-
> thened it. Science, its basic sets of mind, its prejudices, gripped the whole
> globe and there was no appeal...individuals with differing inclinations and
> needs from those tolerated by science had to lead silent or prudent lives,
> careful of offending the obligations of the scientific global governing class:
> in the service of national governments and therefore of war – an invisible
> global ruling caste, obedient to the warmakers."

That this page from the history of Shikasta may be a warning and not a
prophecy is a formidable challenge to non-governmental and intergovern-
mental elements of the international community. Unesco, in collaboration
with the scientific communities of its Member States and with organizations such as Pugwash, will continue to apply international co-operation in
meeting this challenge.

References

1. From a speech by Roger Caillois quoted in Richard Hoggart, *An Idea and its Servants. Unesco from Within*, London, Chatto & Windus, 1978, p.26.
2. Constitution of Unesco, Preamble.
3. *Ibid.*
4. *Ibid.*
5. *Ibid.*, Article 1, para. 1.
6. *Ibid.*, Article 1, para. 2(c).
7. Reinhold Niebuhr, for example, wrote in 1949, "If 'peoples speak to peoples' this communication must finally include debate on the ultimate issues of life and not meaningless agreement on shallow generalities about the unity of mankind." Quoted by Hoggart, *op. cit.*, p.23.
8. The project was launched by the General Conference at its second session (Mexico City, 1947) in resolution 5.1. The achievements of this project were recapitulated in *The Nature of Conflict* (International Sociological Association, Unesco, 1959), pp. 9-32.
9. *Social implications of the peaceful uses of nuclear energy*, edited by Otto Klineberg, Unesco, 1964, 169 pages.
10. A historical review up to 1971 is given in Victor Kovda, "Science" in *In the Minds of Men. Unesco 1946 to 1971*, published for the twenty-fifth anniversary of Unesco, Unesco; Paris, 1972, pp.69-94.
11. Unesco, *Medium-Term Plan (1977-1982)*, Document 19 C/4, 1977, p.41.
12. *Ibid*, p.44.
13. The paper, by Marek Thee, was subsequently published under the title "The Dynamics of the Arms Race, Military R&D and

Disarmament" in *International Social Science Journal*, vol. XXX, No. 4, 1978. A special issue of the *International Social Science Journal* was devoted to "The Infernal Cycle of Dynamics" in 1976, (vol. XXVIII, No. 2).

14. See the book *Obstacles to disarmament and ways of overcoming them*, Swadesh Rana, editor, The Unesco Press, collection "Insights", Paris, 1981, 233 pp.

15. Subsequently published by Unesco in the brochure *The Will for Peace*, Unesco, Paris, 1978.

16. Final Document of the Tenth Special Session of the General Assembly (S-10/2), paragraphs 99-102 and 123.

17. *Ibid*, paragraphs 103 and 123.

18. *Ibid*, paragraphs 104 and 106.

19. *Ibid*, paragraphs 106 and 107.

20. Resolution 21 C/11.1, adopted on 24 October 1980, paragraph 3 (h).

21. *Disarmament Education, World Congress on Disarmament Education, Report and Final Document*, Unesco 1980. A selection of the papers of the Congress was published in the *Bulletin of Peace Proposals*, vol. II, No. 3, 1980 and the September 1980 issue of the *Unesco Courier* was devoted to Congress. The final report and document of the World Congress also appear in Swadesh Rana (ed.) *Obstacles to Disarmament and Ways of Overcoming Them*, Unesco, 1981, pp. 218-228 and *Unesco Yearbook on Peace and Conflict Studies 1981* (forthcoming). Other materials may be found in M. Thee (ed.) *Armaments, Arms Control and Disaarmament*, Unesco, 1981, Part VI.

22. The Final Report of the Consultation, containing elements for a phased action plan for disarmament education, is contained in Unesco document SS-82/WS/5.

23. Resolution 21 C/11.1, adopted on 24 October 1980. The full text of this resolution appears in the *United Nations Disarmament Yearbook*, Vol. 5, 1980, pp.458-460 and S. Rana, *op. cit.*, pp. 229-233.

24. Reference to this appeal of the Manifesto is made explicitly in the preface of the Unesco publication *Obstacles to Disarmament and Ways of Overcoming Them*, Paris, 1981, p.11, and in the introduction to the publication of selected papers from the World Congress on Disarmament Education. See Marks, The Imperative of Disarmament Education, *Bulletin of Peace Proposals*, vol. II, No. 3, 1980, p.199.

25. *Military Research and Development: its relation to the Arms Race and Development*, edited by Raimo Väyrynen, Unesco (forthcoming).

26. Amadou Mahtar M'Bow, *The Will for Peace*, Unesco, 1978, p.19.

27. Resolution 21 C/12.1, paragraph 1 (a).

28. *Programme and Budget for 1981-1983* Unesco, 1981, paragraph 3216

29. Declaration on Fundamental Principles concerning the Contribution

of the Mass Media to Strengthening Peace and International Understanding, to the Promotion of Human Rights and to Countering Racialism, Apartheid and Incitement to War, adopted by the General Conference at its twentieth session, on 22 November 1978.

30. For example the April 1979 issue of the *Unesco Courier* was based on the United Nations study on "the economic and social consequences of the arms race and of military expenditure" and the March 1982 issue is based on the UN study on "the relationship between disarmament and development."

31. *Einstein on Peace*, edited by Otto Nathan and Heinz Norden, Simon and Schuster, New York, 1960, p.105.

32. Doris Lessing, *Shikasta*, Vintage Books, New York, 1979, pp.87-88.

Chapter 17. The Second Disarmament Decade

Olu Adeniji

Introduction

In writing about the Second Disarmament Decade, it is essential to make a brief historical recollection of the genesis of Disarmament Decades. Obviously when the United Nations took up disarmament where the League of Nations left it, the main preoccupation was the reduction of armaments, not general and complete disarmament. Any idea of phasing the time required into decades was not an immediate factor. The League of Nations' Conference for the Reduction and Limitation of Armaments 1932–35 was primarily concerned with an immediate agreement on a Treaty for the control of armaments. This agreement was to have emerged from the Conference itself and be implemented as soon as the Treaty was signed and ratified by the requisite number of Parties.

The same attitude to the possible control of armaments was carried over to the efforts of the years immediately after the Second World War. This was reflected in the provisions of the Charter of the United Nations. Article 26 of the Charter provides that the Security Council shall be responsible for formulating, with the assistance of the Military Staff Committee plans to be submitted to members of the United Nations for the establishment of a system for the regulation of armaments. Article 47 lists one of the functions of the Military Staff Committee as being to advise and assist the Security Council on the regulation of armaments and possible disarmament.

It was not until 1959 that the United Nations set the basic goal of all its efforts in relation to armaments as general and complete disarmament. After discussion of the item on the Agenda of the XIVth Session entitled General and Complete Disarmament, the General Assembly on November 20, 1959 adopted resolution 1378 (XIV) the essential elements of which are as follows:

"The General Assembly

> Considering that the question of general and complete disarmament is the most important one facing the world today.
>
> Expresses the hope that measures leading towards the goal of general and complete disarmament under effective international control will be worked out in detail and agreed upon in the shortest possible time."

The national and international impact of disarmament became the focus of attention in the General Assembly following the adoption of this resolution. Though there was no immediate agreement on ways and means of carrying it out (as interpretations differ) it is worthy to note that in the joint Soviet – United States statement of Agreed Principles issued in 1961 as a basis for disarmament negotiations, the first principle stated:

> "the goal of negotiations is to achieve agreement on a programme which will ensure that disarmament is general and complete and war is no longer an instrument for settling international problems."

The machinery created for negotiation in the following year, the Eighteen Nation Disarmament Committee, was immediately faced with two draft Treaties on general and complete disarmament, proposed by the Soviet Union and the United States respectively. Both drafts envisaged the accomplishment of general and complete disarmament in less than ten years, phased into three stages. The difference in approach evident in the two drafts made immediate reconciliation impossible and no progress was therefore made in the negotiation. An alternative approach of negotiation in stages began to emerge following the impasse on negotiating a treaty on general and complete disarmament. It was in the context of arms control negotiations that proposals were first made in the Eighteen Nation Disarmament Committee for the adoption of "an organic disarmament programme" and for the "proclamation of a United Nations Disarmament Decade 1970-1980".

United Nations Disarmament Decade: Secretary-General's comments and proposal

The Secretary-General of the United Nations, U Thant, formally brought the idea of the Disarmament Decade to the attention of the General Assembly. In the customary introduction to his annual report on the work of the United Nations 1968-69, U Thant expressed grave concern at the ever escalating arms race, the continued stockpiling of both nuclear and conventional weapons and the continued growth of military expenditure. The world, he said, stood at a most critical crossroads. It could either pursue the arms race at a terrible price to the security and progress of the peoples of the world, or it could move ahead towards the goal of general and complete disarmament, a goal that was set in 1959 by a unanimous decision of the General Assemby on the eve of the decade of the 1960s. He went on to observe that the diversion of enormous resources and energy both human and material from peaceful economic and social pursuits to unproductive and uneconomic military purposes was an important factor in the failure to make greater progress in the advancement of the developing countries during the First United Nations Development Decade. It was his belief that should the world decide to reverse the trend of the arms race and move towards the goal of general and complete disarmament, the security, the economic well-being, and the progress not only of the developing countries, but also of the developed countries and of the entire world would be tremendously enhanced.

Secretary-General U Thant then made a proposal:

> "I would accordingly propose that the Members of the United Nations decide to dedicate the decade of the 1970s which has already been designated as the Second United Nations Development Decade as a Disarmament Decade. I would hope that the members of the General Assembly could establish a specific programme and timetable for dealing with all aspects of the problem of arms control and disarmament..."

The Secretary-General's proposal received wide support in the General Assembly. In its resolution 2499 (XXIV) 31 October 1969, concerning the celebration of the 25th anniversary of the United Nations, the Assembly endorsed the proclamation of a Disarmament Decade to coincide with the Second United Nations Development Decade and entrusted the competent bodies of the Organization with the task of presenting concrete proposals to the General Assembly at its 25th Session.

On 16 December 1969, the General Assembly adopted resolution 2602E (XXIV) by which it:

1. Declares the decade of the 1970s a Disarmament Decade;
2. Calls upon Governments to intensify without delay their concerted and concentrated efforts for effective measures relating to the cessation of the nuclear arms race at an early date and to nuclear disarmament and the elimination of other weapons of mass destruction, and for a treaty on general and complete disarmament under strict and effective international control.

The resolution further requested the Conference of the Committee on Disarmament to work out a Comprehensive Programme of Disarmament, and recommended that consideration be given to channelling a substantial portion of the savings as a result of disarmament measures into economic and social programmes.

Review of the First Disarmament Decade

In retrospect, the experiment of the Disarmament Decade for the 1970s failed to achieve its objectives, just as the Second Development Decade was a failure. Though this was the period of détente, which witnessed improved relations between the United States and the Soviet Union, all the hope that this improved climate would manifest itself in the area of arms limitation and disarmament failed to materialize. In 1972, the Soviet Union and the United States of America signed the SALT I agreement, with an undertaking to begin negotiations on SALT II. As it turned out these negotiations were protracted and SALT II was not signed until June 1979. However, it has not been put into force and the chances are very slim that it will be ratified by the American side.

As for multilateral negotiations on disarmament, little progress was made. Through the agreement reached in 1969, the ENDC became the 26-mem' er Conference of the Committee on Disarmament. Throughout the 1970s, the Committee concluded negotiations on only three instruments, namely, the Treaty on the Prohibition of the Emplacement of Nuclear Weapons and other Weapons of Mass Destruction on the Sea-bed and Ocean floor and in the Sub soil thereof (1971); the convention on the Prohibition of the Development, Production and Stockpiling of Bacteriological (Biological) and Toxin Weapons and on their destruction (1972); and the Convention on the Prohibition of Military or any other Hostile Use of Environmental Modification Techniques (1977).

Meanwhile the results of military research and development were increasingly evident in the production and deployment of nuclear weapons of greater yield and vastly improved accuracy. Concentration by the multilateral negotiating body on collateral measures in the circumstances was an indication of the powerlessness of that body under the joint United States/Soviet Union control as co-chairmen. Though the one specific element of the Declaration required the Conference of the Committee for Disarmament to work out a Comprehensive Programme of Disarmament, no agreement was reached on the nature of this assignment until 1979 when the Committee set up a Working Group. As there was no substantial measure of disarmament put into effect, there could not have been any diversion of savings to economic and social purposes. Rather, military expenditures grew in constant 1978 prices from 375 billion US dollars to $455 billion during the course of the decade.

First Special Session on Disarmament

The anxiety of the Non Aligned Countries over the escalating arms race, and their distress at the seeming unwillingness of the superpowers to embark on serious disarmament negotiations, led to the call for the convening of a Special Session of the General Assembly devoted to disarmament. Held from 23 May to 1 July 1978 at the United Nations headquarters, the first Special Session devoted to disarmament (Tenth General Assembly Special Session) was quick to deliver a verdict on the Disarmament Decade of the 1970s. In its Final Document the Special Session observed:

> "the Disarmament Decade solemnly declared in 1969 by the United Nations is coming to end. Unfortunately, the objectives established on that occasion by the General Assembly appear to be as far away today as they were then, or even further because the arms race is not diminishing but increasing and outstrips by far the efforts to curb it. While it is true that some limited agreements have been reached, 'effective measures relating to the cessation of the arms race at an early date and to nuclear disarmament' continue to elude man's grasp".

The Special Session did not, however, decide upon a follow-up to the Disarmament Decade which was then coming to an end. Any indication of a time frame for the implementation of the Programme of Action agreed upon at the Special Session was couched in vague terms thus: "the present Programme of Action enumerates the specific measures of disarmament which should be implemented over the next few years". A few months after the Special Session, during the 33rd regular session of the General Assembly, an initiative was taken under the regular item "Effective measures to implement the purposes and objectives of the Disarmament Decade". That item had, since 1975, provided the General Assembly with an opportunity to underline the need for the elaboration of the Comprehensive Programme of Disarmament. At the 33rd Session of the General Assembly, however, on the initiative of some Non-Aligned countries, the resolution 33/62, adopted under the item contained an additional element in its para. 3:

> "Takes note of the preparations for the third United Nations Development Decade and stresses the need to continue to promote the link between the strategy for disarmament and the strategy for development in view of the close relationship between disarmament and development affirmed by the General Assembly at its Tenth Special Session".

In the final paragraph of the same resolution, the General Assembly decided to include in the provisional agenda of its 34th Session an item entitled "Consideration of the declaration of the 1980s as a disarmament decade".

Opinion in the General Assembly on the Declaration of another Disarmament Decade was by no means unanimously favourable. There were many representatives who expressed doubt as to the usefulness of another "Decade", which would raise expectations that in the end might not be fulfilled. Behind such arguments lay the reluctance to set a deadline for the achievement of specific disarmament measures, evident in the course of the negotiations of the Final Document of the Special Session on Disarmament. They opposed the fixing of the target dates for such highly sensitive and very complicated negotiations in the field of disarmament as being unrealistic and counter-productive. These arguments were to be repeated again during the negotiations of the Elements of the Declaration of the 1980s as of the Second United Nations Disarmament Decade by the United Nations Disarmament Commission in 1979.

The overwhelming majority of members, however, were in favour of a second Disarmament Decade. The Non-Aligned countries were particularly anxious to press forward the inter-relationship between disarmament and development, notwithstanding the denial of such link by some militarily significant states. The lack of progress in attaining the objectives of the Disarmament Decade in the 1970s was seen by the Non-Aligned as the result of the lack of political will to reverse the trend of the arms race by the military alliances. The same lack of political will could be discerned as the major obstacle to progress in the implementation of the objectives and the targets of the Second Development Decade. Though the target of the Decade on the transfer of resources in the form of Official Development Assistance was fixed at 0.7 per cent of GNP of each developed country, this figure was not met by the overwhelming majority of those countries. Average annual resources available for multilateral development assistance, as reflected in pledges to the United Nations Development Programme, were $250 million, which represented little more than the average military expenditure every 6 hours during the course of the Decade. As long as military spending escalated, the chances of satisfying national and international economic and social requirements would continue to be severely diminished. Disarmament Decades would therefore continue to be relevant as one of the contributory factors to development on a universal basis.

Consideration at the 34th General Assembly

As its 34th Session in 1979, the General Assembly had a fuller exchange of views on the Disarmament Decade under the item: Consideration of the declaration of the 1980s as the Second Disarmament Decade.

The reservations of the previous year on the necessity for another decade had by and large given way to widespread support of the proposal as an important element in the strategy for disarmament. By resolution 34/75 adopted on 11 December 1979 the General Assembly:

"1.   Decides to declare the decade of the 1980s as the Second Disarmament Decade.
2.   Directs the Disarmament Commission at its substantive Session in 1980 to prepare elements of a draft resolution entitled Declaration of the 1980s as the Second Disarmament Decade and submit them to the General Assembly at its 35th Session for consideration and adoption.
3.   Determines that the Draft resolution should embody *inter alia* an indication of targets during the Second Disarmament Decade for accomplishing the major objectives and goals of disarmament as well as ways and means of mobilizing world public opinion in this regard."

The terms of reference given the United Nations Disarmament Commission in resolution 34/75 showed several departures from the procedure for the declaration of the First Disarmament Decade. The General Assembly was determined that the declaration of the 1980s should embody an indicative programme of measures to be accomplished during the decade. Moreover, it was clearly indicated that in addition to the negotiating process which remains the primary means of progress in disarmament, due importance is also to be given to mobilizing world public opinion through education and information. The Special Session on Disarmament (10th UNGA Special Session 1978) had given recognition to the role which public awareness of the true nature of, and the danger implicit in the arms race could play in making world opinion at large aware of the necessity for disarmament. Indeed, paragraphs 99–108 of the Final Document of the Special Session listed a number of measures aimed at mobilizing world public opinion in favour of disarmament. Among such measures were:

call on governmental and non-governmental information organs and those of the United Nations and its Specialized Agencies to give priority to the preparation and distribution of printed and audio-visual material relating to the danger represented by the armaments race as well as to the disarmament efforts;
call on the United Nations Centre for Disarmament and UNESCO to intensify their activities in the presentation of information, in facilitating research and publication on disarmament;
call on Governments, governmental and non-governmental organizations, to develop programmes of education for disarmament and peace studies at all levels;
call on UNESCO to step up its programmes aimed at the development of disarmament education as a distinct field study;
establishment by the United Nations of a programme of fellowships on disarmament "in order to promote expertise in disarmament in more member states, particularly in the developing countries."

The Declaration

The negotiations for the Declaration took place in the United Nations Disarmament Commission at its May 1980 session. Two approaches were noticeable in the written views submitted by members on possible elements for the Declaration. One approach sought to make governments undertake binding commitment to undertake negotiations and conclude instruments on specific disarmament issues to be identified in the Declaration. Such activities would be phased during the decade, earmarking those to be completed in the first half and those for the second half. The priority issue of nuclear disarmament was particularly stressed, and discernible progress was to be made in the first half of the Decade on specific and identified areas. The second approach sought to identify only in general terms those measures on which negotiations should continue or commence without a prior commitment as to their conclusion. Naturally, according to this latter view there could be no prior fixing of the time for the completion of the negotiation, nor could there be a phasing of the items during the decade. The proponents of this view believed that the fixing of a timeframe would be unrealistic in light of the many imponderables that affect disarmament negotiations, such as the complexity of any given negotiation, the issue of verification, and the international situation, especially the political relationship between the two superpowers. Given such complexities, rigid targets would only result in unfulfilled expectations. On the other hand, it was argued that while rigidity certainly ought to be avoided, it was necessary, for the guidance of negotiators, to provide a timeframe within which they would be expected to conclude negotiations of specific items. Moreover, it was argued that the indication of such a timeframe would be a sign of the commitment of states to make substantive progress in the field of disarmament. The difference between the Programme of Action of the Special Session on Disarmament (10th UNGA Special Session 1978) and the activities of the Decade should lie in part in the timeframe. While there was no specific timeframe designated for the implementation of the former, the latter was to be over a ten year period. Within the overall period, it should be possible to envisage the phasing of negotiations in such a manner that there would be a continuous flow of activities throughout the decade. As will be seen later, a compromise was forged between the two positions.

A marked novel feature of the Declaration of the Second Disarmament Decade is that it took the form of a strategy for disarmament in the period of the 1980s, similar to the strategy for development. While therefore avoiding a duplication of the Final Document of the Special Session on Disarmament, it nevertheless was elaborated as a self-contained document complete with its own Introduction, Goals and Principles, Activities, and Review and Appraisal Mechanism. Naturally, it is not as extensive as the Programme of Action of the Final Document of the Special Session on Disarmament; it would have been unrealistic if it were to assume that all the elements for the accomplishment of general and complete disarmament could be completed in the 1980s. Nevertheless, it went far beyond the very modest declaration for the 1970s as contained in resolution 2602(e) (XXIV), which left the decision on issues to be negotiated to states themselves, with very little guidance.

The strategy for the Second Disarmament Decade is divided into four parts. The introductory part needs no comments. The second part deals with Principles and Goals. In order to avoid a repetition of the lengthy negotiations during the preparatory stages, as well as at the Special Session on Disarmament, on the Principles that should govern disarmament negotiations, the Declaration of the 1980s confined itself to a reaffirmation of those Principles. Within the overall objective of general and complete disarmament under effective international control, the specific goals set for the Second Disarmament Decade are five-fold:

i.   Halting and reversing the arms race, particularly the nuclear arms race.
ii.   The conclusion and implementation of effective agreements which will contribute significantly to the achievement of general and complete disarmament under effective international control.
iii. Development on an equitable basis of the limited results obtained in the field of disarmament in the 1970s in accordance with the provisions of the Final Document of the Special Session devoted to Disarmament.
iv.   Strengthening international peace and security in accordance with the Charter of the United Nations.
v.   Making available a substantial part of the resources released by disarmament measures to promote the attainment of the objectives of the Third United Nations Development Decade and in particular the economic and social development of developing countries so as to accelerate the progress towards the New International Economic Order.

Activities in the Second Decade

The activities earmarked for the Decade include both those to be negotiated in the multilateral disarmament forum – the Committee on Disarmament – as well as those negotiations of a bilateral, regional or multilateral nature conducted outside the Committee on Disarmament. This was to emphasize the essential unity of disarmament negotiations irrespective of the forum. Thus Part III of the Declaration began as follows:

"The Decade of the 1980s should witness renewed intensification by all Governments and the United Nations of their efforts to reach agreement and to implement effective measures that will lead to discernible progress towards the goal of general and complete disarmament under effective international control. In this connection, special attention should be focussed on certain identifiable elements in the Programme of Action as adopted by the General Assembly at its Tenth Special Session which should as a minimum be accomplished during the Second Disarmament Decade both through negotiations in the mutilateral negotiating forum, the Committee on Disarmament, and in other appropriate forums...".

Though consensus could not be reached on the proposal to group the measures to be accomplished during the decade into those for the first half up to 1985 and those for the following second half, it was possible nevertheless to indicate some degree of priority as well as a timeframe for accomplishment, albeit in a flexible manner. Thus, the first identifiable period can be said to be 1980-82, the latter year being the year when the Second Special Session devoted to disarmament will be held. The elaboration of the blueprint for disarmament, the Comprehensive Programme for Disarmament, was placed first on the list of measures to be accomplished during the decade. It is a mark of the importance attached to the Comprehensive Programme that it is the only measure for which "a rigid timeframe", was accepted. It is to be completed and adopted in 1982 during the Second Special Session on disarmament. The programme is to encompass all measures thought to be advisable in order to ensure "that the goal of general and complete disarmament under effective international control becomes a reality in a world in which international peace and security prevail and in which the new international economic order is strengthened and consolidated..."

The first group of concrete disarmament measures identified as worthy of priority negotiations by the multilateral negotiating organ ought to have belonged to the same category as the Comprehensive Programme of Disarmament. However, owing to objections on the fixing of a rigid timetable, these measures were recommended as those whose accomplishment would create a very favourable international climate for the second Special Session of the General Assembly devoted to disarmament. "All efforts should be exerted therefore by the Committee on Disarmament urgently to negotiate with a view to reaching agreement, and to submit agreed texts where possible before the second special session devoted to disarmament." Such measures are:

(a) a comprehensive nuclear test ban treaty;
(b) a treaty on the prohibition of the development, production and stockpiling of all chemical weapons and on their destruction;
(c) convention on radiological weapons;
(d) security assurances to non-nuclear weapon states against use or threat of use of nuclear weapons

These are measures of a basic character, that have been under negotiation in the multilateral negotiating body, the Conference of the Committee on Disarmament (CCD) and its successor, the Committee on

Disarmament (CD). Considering the many detailed studies that have been carried out, and the equally detailed discussions that have been held on some of these subjects, it was the opinion of many that their early conclusion might well determine the will of states, particularly the militarily significant states to achieve concrete disarmament results in the decade of the 1980s. A particularly sensitive area in the decade will be the issue of nuclear proliferation. It is now obvious that the most important element in the nuclear non-proliferation regime – the Non-Proliferation Treaty (NPT) – has been under severe pressure both by Parties and Non-Parties alike. Its essentially discriminatory nature, its "approval" of the possession of nuclear weapons, and the lack of progress in steps for nuclear disarmament, are some of the criticisms made of the NPT. The failure of the Parties to the Treaty to agree on a document at the Second Review Conference in August 1980 was a manifestation of the wide crack that has appeared in the NPT wall.

At the same time reports that various countries are on the threshold of nuclear weapon capability have persisted. In the case of one of such countries – South Africa – it was known to have made detailed preparations for exploding a nuclear device in 1977, and believed to have actually detonated one in 1979. In view of these pressures, the need for early progress in developing an international consensus of ways and means to prevent the proliferation of nuclear weapons becomes urgent. It is in this context that the importance and priority nature attached to the Comprehensive Nuclear Test Ban Treaty emerges. It will, on the one hand, make a significant contribution to the aim of ending the further refinement of nuclear weapons and expansion of the stockpile, as well as the development of new types of such weapons. On the other hand, it will prevent the proliferation of nuclear weapons by providing an egalitarian alternative to those countries that have stayed outside the regime of the NPT because of the complaint of its discriminatory character. Even if the Comprehensive Test Ban Treaty cannot by itself alone sustain a Non Proliferation regime for the 1980s, it will be a more reliable first element for Nuclear Non Proliferation. The political will of the nuclear weapon states is the one crucial missing element in the conclusion of the Treaty. Once that will is demonstrated, this basic but crucial measure can be accomplished early in the decade of the 1980s.

Side by side with the priority instruments under negotiation in the multilateral negotiating forum, the disarmament strategy for the 1980s lists a number of measures on which equally early progress should be made and which are either being negotiated on a bilateral or regional level or, having been already negotiated, are yet to be brought fully into force. These measures are:

Ratification of the Strategic Arms Limitation Treaty (SALT II) signed by the United States and the Soviet Union in 1979.

Negotiations by the United States and the Soviet Union of further limitation of Strategic Arms to result in SALT III.

Strengthening of the Treaty for the Prohibition of Nuclear Weapons in Latin America (Treaty of Tlatelolco) through the ratification of its Additional Protocol I.

Signature and Ratification of the Treaty and Protocols adopted by the United Nations Conference on Prohibitions or Restrictions of use of certain Conventional Weapons which may be deemed to be excessively Injurious or to have Indiscriminate Effects. The Protocols relate to Fragments not detectable by X-rays, Mines and Booby Traps and Incendiary Weapons.

Agreement on Mutual and Balanced Reduction of Arms and Armed Forces in Central Europe.

It is natural that at the top of the list of these measures is the SALT process. Notwithstanding the SALT I agreement concluded in 1972, and the undertaking to negotiate SALT II, both the United States and the Soviet Union took major steps in the development and deployment of strategic nuclear weapons in the 1970s. Given the growing danger represented by these weapons in the light of their greatly improved accuracy as well as explosive yield, the negotiations for their limitation attracted universal interest. The Special Session on Disarmament held by the United Nations General Assembly in 1978 devoted considerable attention to the SALT process. The consensus reached was reflected in paragraph 52 of its Final Document which called upon the USSR and the United States of America to conclude at the earliest possible date their talks on SALT II. The two Powers were invited to follow SALT II promptly by further negotiations on strategic arms limitation "leading to agreed significant reductions of, and qualitative limitations on strategic arms."

The signing of SALT II in 1979 was greeted with some relief world-wide, notwithstanding the doubts raised in many quarters about its immediate value for limitation of strategic arms. The subsequent refusal by the new American Administration to ratify it, and the gigantic modernization proposals for the 1980s, open the prospect for another round of the strategic weapons race. The important place accorded to negotiations on this category of weapons has become all the more justified. Concerted international pressure is therefore necessary to ensure early resumption of these negotiations with a view to a real limitation of strategic weapons. A related area concerns theatre nuclear weapons in Europe. The deployment of the Soviet SS-20 missiles and the consequent NATO decision to deploy new American cruise and Pershing missiles, open the possibility of a dangerous escalation of the nuclear confrontation in Europe. Commencement of negotiations in the early years of the Second Disarmament Decade may yet obviate the necessity for another round of competition which obviously the Europeans wish to avoid.

The final list of measures "to be pursued as rapidly as possible during the Second Disarmament Decade" included many important items in both nuclear and conventional weapons as well as confidence building. These items are listed in more general terms, partly because of the continuing disagreement on the modalities and prior conditions for their negotiation, and partly because of the necessity for further studies. At the top of this list is the question of nuclear disarmament, in which general areas, identified in the Programme of Action of the First Special Session on Disarmament, were again repeated. Negotiations of agreements at appropriate stages together with adequate measures of verification satisfactory to the States concerned are to be conducted for:

- cessation of qualitative improvement and development of nuclear weapon systems;
- cessation of the production of all types of nuclear weapons and their means of delivery as well as the production of fissionable material for weapons purposes;
- a comprehensive phased programme with agreed timeframes, whenever feasible, for progressive and balanced reduction of stockpiles of nuclear weapons and their means of delivery leading to their ultimate and complete elimination at the earliest possible time.

Alongside of these negotiations, further measures are to be taken for the prevention of the proliferation of nuclear weapons. The development of the Safeguards system of the International Atomic Energy Agency, and the creation of other Nuclear-Weapon-Free Zones are among the steps envisaged. Proposals have already been made and supported by the United Nations General Assembly for nuclear-weapon-free zones in Africa, the Middle East and South Asia. Increasingly, also, suggestions are being made for the establishment of a nuclear-weapon-free zone in central Europe to eliminate once and for all the dangerous situation created by the concentration and modernization of Soviet and NATO nuclear weapons in the area. As a further step to save mankind from the danger of nuclear weapons, it is envisaged during the Decade to adopt measures for the avoidance of the use of nuclear weapons and the prevention of nuclear war through the adoption of confidence-building measures.

In the area of conventional weapons, multilateral, regional and bilateral measures are to be taken on the limitation and reduction of conventional weapons and armed forces in accordance with the relevant provisions of the Final Document of the First Special Session on Disarmament. The importance of steps in the area of conventional weapons derives partly from their universal effect, since all recent conflicts have involved these weapons, partly from the enormous expenditure they consume (about 80 per cent of world-wide military expenditure), and partly from their susceptibility to regional control. Without, therefore, diluting the priority attached to nuclear disarmament, due to the danger to mankind's existence which nuclear weapons pose, and mindful of the need for states to protect their sovereignty and territorial integrity, appropriate steps towards the reduction of conventional weapons and armed forces will contribute to the achievement of the objectives of the Decade. Resolution 35/156A, adopted by the General Assembly in 1980, in which it requested the Secretary-General to carry out a study on all aspects of the conventional arms race and on disarmament relating to conventional weapons and armed forces, was a useful first step.

Practical steps towards the reduction of military expenditure, especially by the militarily significant states, will have an immediate impact in the area of conventional disarmament, will be a good example to other states, and will contribute to fostering the inter-relationship between disarmament and development. Peace and development being indivisible, progress in one will benefit the other. The existence side by side of mass poverty and desperate living conditions in the developing countries on the one hand, with affluence and often lavish life style in the developed countries on the other, is recognized as a potential threat to international peace and security. Improvement of the quality of life and the general economic well-being of the peoples of the developing countries requires a combination of internal measures as well as a much-improved international economic co-operation. The economic difficulties in many of the developed countries in the latter part of the 1970s have reverberated in their contributions to international development. These contributions have declined in real terms; yet expenditures on armaments have consistently increased, even at the expense of social programmes within countries.

Bearing in mind the relationship between expenditure on armaments and economic and social development, the First Special Session on Disarmament emphasized the need to release real resources used for military purposes to economic and social development in the world, particularly for the benefit of the developing countries. A study which was commissioned on this subject has focussed on three issues: present-day utilization of resources for military purposes; economic and social effects of a continuing arms race and of the implementation of disarmament measures; and conversion and redeployment of resources released from military purposes through disarmament measures to economic purposes. With its forward-looking and policy-oriented approach, the study can be a stimulus to the necessity for disarmament and the consequential advantages of conversion and redeployment of resources from armaments to economic and social programmes. This process may well facilitate the establishment of the New International Economic Order.

Disarmament and international security

The process of disarmament is both cause and effect of the general global situation, especially the relationships among the most advanced military powers. In a period of détente among these powers, disarmament and arms limitation gain added impetus; the lack of détente creates a situation where trust is less but the need for disarmament is even greater, rather than less. In order, therefore, to create the right atmosphere for sustained disarmament measures during the Second Disarmament Decade, it is indispensable that the major Powers refrain from actions that will increase international tension and threaten the sovereignty and territorial integrity of states, and the right of peoples under colonial or foreign domination to self-determination and national independence. Strict adherence to the provisions of the Charter of the United Nations on non-intervention in the internal affairs of states will be necessary to create the right atmosphere. So also will the development by the United Nations of its capacity for peace-making and peace-keeping. The institution of confidence-building measures globally, and as appropriate to particular regional conditions, should be a continuing process during the Decade.

Public awareness

An important area which was neglected during the First Disarmament Decade was the popularization of disarmament discussions in such a way that those outside the immediate circle of policy makers and negotiators would take an interest. The First Special Session on Disarmament was the first major attempt to democratize disarmament deliberations and negotiations. That session also aroused a world-wide interest in this otherwise exclusive subject, which most people had been prepared to leave to the experts. If war is too important to leave to generals alone, so is disarmament too important to leave to the policy makers alone. It is essential that not only governments, but also the peoples of the world recognize and understand the dangers of the arms race. The programme of information, education and research launched by the First Special Session has already yielded some dividends. The United Nations Centre for Disarmament has widely diversified its publications on disarmament issues, as well as the results of studies carried out in this field. It has also undertaken a training programme for young diplomats through the United Nations Fellowship Programme on Disarmament. Disarmament Week is widely observed annually in United Nation member states. Unesco, which in 1980 held a World Congress on Disarmanent Education, has proceeded along the way to develop disarmament-related activities during the Decade, including the development of disarmament education. A series of regional training seminars has been planned by Unesco for university teachers. Similarly, the United Nations Centre for Disarmament has been charged by the General Assembly with sponsoring seminars in the different regions of the world at which issues relating to world disarmament in general, and to the particular region concerned will be extensively discussed.

The Role of scientists

The role of science and technology is crucial to the maintenance of the arms race. It has been estimated that at least a quarter, and probably much more of the resources, intellectual and financial, available for research in all areas of human activity is devoted to military research and development. This enormous concentration of human and material resources ensures constant sophistication and frequent changes in military technology. By contrast, some of the most devastating scourges of mankind (cancer and malaria, to mention just two), into which research ought to be urgently stepped up, often run into problems of attracting the necessary resources. Thus, military research and technology not only contribute to the further insecurity of the world, but also encourage the diversion of intellectual and material resources available from areas more important for the enhancement of the quality of human existence.

No single group is more aware than the scientific community of the destructive capability of the present generation of military hardware, especially nuclear weapons. The ingenuity of man which has created these monster weapons of destruction can be redirected towards their effective control, limitation and ultimate elimination. It is essential that more scientists, individually and collectively, speak out against further development and accumulation of armaments and in favour of disarmament, not as idealists but as realists aware of the danger to present and future generations implicit in the current level of armaments. The annual Pugwash Conferences provide one forum which is increasingly commanding attention. It is encouraging to note that at the 31st Pugwash Conference held in August – September 1981, the participants supported recent proposals for a Committee of distinguished scientists to analyse and make known the dangers of nuclear war. They also agreed to make the expertise of their members available to the many new groups working to mobilize public opinion for disarmament.

To this end, scientists can make significant contributions to the development of verification measures so essential in disarmament agreements. Moreover, social scientists and Peace Research Institutes can, through research, expose the fallacy underlying many of the concepts and ideas which encourage militarism. The United Nations as well as Unesco should continue to encourage such research.

Non-governmental organizations

The role of non-governmental organizations in the campaign for disarmament has been widely recognized. A number of these organizations are already active nationally as well as internationally. The strategy for the Second disarmament Decade called upon all segments concerned with information activities – governmental and non-governmental organs of member states and those of the United Nations and the Specialized Agencies, as well as non-governmental organizations – to undertake further programmes of information relating to the dangers of the armaments race, as well as to disarmament efforts and negotiations and their results.

World Disarmament Campaign

These activities may be co-ordinated in the proposed World Disarmament Campaign. Suggested first by the Secretary-General's Advisory Board on Disarmament Studies, the United Nations General Assembly, in its resolution 35/152 I of December 1980, requested the Secretary-General "to carry out a study on the organization and financing of a World Disarmament Campaign under the auspices of the United Nations". If agreement can be reached on the means of financing it, the World Disarmament Campaign may be launched at the forthcoming Special Session of the General Assembly devoted to Disarmament in 1982.

***

In conclusion, it should be pointed out that three dates will be important in the context of the implementation of the objectives of the Second Disarmament Decade. The year of the first major event of the

Decade is 1982, when the Second Special Session of the General Assembly devoted to Disarmament will be held. That session is expected to launch the blueprint for disarmament negotiations – the Comprehensive Programme of Disarmament. It should give an added impetus to the process of negotiations in the multilateral negotiating body, the Committee on Disarmament, as well as in other forums of negotiation. It should also see the launching of the World Disarmament Campaign, whereby all segments of the world population – men, women, students, professionals, parliamentarians, religious leaders, labour unions – would be included in the disarmament constituency. The second important date is 1985, the mid-term year when the General Assembly will undertake a review and appraisal of the implementation of the measures identified in the Declaration of the 1980s as the Second Disarmament Decade. The third date, 1990, will not only mark the end of the Second Disarmament Decade but, hopefully, will mark the half-way stage in the achievement of the general objective of general and complete disarmament under effective international control. In the course of negotiating the Comprehensive Programme for Disarmament, the trend has been strongly in favour of a twenty-year timeframe. If that trend holds, the world may witness no more than another and final Disarmament Decade after the current one. Such an eventuality will lend credibility to the determination of the member states of the United Nations to live by the obligation they assumed in declaring Decades for the achievement of disarmament.

Chapter 18. Towards a comprehensive programme of disarmament

Alfonso Garcia-Robles

Introduction

The convening of a second special session on disarmament of the United Nations General Assembly (UNSSOD II) was decided by the first special session of the same nature (UNSSOD I) whose Final Document, approved by consensus, stated in its paragraph 119:

> "A second special session of the General Assembly devoted to disarmament should be held on a date to be decided by the Assembly at its thirty-third session."

As contemplated in this paragraph, the Assembly subsequently adopted, on 14 December 1978, resolution 33/71 H whereby it decided that UNSSOD II should convene in 1982 at United Nations headquarters in New York, and that a preparatory committee for such a special session should be set up at its thirty-fifth session.

On 3 December 1980, the preparatory committee was established by resolution 35/47 with a composition of seventy-eight Member States appointed by the President of the General Assembly on the usual basis of "equitable geographic distribution".

The Committee held a brief organizational session of three working meetings on 4-5 December 1980 and a second session – which has been the first devoted to substantive questions – on 4 – 15 May 1981. At this session, the Committee began the consideration of the possible content of the provisional agenda of UNSSOD II. This was the task of the next session, 6-16 October 1981, since the Committee had been asked by the above-mentioned resolution to submit to the General Assembly at its thirty-sixth session its recommendations thereon.

Agenda for UNSSOD II

The Preparatory Committee had no difficulty in reaching agreement with regard to the inclusion on the provisional agenda of a series of those items that may be defined as ritual, such as the opening of the session, the holding of a minute of silent prayer or meditation, the election of the President and the adoption of the agenda.

When the discussion went beyond those traditional items, the many different views advanced could be broadly classified in two categories.

The first would comprise all those put forward by delegations which suggested for inclusion on the provisional agenda of the Assembly a large variety of items – some of them embracing various sub-items – which comprised mainly the following:

Review of the implementation of the decisions and recommendations of the first special session devoted to disarmament.

Consideration of initiatives and proposals of Member States.

Implementation of the declaration of the 1980s as the second disarmament decade.

Consideration and adoption of the comprehensive programme of disarmament.

Strengthening of the role of the United Nations in the field of disarmament.

The main exponent of the second category of views was the Delegation of Mexico which, in addition to the eight ritual procedural items and to a closing one devoted to the "Adoption of the Final Act of the Session", proposed that the agenda should follow the example of UNSSOD I (which, as is well known, had on its agenda only three substantive items dealing with the three main chapters of what was to become its Final Document: a Declaration on disarmament; a Programme of Action for disarmament, and a Machinery for disarmament) and concentrate its efforts on the consideration and adoption of the comprehensive programme of disarmament specifically requested in paragraph 109 of the Final Document and whose draft is being elaborated by the Committee on Disarmament since 1980.

In support of its proposal the Mexican delegation submitted a working paper in which it noted *inter-alia* the following:

"The experience of the General Assembly at its first special session devoted to disarmament underscored how useful it is, in dealing with a wide-ranging item whose various elements are closely interrelated, to do everything possible to prevent a dissipation of effort, and to seek instead a concentration of effort, with a view to maximum co-ordination.

This experience will be very valuable for the second special session; the lessons of the experience must be turned to full account. Such an approach is particularly advisable considering that the key item on the agenda will undoubtedly be the comprehensive programme of disarmament; the programme's structure and content are in several respects similar to those of the Final Document. Even more than the latter, they will require a sustained unity and the necessary correlation between the various components.

It thus appears most desirable to avoid a proliferation of items on the agenda of the forthcoming second session, which would rob it of its distinctiveness as a 'special' session and make it rather like a regular session. That would be all the more regrettable considering the frequency of regular sessions: the thirty-sixth session will take place six months before the second special session, and the thirty-seventh session barely three months or so after the end of the special session.

On the other hand, since the comprehensive programme of disarmament has to be 'self-contained', a thorough examination and analysis of the content of the programme by the Assembly at its special session, a *sine qua non* for the adoption of the programme by consensus, would, far from preventing consideration of other less important related items, make such consideration indispensible."

That this view is well-founded becomes evident if one bears in mind that the elaboration of the comprehensive programme of disarmament was expressly provided for in the Final Document of the first special session of the General Assembly devoted to disarmament. In paragraph 109 of that Document, the General Assembly agreed that the programme should encompass:

"All measures thought to be advisable in order to ensure that the goal of general and complete disarmament under effective international control becomes a reality in a world in which international peace and security prevail and in which the new international economic order is strengthened and consolidated."

Subsequently, the Committee on Disarmament, in its report to the General Assembly at its thirty-fifth session (a report welcomed by the Assembly), affirmed that the comprehensive programme would have to be "self-contained".

In the light of those statements, borne out by the structure and content of the programme, which are in general similar to those of the Final Document of UNSSOD I, it seems obvious, on the one hand, that the key item on the agenda of the second special session will be the comprehensive programme of disarmament and, on the other hand, that the programme itself, by virtue of its "comprehensiveness", will not only encompass all the elements included in the Final Document, but will go further than the Final Document in some respects.

Appropriate consideration of the draft comprehensive programme prepared by the Committee on Disarmament will therefore require, *inter alia*, a review of the implementation of the decisions and recommendations of the previous special session, and a review of the status of disarmament negotiations envisaged in the Programme of Action, particularly those relating to nuclear disarmament. It will also be necessary to consider the recommendations made by the Assembly at the previous special session, the follow-up to studies initiated by it during or after that session, the initiatives and proposals of Member States, and the manner of implementation of the declaration of the 1980s as the Second Disarmament Decade.

It will certainly be essential for the General Assembly to consider another question during its deliberations on the comprehensive programme: the strengthening of the role of the United Nations in the field of disarmament, including the functioning of deliberative organs, ways of enhancing the effectiveness of the Committee on Disarmament as the sole multilateral negotiating body in the field of disarmament, and the consideration of other such institutional arrangements as the possible convening of a world disarmament conference. Similarly, the World Disarmament Campaign – on which a study is at present being finalized – will undoubtedly have to be accorded a rightful place in the work of the General Assembly, like such other educational and information activities on disarmament as the holding of seminars and the fellowship programme.

Nevertheless, if all those questions will require attentive consideration by the General Assembly, they should not be examined in a haphazard manner as unconnected subjects, but in a coherent and co-ordinated way as elements of the comprehensive programme of disarmament and within its framework.

Achievements of UNSSOD I

For a better understanding of what should be the role of UNSSOD II, it seems appropriate to recall briefly some of the main achievements of UNSSOD I, which took place in May – June 1978.

First and foremost among those achievements was undoubtedly the adoption, by consensus, of a Final Document comprising four sections – Introduction, Declaration, Programme of Action and Machinery – closely intertwined. Its contents, of a much broader scope than anything previously approved by the United Nations, provides the elements for what could be called a new disarmament strategy.

Among these elements, perhaps the most prominent place belongs to a series of well-founded declarations, and to several fundamental purposes, principles and priorities which are clearly defined in the Final Document.

From among them it may be useful to recall as illustrative examples the following.

Concerning international security, which so often has been advanced as a pretext to reject or postpone disarmament, the General Assembly proclaimed that "the increase in weapons, especially nuclear weapons, far from helping to strengthen international security, on the contrary weakens it", and added later on that "enduring international peace and security cannot be built on the accumulation of weaponry by military alliances nor be sustained by a precarious balance of deterrence or doctrines of strategic superiority".

With regard to the dangers involved in the existing situation, the Assembly, after expressing its alarm about "the threat to the very survival of mankind by the existence of nuclear weapons and the continuing arms race", went on to say that "mankind today is confronted with an unprecedented threat of self-extinction arising from the massive and competitive accumulation of the most destructive weapons ever produced" and concluded that: "Removing the threat of a world war – a nuclear war – is the most acute and urgent task of the present day. Mankind is confronted with a choice: we must halt the arms race and proceed to disarmament or face annihiliation".

As a corollary of the above pronouncements, the Final Document included several provisions intended to underline that "all peoples of the world have a vital interest in the success of disarmament negotiations", that "all States have the right to participate" in such negotiations; and that "it is essential that not only Governments but also the peoples of the world recognize and understand the dangers in the present situation".

The Assembly also concluded that "it is essential to halt and reverse the nuclear arms race in all its aspects in order to avert the danger of war involving nuclear weapons"; that "the ultimate goal in this context is the complete elimination of nuclear weapons"; that the final goal of "the efforts of States in the disarmament process is general and complete disarmament under effective international control"; and that "progress towards this objective requires the conclusion and implementation of agreements on the cessation of the arms race and on genuine measures of disarmament" which should take place in stages and in such an equitable and balanced manner as to ensure at any stage to each State or group of States "undiminished security at the lowest possible level of armaments and military forces".

In addition to these few illustrative examples, which should rightly be granted priority in any recapitulation of disarmament principles and objectives approved by UNSSOD I, it seems advisable to bear in mind that the Final Document contains many other provisions of the same nature which cover exhaustively all other aspects of this complex matter, such as the following.

Obligation to strictly observe the principles of the UN Charter; negative effect of the arms race on the relaxation of international tension as well as on the exercise of the right of self-determination; necessity to build confidence among States; recognition of the central role of the

United Nations in the sphere of disarmament and of the need to strengthen it; affirmation that effective measures of nuclear disarmament and the prevention of nuclear war have the highest priority; elimination of the use or the threat of use of force from international life; effective implementation of the security system provided for in the UN Charter and recourse to procedures of peaceful settlement of disputes; strict observance of an acceptable balance of mutual responsibilities and obligations for nuclear and non-nuclear-weapon States; primary responsibility of nuclear-weapon States, together with other militarily significant States for halting and reversing the arms race; advantages of the creation of nuclear-weapon-free zones and of zones of peace; adequate measures of verification to be included in disarmament agreements; definition of the following priorities for disarmament negotiations – nuclear weapons, chemical weapons and other weapons of mass destruction, conventional weapons and reduction of armed forces; close relationship between disarmament and development and incompatibility of the economic and social consequences of the arms race with the implementation of the new international economic order, based on justice, equity and co-operation; urgency to mobilize world public opinion on behalf of disarmament and, to that end, to avoid dissemination of false and tendentious information concerning armaments and to concentrate on a campaign of education and information on the danger of escalation of the arms race and the need for general and complete disarmament under effective international control.

There is no doubt that those and all other similar provisions approved by consensus at UNSSOD I have today the same or even greater validity and will not be in need of any modification by UNSSOD II.

What has just been said regarding principles, objectives and priorities approved by UNSSOD I, is to some extent equally true in connection with the provisions of the Final Document included in its section entitled "Machinery" which are briefly described below.

The General Assembly began by stating the need to "revitalize" the existing disarmament machinery and by rightly pointing out that two kinds of bodies are requested in the field of disarmament, deliberative and negotiating, and that "all Member States" should be represented on the former, "whereas the latter, for the sake of convenience, should have a relatively small membership".

With regard to deliberation, it was declared in the Final Document that the General Assembly had been and should remain "the main deliberative organ of the United Nations", and that its First Committee should deal in the future "only with questions of disarmament and related international security questions". The General Assembly also established, as one of its subsidiary organs, a Disarmament Commission composed of all States Members of the United Nations, which should be a deliberative body and meet every year for a period of four weeks.

Finally, it was also agreed that a second special session of the General

Assembly devoted to disarmament should be held at a date to be decided later, and which at present will be June – July 1982.

Concerning negotiations, UNSSOD I declared to be "deeply aware of the continuing requirement for a single multilateral disarmament negotiating forum of limited size taking decisions on the basis of consensus". As a result of this and other related provisions the Committee on Disarmament was constituted with a membership of forty: the five nuclear weapon States and thirty-five other States.

From the procedural stand-point the decisions of UNSSOD I relating to machinery, be it deliberative or negotiating, have proved generally adequate. The fact that both types of organs have been, although with some exceptions, working smoothly, does not mean that there has been progress on disarmament. The absence of political will of the nuclear weapon States – even if in some cases it has been only of some of them – gives full validity to the appraisal made in the Final Document. It is a fact that there are now even more reasons than in 1978 to affirm that the disarmament objectives "appear to be as far away today as they were then, or even further because the arms race is not diminishing but increasing and outstrips by far the efforts to curb it".

It should also be recalled that UNSSOD I, bearing in mind that the United Nations "has a central role and primary responsibility in the sphere of disarmament", stressed the necessity of keeping the world organization "duly informed... of all disarmament efforts outside its aegis", whether they are "unilateral, bilateral, regional, or multilateral". The observance of these provisions has so far left much to be desired.

It is in connection with questions such as these, as well as with the mobilization of "world public opinion on behalf of disarmament", also expressly contemplated in the Final Document, that UNSSOD II may perform a most useful task when it reviews the existing disarmament machinery and procedures. Thus, for instance, it could be made mandatory for any President, Chairman or Secretary of a meeting on disarmament held outside the United Nations to send two complete sets of all relevant documents to the UN Secretary-General for transmission to the General Assembly and to the Committee on Disarmament, respectively. The second special session, would likewise provide an excellent opportunity for the solemn launching of the "World Disarmament Campaign" for whose organization and financing the Secretary-General is presently carrying out a thorough study with the assistance of qualified experts, as requested by the thirty-fifth session in 1980. The Assembly could also devise ways and means to prevent paralysis of the negotiating function of the Committee through the abuse of the "consensus" rule on procedural questions.

Nevertheless, whatever may be the significance of any developments and improvements which UNSSOD II may approve on the various types of machinery and procedure briefly outlined above, it seems axiomatic that it is on what was called in the Final Document of 1978 a "Programme of

Action" that the forthcoming Assembly should particularly endeavour to secure effective results.

Indeed, none of the priority measures relating to nuclear arms control, not to mention those pertaining to nuclear disarmament, has received even a token implementation.

Comprehensive Programme of Disarmament

In the light of what has happened during the last three years, and of the present alarming conditions of the arms race, pledges like those enshrined in paragraphs 17 ("The pressing need now is to translate into practical terms the provisions of this Final Document and to proceed along the road of binding and effective international agreements in the field of disarmament"), and 42 ("Since prompt measures should be taken in order to halt and reverse the arms race, Member States hereby declare that they will respect the objectives and principles stated above and make every effort faithfully to carry out the Programme of Action") of the Final Document of UNSSOD I, acquire today an ironic flavour. Consequently, it seems imperative that UNSSOD II concentrates its efforts in adopting an all-embracing and specific programme of disarmament, and in securing a binding commitment of all participant States to its faithful implementation.

Fortunately, the Assembly, since the moment when it held its first special session devoted to disarmament, had foreseen this need. Thus, in paragraph 109 of its Final Document it is explicitly provided that "concurrently with negotiations on partial measures of disarmament" it would be necessary to conduct "negotiations on general and complete disarmament", which remains "the ultimate goal of all efforts exerted in the field of disarmament", as emphatically affirmed by the Assembly that adopted at the same time the following far-sighted decision:

> "With this purpose in mind, the Committee on Disarmament will undertake the elaboration of a comprehensive programme of disarmament encompassing all measures thought to be advisable in order to ensure that the goal of general and complete disarmament under effective international control becomes a reality in a world in which international peace and security prevail and in which the new international economic order is strengthened and consolidated".

It is in compliance with this decision that the Committee on Disarmament established in March 1980 an *ad hoc* working group "to initiate negotiations on the Comprehensive Programme of Disarmament... with a view to completing its elaboration before the second special session of the General Assembly devoted to disarmament".

The working group has met regularly since then. It held ten meetings in 1980 and more than twenty in 1981. Since 1980, at an early stage of its deliberations, the working group agreed on a structure for the Comprehensive Programme which is very similar to that of the Final Document, inasmuch as it comprises, in addition to an Introduction or Preamble, sections or chapters devoted to Objectives, Principles and Priorities, Measures with indication of Stages of Implementation, and Machinery and Procedure.

Subsequently, the Committee on Disarmament, in its report to the thirty-fifth session of the General Assembly (a report welcomed by the Assembly) affirmed that the Comprehensive Programme would have to be "self-contained". Bearing this in mind, as well as the "comprehensiveness" which will have to be one of its essential characteristics, it is clear that the Programme will not only encompass all the elements included in the Final Document but will go further than the latter in some respects. In view of this and of the pressing need to adopt new methods and register appropriate undertakings which permit the implementation of effective disarmament measures, it seems obvious that the key item in the agenda of UNSSOD II will be the Comprehensive Programme of Disarmament.

In the light of the tentative conclusion reached as a result of a "first reading" consideration of all material available to the working group until the middle of July, 1981, it would seem probable that the Comprehensive Programme of Disarmament may comprise four "stages of implementation" of the numerous measures it is going to embrace and the realization of which would have to culminate, as explicitly directed by the Assembly, in general and complete disarmament under effective international control.

As a working hypothesis, the group has provisionally accepted a duration of five years for each of those four stages. This would mean the completion of the Programme by the end of the century, it being understood that, at the end of each stage, a special session of the General Assembly should be convened to review the implementation of the Programme and to make the necessary adjustments for the next stages.

The timeframes thus contemplated, should not however be interpreted as the equivalent of rigid timetables, but rather as the indication of agreed deadlines which represent desirable goals to be aimed at, and for whose attainment all States would thus be accepting a binding undertaking to make every possible effort within their reach.

It is too early to have a clear picture of the results of the *ad hoc* working group deliberations and negotiations. Nevertheless, it may be safely concluded, in the light of all that has been stated in the present paper, that success or failure of the second special session of the General Assembly devoted to disarmament will rest on whether or not it is able to adopt an adequate Comprehensive Programme of Disarmament which, if it is to be effective, should present the following characteristics.

The Programme must fit the description made of it in paragraph 109 of the Final Document as an instrument which should ensure that the goal of general and complete disarmament under effective international control becomes a reality in a world in which international peace and security prevail, and in which the new international economic order is strengthened and consolidated.

With this purpose in mind, the Programme should encompass all measures thought to be advisable for its achievement and which could be divided into two broad categories. The first would cover what is normally called in the United Nations "Disarmament measures", embracing all types of measures dealing with disarmament, whether they be for the prevention, the limitation, the reduction or the elimination of armaments, or for the reduction of armed forces. The second category would comprise all other relevant measures – which could be listed under the general heading "Associated measures" – such as those aimed at ensuring that disarmament makes an effective contribution to economic and social development and, in particular, to full realization of the new international economic order; those intended to contribute to the strengthening of international procedures and institutions for the peaceful settlement of disputes and for the maintenance of peace and security in accordance with the Charter of the United Nations; those whose main purpose would be to mobilize world public opinion in favour of disarmament through a well organized world disarmament campaign, directed and co-ordinated by the United Nations Secretary-General; and those which are usually referred to as confidence-building measures.

While the Comprehensive Programme would thus contain measures of identical nature to those included in the Final Document, the two documents would, however, present some substantial differences: e.g. due to its comprehensiveness, the measures to be included in the Programme would be more numerous than those contained in the Final Document; the measures would be enunciated in a more concrete manner and described more specifically than they are in the Final Document, and they should be assembled in some – perhaps four – stages in order to ensure that the adoption of disarmament measures is carried out in "an equitable and balanced manner" in such a way that the security of all States is guaranteed at progressively lower levels, both qualitative and quantitative, of armaments.

With regard to machinery, some improvements may also be sought, such as longer annual sessions for the Committee on Disarmament and procedural ways and means to avoid the abuse of the consensus rule to paralyse negotiations in the Committee, as well as to secure the practical application of past decisions for keeping the United Nations duly informed of all disarmament efforts outside its aegis.

It would also be most desirable to upgrade the UN Secretariat unit in charge of disarmament matters – the "UN Centre for Disarmament" – converting it into a "Department of Disarmament Affairs" which should be placed on the same level as the Department of Political and Security Council Affairs and the Department of International Economic and Social Affairs.

The objectives to be pursued, as well as the principles and priorities for the implementation of the measures which were approved by consensus at UNSSOD I, have today, as already stated, the same or even greater, validity than in 1978. It is therefore safe to assume that those which may be included in the Comprehensive Programme will have to be essentially identical to those contained in the Final Document.

At the outset of the Comprehensive Programme there must certainly be included some introductory material which probably will consist of a descriptive introduction *strictu sensu* and an analytical preamble. But perhaps one of the most important features, for whose inclusion in the Programme no effort should be spared, would consist of a firm undertaking of all participant States to abide strictly by the provisions of the programme and of their recognition of some kind of binding force to such provisions. In this respect it should be recalled that the Final Document of 1978, which, in theory, is an outstanding document, has in practice remained a dead letter because of the absence of political will of the nuclear-weapon States, or at least of some of them. It seems therefore indispensable to avoid, in connection with the Comprehensive Programme of Disarmament, the repetition of such a sad experience. The second special session of the United Nations General Assembly devoted to disarmament is entitled – as are all the people of the world – not to be deceived once again.

Appendix 1

The Russell-Einstein Manifesto

In the tragic situation which confronts humanity, we feel that scientists should assemble in conference to appraise the perils that have arisen as a result of the development of weapons of mass destruction, and to discuss a resolution in the spirit of the appended draft.

We are speaking on this occasion, not as members of this or that nation, continent, or creed, but as human beings, members of the species Man, whose continued existence is in doubt. The world is full of conflicts; and, overshadowing all minor conflicts, the titanic struggle between Communism and anti-Communism.

Almost everybody who is politically conscious has strong feelings about one or more of these issues; but we want you, if you can, to set aside such feelings and consider yourselves only as members of a biological species which has had a remarkable history, and whose disappearance none of us can desire.

We shall try to say no single word which should appeal to one group rather than to another. All, equally, are in peril, and, if the peril is understood, there is hope that they may collectively avert it.

We have to learn to think in a new way. We have to learn to ask ourselves, not what steps can be taken to give military victory to whatever group we prefer, for there no longer are such steps; the question we have to ask ourselves is: what steps can be taken to prevent a military contest of which the issue must be disastrous to all parties?

The general public, and even many men in position of authority, have not realized what would be involved in a war with nuclear bombs. The general public still thinks in terms of the obliteration of cities. It is understood that the new bombs are more powerful than the old, and that, while one A-bomb could obliterate Hiroshima, one H-bomb could obliterate the largest cities, such as London, New York, and Moscow.

No doubt in an H-bomb war great cities would be obliterated. But this is one of the minor disasters that would have to be faced. If everybody in London, New York, and Moscow were exterminated, the world might, in the course of a few centuries, recover from the blow. But we now know, especially since the Bikini test, that nuclear bombs can gradually spread destruction over a very much wider area than had been supposed.

It is stated on very good authority that a bomb can now be manufactured which will be 2,500 times as powerful as that which destroyed Hiroshima. Such a bomb, if exploded near the ground or under water, sends radioactive particles into the upper air. They sink gradually and reach the surface of the earth in the form of a deadly dust or rain. It was this dust which infected the Japanese fishermen and their catch of fish.

No one knows how widely such lethal radio-active particles might be diffused, but the best authorities are unanimous in saying that a war with H-bombs might quite possibly put an end to the human race. It is feared that if many H-bombs are used there will be universal death – sudden only for a minority, but for the majority a slow torture of disease and disintegration.

Many warnings have been uttered by eminent men of science and by authorities in military strategy. None of them will say that the worst results are certain. What they do say is that these results are possible, and no one can be sure that they will not be realized. We have not yet found that the views of experts on this question depend in any degree upon their politics or prejudices. They depend only, so far as our researches have revealed, upon the extent of the particular expert's knowledge. We have found that the men who know most are the most gloomy.

Here, then, is the problem which we present to you, stark and dreadful and inescapable: Shall we put an end to the human race; or shall mankind renounce war?* People will not face this alternative because it is so difficult to abolish war.

The abolition of war will demand distasteful limitations of national sovereignty.** But what perhaps impedes understanding of the situation more than anything else is that the term "mankind" feels vague and abstract. People scarcely bring themselves to grasp that they, individually, and those whom they love are in imminent danger of perishing agonizingly. And so they hope that perhaps war may be allowed to continue provided modern weapons are prohibited.

This hope is illusory. Whatever agreements not to use H-bombs had been reached in time of peace, they would no longer be considered binding in time of war, and both sides would set to work to manufacture H-bombs as soon as war broke out, for, if one side manufactured the bombs and the other did not, the side that manufactured them would inevitably be victorious.

Although an agreement to renounce nuclear weapons as part of a general reduction of armaments*** would not afford an ultimate solution, it would serve certain important purposes. First: any agreement between East and West is to the good insofar as it tends to diminish tension. Second: the abolition of thermonuclear weapons, if each side believed that the other had carried it out sincerely, would lessen the fear of a sudden attack in the style of Pearl Harbour, which at present keeps both sides in a state of nervous apprehension. We should, therefore, welcome such an agreement, though only as a first step.

Most of us are not neutral in feeling, but as human beings, we have to remember that, if the issues between East and West are to be decided in any manner that can give any possible satisfaction to anybody, whether Communist or anti-Communist, whether Asian or European or American, whether White or Black, then these issues must not be decided by war. We should wish this to be understood, both in the East and in the West.

There lies before us, if we choose, continual progress in happiness, knowledge and wisdom. Shall we instead, choose death, because we cannot forget our quarrels? We appeal, as human beings, to human beings: remember your humanity, and forget the rest. If you can do so, the way lies open to a new Paradise; if you cannot, there lies before you the risk of universal death.

---

*Professor Joliot-Curie wishes to add the words: "as a means of settling differences between States."

**Professor Joliot-Curie wishes to add that these limitations are to be agreed by all and in the interests of all.

***Professor Muller makes the reservation that this be taken to mean "a concomitant balanced reduction of all armaments."

Resolution

We invite this Congress, and through it the scientists of the world and the general public, to subscribe to the following resolution:

"In view of the fact that in any future world war nuclear weapons will certainly be employed, and that such weapons threaten the continued existence of mankind, we urge the Governments of the world to realize, and to acknowledge publicly, that their purpose cannot be furthered by a world war, and we urge them, consequently to find peaceful means for the settlement of all matters of dispute between them".

Professor Max Born (Professor of Theoretical Physics at Berlin, Frankfurt, and Göttingen, and of Natural Philosophy, Edinburgh; Nobel Prize in physics).

Professor P.W. Bridgman (Professor of Physics, Harvard University; Nobel Prize in physics).

Professor Albert Einstein.

Professor L. Infeld (Professor of Theoretical Physics, University of Warsaw).

Professor J.F. Joliot-Curie (Professor of Physics at the Collège de France; Nobel Prize in chemistry).

Professor H.J. Muller (Professor of Zoology at University of Indiana; Nobel Prize in physiology and medicine).

Professor Linus Pauling (Professor of Chemistry, California Institute of Technology; Nobel Prize in chemistry).

Professor C.F. Powell (Professor of Physics, Bristol University; Nobel Prize in physics).

Professor J. Rotblat (Professor of Physics, University of London, Medical College of St. Bartholomew's Hospital).

Bertrand Russell.

Professor Hideki Yukawa (Professor of Theoretical Physics, Kyoto University; Nobel Prize in physics).

Appendix 2

Recommendation on the Status of Scientific Researchers

The General Conference of the United Nations Educational, Scientific and Cultural Organization (Unesco), meeting in Paris from 17 October to 23 November 1974 at its eighteenth session... Adopts this recommendation this twentieth day of November 1974.

I.   SCOPE OF APPLICATION

The General Conference recommends that Member States should apply the following provisions by taking whatever legislative or other steps may be required to apply within their respective territories the principles and norms set forth in this recommendation.

The General Conference recommends that Member States should bring this recommendation to the attention of the authorities, institutions and enterprises responsible for the conduct of research and experimental development and the application of its results, and of the various organizations representing or promoting the interests of scientific researchers in association, and other interested parties.

*   *   *

II.   SCIENTIFIC RESEARCHERS IN THE CONTEXT OF NATIONAL POLICY-MAKING

4.   Each Member State should strive to use scientific and technological knowledge for the enhancement of the cultural and material well-being of its citizens, and to further the United Nations ideals and objectives. To attain this objective, each Member State should equip itself with the personnel, institutions and mechanisms necessary for developing and putting into practice national science and technology policies aimed at directing scientific research and experimental development efforts to the achievement of national goals while according a sufficient place to science *per se*. By the policies they adopt in respect of science and technology, by the way in which they use science and technology in policy-making generally, and by their treatment of scientific researchers in particular, Member States should demonstrate that science and technology are not activities to be carried out in isolation but part of the nations' integrated effort to set up a society that will be more humane and really just.

5.   At all appropriate stages of their national planning generally, and of their planning in science and technology specifically, Member States should:

(a) treat public funding of scientific research and experimental development

305

as a form of public investment the returns on which are, for the most part, necessarily long term; and

(b)take all appropriate measures to ensure that the justification for, and indeed the indispensability of such expenditure is held constantly before public opinion.

6. Member States should make every effort to translate into terms of international policies and practices, their awareness of the need to apply science and technology in a great variety of specific fields of wider than national concern: namely, such vast and complex problems as the preservation of international peace and the elimination of want and other problems which can only be effectively tackled on an international basis, such as pollution monitoring and control, weather forecasting and earthquake prediction.

7. Member States should cultivate opportunities for scientific researchers to participate in the outlining of national scientific research and experimental development policy. In particular, each Member State should ensure that these processes are supported by appropriate institutional mechanisms enjoying adequate advice and assistance from scientific researchers and their professional organizations.

8. Each Member State should institute procedures adapted to its needs for ensuring that, in the performance of publicly-supported scientific research and experimental development, scientific researchers respect public accountability while at the same time enjoying the degree of autonomy appropriate to their task and to the advancement of science and technology. It should be fully taken into account that creative activities of scientific researchers should be promoted in the national science policy on the basis of utmost respect for the autonomy and freedom of research necessary to scientific progress.

9. With the above ends in view, and with respect for the principle of freedom of movement of scientific researchers, Member States should be concerned to create that general climate, and to provide those specific measures for the moral and material support and encouragement of scientific researchers, as will:

(a)ensure that young people of high calibre find sufficient attraction in the vocation, and sufficient confidence in scientific research and experimental development as a career offering reasonable prospects and a fair degree of security, to maintain a constantly adequate regeneration of the nation's scientific and technological personnel;

(b)facilitate the emergence and stimulate the appropriate growth, among its own citizens, of a body of scientific researchers regarding themselves and regarded by their colleagues throughout the world as worthy members of the international scientific and technological community;

(c)encourage a situation in which the majority of scientific researchers or young people who aspire to become scientific researchers are provided with the necessary incentives to work in the service of their country and to return there if they seek some of their education, training or experience abroad.

III. THE INITIAL EDUCATION AND TRAINING OF SCIENTIFIC RESEARCHERS

10. Member States should have regard for the fact that effective scientific research calls for scientific researchers of integrity and maturity, combining high moral and intellectual qualities.

11. Among the measures which Member States should take to assist the emergence of scientific researchers of this high calibre are:

(a) ensuring that, without discrimination on the basis of race, colour, sex, language, religion, political or other opinion, national or social origin, economic condition or birth, all citizens enjoy equal opportunities for the initial education and training needed to qualify for scientific research work, as well as ensuring that all citizens who succeed in so qualifying enjoy equal access to available employment in scientific research;

(b) encouragement of the spirit of community service as an important element in such education and training for scientific workers.

12. So far as is compatible with the necessary and proper independence of educators, Member States should lend their support to all educational initiatives designed to foster that spirit, such as:

(a) the incorporation or development, in the curricula and courses concerning the natural sciences and technology, of elements of social and environmental sciences;

(b) the development and use of educational techniques for awakening and stimulating such personal qualities and habits of mind as:

(i) disinterestedness and intellectual integrity;

(ii) the ability to review a problem or situation in perspective and in proportion, with all its human implications;

(iii) skill in isolating the civic and ethical implications, in issues involving the search for new knowledge and which may at first sight seem to be of a technical nature only;

(iv) vigilance as to the probable and possible social and ecological consequences of scientific research and experimental development activities;

(v) willingness to communicate with others not only in scientific and technological circles but also outside those circles, which implies willingness to work in a team and in a multi-occupational context.

IV. THE VOCATION OF THE SCIENTIFIC RESEARCHER

13. Member States should bear in mind that the scientific researchers' sense of vocation can be powerfully reinforced if he is encouraged to think of his work in terms of service both to his fellow countrymen and to his fellow human beings in general. Member States should seek, in their treatment of and attitude towards scientific researchers, to express encouragement for scientific research and experimental development performed in this broad spirit of community service.

The civic and ethical aspect of scientific research

14. Member States should seek to encourage conditions in which scientific

researchers, with the support of the public authorities, have the responsibility and the right:

(a) to work in a spirit of intellectual freedom to pursue, expound and defend the scientific truth as they see it;

(b) to contribute to the definition of the aims and objectives of the programmes in which they are engaged and to the determination of the methods to be adopted which should be humanely, socially and ecologically responsible;

(c) to express themselves freely on the human, social or ecological value of certain projects and in the last resort withdraw from those projects if their conscience so dictates;

(d) to contribute positively and constructively to the fabric of science, culture and education in their own country, as well as to the achievement of national goals, the enhancement of their fellow citizens' well-being, and the furtherance of the international ideals and objectives of the United Nations;

it being understood that Member States, when acting as employers of scientific researchers, should specify as explicitly and narrowly as possible the cases in which they deem it necessary to depart from the principles set out in paragraphs (a) to (d) above.

15.   Member States should take all appropriate steps to urge all other employers of scientific researchers to follow the recommendations contained in paragraph 14.

The international aspect of scientific research

16.   Member States should recognize that scientific researchers encounter, with increasing frequency, situations in which the scientific research and experimental development on which they are engaged has an international dimension; and should endeavour to assist scientific researchers to exploit such situations in the furtherance of international peace, co-operation and understanding, and the common welfare of mankind.

17.   Member States should in particular provide all possible support to the initiatives of scientific researchers undertaken in search of improved understanding of factors involved in the survival and well-being of mankind as a whole.

18.   Each Member State should enlist the knowledge, industry and idealism of those of its citizens who are scientific researchers, especially of the younger generation, in the task of furnishing as generous a contribution as its resources can permit to the world's scientific and technological research effort. Member States should welcome all the advice and assistance scientific researchers can provide, in socio-economic development efforts that will contribute to the consolidation of an authentic culture and of national sovereignty.

19.   In order that the full potentialities of scientific and technological knowledge be promptly geared to the benefit of all peoples, Member States should urge scientific researchers to keep in mind the principles set out in paragraphs 16, 17 and 18.

V. CONDITIONS FOR SUCCESS ON THE PART OF SCIENTIFIC RE-SEARCHERS

20.   Member States should:
(a) bear in mind that the public interest, as well as that of scientific researchers, requires moral support and material assistance conducive to successful performance in scientific research and experimental development by scientific researchers;
(b) recognize that in this respect they have, as employers of scientific researchers, a leading responsibility and should attempt to set an example to other employers of such researchers;
(c) urge all other employers of scientific researchers to pay close attention to the provision of satisfactory working conditions for scientific researchers, notably in respect of all the provisions of the present Section;
(d) ensure that scientific researchers enjoy conditions of work and pay commensurate with their status and performance without discrimination on the basis of sex, language, age, religion or national origin.

Adequate career development prospects and facilities

21.   Member States should draw up, preferably within the framework of a comprehensive national manpower policy, policies in respect of employment which adequately cover the needs of scientific researchers, in particular by:
(a) providing scientific researchers in their direct employment with adequate career development prospects and facilities though not necessarily exclusively in the fields of scientific research and experimental development: and encouraging non-governmental employers to do likewise;
(b) making every effort to plan scientific research and experimental development in such a way that the scientific researchers concerned are not subjected, merely by the nature of their work, to avoidable hardship;
(c) considering the provision of the necessary funds for facilities for readaptation and redeployment in respect of the scientific researchers in their permanent employ, as an integral part of scientific research and experimental development planning, especially, but not exclusively, in the case of programmes or projects designed as limited duration activities; and where these facilities are not possible, by providing appropriate compensatory arrangements;
(d) offering challenging opportunities for young scientific researchers to do significant scientific research and experimental development, in accordance with their abilities.

Permanent self re-education

22.   Member States should seek to encourage that:
(a) like other categories of workers facing similar problems, scientific researchers enjoy opportunities for keeping themselves up to date in their own and in related subjects, by attendance at conferences, by free access to libraries and other sources of information, and by participation in educational or vocational courses; and where necessary, scientific researchers should have the opportunity to undergo further scientific training with a view to transferring to another branch of scientific activity;
(b) appropriate facilities are provided for this purpose.

Mobility in general and the civil service in particular

23.   Member States should take measures to encourage and facilitate, as part of a comprehensive national policy for highly-qualified manpower, the interchange or mobility of scientific researchers as between scientific research and experimental development service in the government and in the higher education and productive enterprise contexts.

24.   Member States should also bear in mind that the machinery of government at all levels can benefit from the special skills and insights provided by scientific researchers. All Member States could therefore profitably benefit from a careful comparative examination of the experience gained in those Member States which have introduced salary scales and other conditions of employment specially designed for scientific researchers, with a view to determining to what extent such schemes would help meet their own national needs. Matters which appear to require particular attention in this respect are:

> (a) optimum utilization of scientific researchers within the framework of a comprehensive national policy for highly-qualified manpower;
> (b) the desirability of providing procedures with all the necessary guarantees allowing for the periodic review of the material conditions of scientific researchers to ensure that they remain equitably comparable with those of other workers having equivalent experience and qualifications and in keeping with the country's standard of living;
> (c) the possibility of providing adequate career development prospects in public research bodies; as well as the need to give scientifically or technologically qualified researchers the option of transferring from scientific research and experimental development positions to administrative positions.

25.   Member States should furthermore turn to advantage the fact that science and technology can be stimulated by close contact with other spheres of national activity, and vice versa. Member States should accordingly take care not to discourage scientific researchers whose predilections and talents, initially cultivated in the scientific research and experimental development context proper, lead them to progress into cognate activities. Member States should on the contrary be vigilant to encourage those scientific researchers, whose original scientific research and experimental development training and subsequently acquired experience reveal potentialities lying in such fields as management of scientific research and experimental development or the broader field of science and technology policies as a whole, to develop to the full their talents in these directions.

Participation in international scientific and technological gatherings

26.   Member States should actively promote the interplay of ideas and information among scientific researchers throughout the world, which is vital to the healthy development of science and technology; and to this end should take all measures necessary to ensure that scientific researchers are enabled, throughout their careers, to participate in international scientific and technological gatherings and to travel abroad.

27.   Member States should furthermore see to it that all governmental or quasi-governmental organizations in which or under whose authority scientific research and experimental development are performed, regularly devote a portion

of their budget to financing the participation at such international scientific and technological gatherings, of scientific researchers in their employ.

Access by scientific researchers to positions of greater responsibility with corresponding rewards

28.   Member States should encourage in practice that decisions as to access by scientific researchers in their employ to positions of greater responsibility and correspondingly higher rewards, are formulated essentially on the basis of fair and realistic appraisal of the capacities of the persons concerned, as evidenced by their current or recent performances, as well as on the basis of formal or academic evidence of knowledge acquired or skills demonstrated by them.

Protection of health; social security

29.   (a)Member States should accept that, as employers of scientific researchers, the onus is on them – in accordance with national regulations, and the international instruments concerned with the protection of workers in general from hostile or dangerous environments – to guarantee so far as is reasonably possible the health and safety of the scientific researchers in their employ, as of all other persons likely to be affected by the scientific research and experimental development in question. They should accordingly ensure that the managements of scientific establishments enforce appropriate safety standards; train all those in their employ in the necessary safety procedures; monitor and safeguard the health of all persons at risk; take due note of warnings of new (or possible new) hazards brought to their attention, in particular by the scientific researchers themselves, and act accordingly; ensure that the working day and rest periods are of reasonable length, the latter to include annual leave on full pay.

(b)Member States should take all appropriate steps to urge like practices on all other employers of scientific researchers.

30.   Member States should ensure that provision is made for scientific researchers to enjoy (in common with all other workers) adequate and equitable social security arrangements appropriate to their age, sex, family situation, state of health and to the nature of the work they perform.

Promotion, appraisal, expression and recognition of creativity

Promotion

31.   Member States should be actively concerned to stimulate creative performance in the field of science and technology by all scientific researchers.

Appraisal

32.   Member States should, as regards scientific researchers in their employ:

(a)take due account, in all procedures for appraisal of the creativity of scientific researchers, of the difficulty inherent in measuring a personal capacity which seldom manifests itself in a constant and unfluctuating form;

(b)enable, and as appropriate encourage scientific researchers in whom it appears this capacity might be profitably stimulated:

(i)   either to turn to a new field of science or technology;

(ii) or else to progress from scientific research and experimental

311

development to other occupations in which the experience they have acquired and the other personal qualities of which they have given proof can be put to better use in a new context.

33. Member States should urge like practices upon other employers of scientific researchers.

34. As elements pertinent to appraisal of creativity, Member States should seek to ensure that scientific researchers may:
  (a) receive without hindrance the questions, criticisms and suggestions addressed to them by their colleagues throughout the world, as well as the intellectual stimulus afforded by such communications and the exchanges to which they give rise;
  (b) enjoy in tranquility international acclaim warranted by their scientific merit.

Expression by publication

35. Member States should encourage and facilitiate publication of the results obtained by scientific researchers, with a view to assisting them to acquire the reputation which they merit as well as with a view to promoting the advancement of science and technology, education and culture generally.

36. To this end, Member States should ensure that the scientific and technological writings of scientific researchers enjoy appropriate legal protection, and in particular the protection afforded by copyright law.

37. Member States should, in consultation with scientific researchers' organizations and as a matter of standard practice encourage the employers of scientific researchers, and themselves as employers seek:
  (a) to regard it as the norm that scientific researchers be at liberty and encouraged to publish the results of their work;
  (b) to minimize the restrictions placed upon scientific researchers' right to publish their findings, consistent with public interest and the right of their employers and fellow workers;
  (c) to express as clearly as possible in writing in the terms and conditions of their employment the circumstances in which such restrictions are likely to apply;
  (d) similarly, to make clear the procedures by which scientific researchers can ascertain whether the restrictions mentioned in this paragraph apply in a particular case and by which he can appeal.

Recognition

38. Member States should demonstrate that they attach high importance to the scientific researcher's receiving appropriate moral support and material compensation for the creative effort which is shown in his work.

39. Accordingly, Member States should:
  (a) bear in mind that:
    (i)   the degree to which scientific researchers receive credit for and acknowledgement of their proven creativity, may affect their level of perceived job satisfaction;
    (ii)   job satisfaction is likely to affect performance in scientific research

generally, and may affect specifically the creative element in that performance;

(*b*)adopt, and urge the adoption of, appropriate treatment of scientific researchers with respect to their proven creative effort.

40.   Similarly, Member States should adopt, and urge the adoption of, the following standard practices:

(*a*)written provisions to be included in the terms and conditions of employment of scientific researchers, stating clearly what rights (if any) belong to them (and, where appropriate, other interested parties) in respect of any discovery, invention, or improvement in technical know-how which may arise in the course of the scientific research and experimental development which those researchers undertake;

(*b*)the attention of scientific researchers to be always drawn by the employer to such written provisions before the scientific researchers enter employment.

Reasonable flexibility in the interpretation and application of texts setting out the terms and conditions of employment of scientific researchers

41.   Member States should seek to ensure that the performance of scientific research and experimental developments be not reduced to pure routine. They should therefore see to it that all texts setting out terms of employment for, or governing the conditions of work of scientific researchers, be framed and interpreted with all the desirable flexibility to meet the requirements of science and technology. This flexibility should not however be invoked in order to impose on scientific researchers conditions that are inferior to those enjoyed by other workers of equivalent qualifications and responsibility.

The advancement of their various interests by scientific researchers in association

42.   Member States should recognize it as wholly legitimate, and indeed desirable, that scientific researchers should associate to protect and promote their individual and collective interests, in bodies such as trade unions, professional associations and learned societies, in accordance with the rights of workers in general and inspired by the principles set out in the international instruments listed in the annex to this recommendation. In all cases where it is necessary to protect the rights of scientific researchers, these organizations should have the right to support the justified claims of such researchers.

VI.   UTILIZATION AND EXPLOITATION OF THE PRESENT RECOMMEN-
DATION

43.   Member States should strive to extend and complement their own action in respect of the status of scientific researchers, by co-operating with all national and international organizations whose activities fall within the scope and objectives of this recommendation, in particular National Commissions for Unesco; international organizations; organizations representing science and technology educators; employers generally; learned societies, professional associations and trade unions of scientific researchers; associations of science writers; youth organizations.

44.   Member States should support the work of the bodies mentioned above by the most appropriate means.

45.　Member States should enlist the vigilant and active co-operation of all organizations representing scientific researchers, in ensuring that the latter may, in a spirit of community service, effectively assume the responsibilities, enjoy the rights and obtain the recognition of the status described in this recommendation.

VII. FINAL PROVISION

46.　Where scientific researchers enjoy a status which is, in certain respects, more favourable than that provided for in this recommendation, its terms should not be invoked to diminish the status already acquired.

About the authors

Olu Adeniji is Director of the Department of European Affairs of the Nigerian Ministry of External Affairs. He was Nigerian Ambassador to Austria and Switzerland, permanent representative to the United Nations Office in Geneva, and leader of the Nigerian Delegation to the Committee on Disarmament, 1977-81. He is Chairman of the Preparatory Committee of the Second Special Session on Disarmament.

Engelbert Broda is Emeritus Professor of Applied Physical Chemistry and Biophysical Chemistry at the University of Vienna, Austria. During the Second World War he worked on basic research aspects of the nuclear energy programme in the United Kingdom. Later he turned to biophysics, and the production and use of energy by living cells. He is interested in science history and has written biographies of Boltzmann and Einstein.

Francesco Calogero is Professor of Theoretical Physics at the University of Rome, Italy. As part of his research work in Elementary Particle Theory and Nuclear Structure, he visited many countries. Since 1963, he has also been involved in arms control matters on which he published a number of papers as well as on topics of Science and Society. He is a member of the Executive Committee of the Pugwash Council.

Vasily Emelyanov is a Corresponding Member of the Soviet Academy of Sciences and was Chairman of the State Committee for Atomic Energy of the Soviet Union. He was the Soviet Delegate on the Committees of Experts which prepared the United Nations Reports on the effects of nuclear weapons and the consequences of the arms race. He has written many books on nuclear energy topics and on the history of Soviet science since the revolution.

Bernard Feld is Professor of Physics at the Massachusetts Institute of Technology, United States. He is also editor-in-chief of the *Bulletin of the Atomic Scientists*. In both areas he has published numerous papers. During the Second World War he was a member of the Manhattan Project at Los

315

Alamos. He was Secretary-General of Pugwash, 1973–77, and is at present Chairman of its Executive Committee.

Essam Galal is a medical practitioner in Cairo. He held the post of Counsellor at the Ministry of Health of the Egyptian Government, and was Head of the Department of Pharmacology at the Azhar University in Cairo. He is the author of many papers in medical journals and of textbooks. He is a member of the Executive Committee of the Pugwash Council.

Alfonso Garcia-Robles is the Head of the Mexican Delegation at the United Nations. He served as Mexican Ambassador to Brazil and was Minister for Foreign Affairs of the Mexican Government. He was President of the Preparatory Committee for the Denuclearization of Latin America which has led to the Tlatelolco Treaty. He is currently Permanent Representative of Mexico to the Committee on Disarmament.

Allen Greb is research historian in the Program of Science, Technology and Public Affairs at the University of California, San Diego, United States, where he received his doctorate. He is co-author, with Herbert York, of several articles on nuclear weapon systems, defence decision-making and arms control policy. He is the recipient of the University of California Fellowship Award.

Sergei Kapitza is Professor of Physics at the Physical Technical Institute in Moscow, USSR, and a member of the Commission of Scientific Aspects of Disarmament of the USSR Academy of Sciences. One of his main interests is popularization of science and he is moderator of the General Science Programme of Television in the USSR. He received the Kalinga Prize in 1979.

Karlheinz Lohs is Director of the Research Department of Chemical Toxicology in Leipzig, GDR, and a member of the GDR Academy of Sciences. He has published many papers and several books on toxicology, as well as on peace research and history of science. He is a member of the Governing Board of the Stockholm International Peace Research Institute.

Ignacy Malecki is Director-General of the Institute of Fundamental Technical Research in Warsaw, Poland. He is a member of the Polish Academy of Sciences, and served as its Foreign Secretary. He was Director of the Unesco Science Policy Department. He is the author of many papers on acoustics and on Science of Science.

Stephen Marks is a graduate of the Stanford University, United States.

Subsequently, he was awarded a French State doctorate in law. He is Instructor of Human Rights and International Law at a University in Paris. He is a member of the Division of Human Rights and Peace at Unesco.

Sir Mark Oliphant is Professor Emeritus of the Institute of Advanced Studies at Canberra University, Australia; previous to that he was Professor of Physics at the University of Birmingham, England, where he worked on the atom bomb project during the Second World War. He is a Fellow of the Royal Society, and was Governor of South Australia from 1971–76.

Swadesh Rana is Senior Research Associate at the Institute for Defence Studies and Analyses in New Delhi, India. She received her doctorate in political science from the University of New Delhi. At present she holds the post of political affairs officer at the Centre for Disarmament of the United Nations in New York.

Bert Röling is Emeritus Professor of International Law and Polemology at the University of Groningen, Netherlands, where he was Director of the Polemological Institute. He is a former judge of the International Military Tribunal for the Far East. He was Secretary-General of the International Peace Research Association during 1965–71.

Joseph Rotblat is Emeritus Professor of Physics at the University of London, England. During the Second World War, he was a member of the British team working in Los Alamos. Later he worked in the fields of medical physics and radiation biology. He is a founder member of the Pugwash Movement and was its Secretary-General from 1957–73. Among his numerous publications is the official history of Pugwash.

Ivan Supek is Professor of Theoretical Physics and Philosophy at the University of Zagreb, Yugoslavia and Head of the Institute for Philosophy of Science and Peace Research of the Yugoslav Academy of Sciences and Arts. He has published many scientific papers on theoretical physics and on problems of disarmament. He has also written several novels and plays.

Marek Thee is Director of the International Peace Research Institute in Oslo, Norway. His early education was in journalism and political sciences, and he has a doctorate in contemporary history. He is Editor-in-Chief of the Bulletin of Peace Proposals and author of numerous papers.

Herbert York is Director of the Program of Science, Technology and Public Affairs at the University of California, San Diego, United States. He was a member of the President's Science Advisory Committee (under Eisenhower and Johnson) and of the General Advisory Committee for Arms Control

317

and Disarmament. He is the author of *Race to Oblivion*, as well as of other books on the arms race and the role of scientists in it.

John Ziman is Professor of Physics at the University of Bristol, England. He is a Fellow at the Royal Society and Chairman of the Council for Science and Society. His books on social aspects of science include: *Public Knowledge*, *The Force of Knowledge* and *Teaching and Learning about Science and Society*.

Index

322